PARTY POLITICS

PARTY POLITICS
Why We Have Poor Presidents

An inquiry into the decline of the presidency,
the reasons for its deterioration,
and a proposal for its improvement.

LEONARD LURIE

STEIN AND DAY/*Publishers*/New York

First published in 1980
Copyright © 1980 by Leonard Lurie
All rights reserved
Designed by Louis A. Ditizio
Printed in the United States of America
Stein and Day/*Publishers*/Scarborough House
Briarcliff Manor, N.Y. 10510

Library of Congress Cataloging in Publication Data

Lurie, Leonard.
    Party politics, why we have poor Presidents.

    Bibliography: p.
    Includes index.
    1. Political parties—United States.
    2. Presidents—United States.   I. Title.
JK2261.L87   324.273   80-18927
        ISBN 0-8128-2754-6

For my grandchildren,
Alexander, Jordan, Daniel and Rachel:
harbingers of a happy future.
May they always be adorable,
and a continuing source of joy,
to all who know them.

Contents

Preface

I attended my first political convention in 1948 while a political science student at Syracuse University. Henry Wallace's Progressive party was meeting in Philadelphia. I was immediately struck by the paradox of that convention of mavericks: The party was under the control of its left wing, and deviations from its dogma were not to be tolerated; its course from gavel to gavel was completely predictable.

Misled by inexperience, I assumed that controlled political conventions were a touchstone of radical politics. Four years later I went to Chicago with Eisenhower and Nixon to learn that Republicans were no more interested in the democratic process than their adversaries at the other end of the political spectrum.

My first book, *The King Makers,* resulted from this experience in the Midwestern slaughterhouse region. The scholarly journal *Foreign Affairs* detected the direction of my thinking even before I was fully aware of it. They described the book as "A hard-hitting account of the 1952 Republican Convention with particular emphasis on Nixon's relentless pursuit of the Vice-Presidential nomination. The author's main target for criticism, however, is the convention system itself."

It was clear to me, as it is, I suspect, to most Americans, that national party conventions are a mixture of showmanship and sham and are only peripherally concerned about the opinions of the average voter.

As the years passed I became more involved in following the twists and turns in Richard Nixon's obsessive pursuit of the presidency. Although I attended the melodramatic 1968 Democratic Convention in Chicago and the 1972 Democratic Convention in Miami, my concern about this basic institution of the party system abated as fascination with the Nixon phenomenon fastened itself on me. The result was *The Running of Richard Nixon,* a biography of the president, then serving the fourth year of his first term in office; but more than that, it was a detailed analysis of how one man became president. For the central fact of Nixon's adult life was that it was devoted solely to that purpose. His career is a case study of a politician on the make—a politician few people liked or trusted, so that how he achieved his objective was particularly instructive to those who are interested in how American presidents are chosen.

Having spent twenty years attending on his every public word and action, by the time Watergate began to surface, I readily understood the nature of his dereliction of duty.

The Impeachment of Richard Nixon was the result of this understanding. It was the first book about Watergate. Moreover, it advocated his removal from office, fully a year and a half before his resignation. Eventually 500,000 copies were printed. In the months following publication I was continually startled that, although scores of books came out dealing with the president's role in Watergate, none of their authors were willing to urge his impeachment. Some of them wrote about how they had uncovered an aspect of the crimes, others catalogued the events and characters in the conspiracy. I concluded that it was the blinding aura of the presidency that kept so many honest, courageous individuals from speaking up for what they knew was right.

The corrupt activity in Nixon's White House did not impress me, as it did some others, as an aberrant occurrence. The Grant and Harding administrations are part of our political mythology; as an historian, I was aware that charges of dishonesty had been voiced against other holders of that office. The more I considered the matter, the clearer it became that corrupt political activity was a common theme in the history of the presidency after 1840 (a theme heard even more frequently in politics on the state and local level). Furthermore, it was equally obvious that the chief culprit in this sordid business was the party system. Somehow the destiny of our nation had been placed in the hands of a small group of politicians who were least capable of protecting it. How, I wondered, did that happen?

This book is an attempt to demonstrate, by focusing primarily on how presidents achieved their office, that it is the *party* selection process that has created many of the problems which confound and corrupt our political institutions.

Americans have always mistrusted politicians. It therefore surprises me that few voices have been raised to condemn the vehicle that has carried these politicians from one desecration to another. During the last one hundred and forty years, voters have frequently denounced individual politicians while ignoring the fact that they are shaped by their training in the party system. Each reformer, intent on ending the exposed corruptions of some political party, has sought salvation by calling for the creation of another party.

The failure of this remedy has not led to a more penetrating analysis of this endemic problem. It is my hope that the sound of a new drum will draw attention to this problem and that a constructive exchange of ideas may result in a new political arrangement in the means by which we select our future leaders.

July 29, 1980
Manhasset, N.Y.

A Cautionary Note
to the Reader

You may conclude that, in sum, I am suggesting a single solution for all of our political problems. If so, the fault lies in my presentation. For I am certainly not a believer in monocausal explanations of human behavior; and since the book is concerned with politicians, it is clearly not my purpose to discuss possible utopias.

Rather, I have approached the writing of this book in much the manner that a doctor deals with a specific disease. He knows his patient has recovered from serious illnesses in the past without his help. He knows that eventually some relentless malady will end his patient's life regardless of his help. Yet he addresses himself to the current problem with enthusiasm. Even as he applies himself to the conquest of his illness, he may pause momentarily to regret that his cure will not solve the problems of money, matrimony, psychology, or any of several dozen other, perhaps more important, social afflictions plaguing his patient.

It is to the disease of *party* that I have addressed myself.

1

A Nightmare Vision

And of what kind are the men that will strive for this profitable pre-eminence [political appointment], through all the bustle of cabal, the heat of contention, the infinite mutual abuse of parties, tearing to pieces the best of characters? It will not be the wise and moderate; the lovers of peace and good order, the men fittest for the trust. It will be the bold and the violent, the men of strong passions and indefatigable activity in their selfish pursuits. These will thrust themselves into your Government and be your rulers.

Benjamin Franklin, June 2, 1787,
at the sixth working session of
the Constitutional Convention[1]

This nightmare vision of Dr. Franklin came to dominate the America of Richard Nixon. Bold and violent men willing to deal criminally with enormous sums of money, thoroughly selfish in the conduct of their office, did in fact become our rulers.

President Nixon's own edited version of what went on daily in his office, released by him April 30, 1974,[2] revealed that acts of moral corruption were the accepted norm, and acts of criminality were performed with a regularity that suggested experience.

When this successor to Jefferson and Lincoln felt compelled to cry out over nationwide television, "I am not a crook,"[3] a juncture had been reached where only the most morally calloused or mentally incompetent could avoid the conclusion that our democratic society was in trouble.

Yet the ex-president's resignation, followed by the conviction of his closest associates, produced virtually no movement for reform. This lack of response was the most disheartening aspect of America's greatest political scandal.

3

The result has been a growing cynicism.[4] The Nixonian rear guard has deepened this cynicism by insisting that all recent presidents have behaved with equal depravity. Congressional investigations in 1975 lent support to this rationalization when they confirmed that the Central Intelligence Agency had been ordered by Presidents Kennedy and Johnson to violate its charter and keep covert files on Americans.[5] Even more frightening was the evidence that these presidents had authorized plots to murder foreign leaders. Why should Nixon be singled out, his apologists insist, when he was merely living up to the standards of his peers?

H. R. Haldeman, Nixon's Lord High Executioner, supported this view in a March 30, 1975, CBS television interview conducted by Mike Wallace. He started by describing his ex-boss as being "weird," and ended by insisting he differed only in degree from former presidents—the main difference being that he was caught.

As they witnessed the slowness with which Congress responded to Nixon's determination to "tough it out" at any price, the young generalized that he was merely the soiled reflection of a debased society. They were, and are, too ready to feel that the American dream of equality and democratic choice has always been a pitchman's fantasy.

Even those buoyant spirits who insisted on conducting themselves as though they were building the City of God failed to touch the truth of this matter. Henry Steele Commager, Raoul Berger, and Sam Ervin worked without pause for the impeachment of Richard Nixon, but seemed to see no problem greater than the disgrace of a single imperfect president. In limiting their response to this palliative they signalled their good intentions, but speeded ultimate failure of their more enduring commitment to honest, efficient, democratic government. They dealt with a symptom, Richard Nixon, while ignoring an epidemic caused by a defective political organism—a virulent organism which has produced, and continues to be capable of producing, corrupt presidents. Merely to disgrace Nixon, and then avert our eyes, is virtually to guarantee that a new generation of dissolute men can make their way to his vacant, inviting seat.

Ben Franklin, shortly before his death, attempted to perform one last service for his country. There is a beginning of wisdom about

Watergate in what he said. It is a wisdom that has been proclaimed repeatedly since, but whose significance, at this most relevant time, has been, incomprehensibly, overlooked. He spoke of the dangers the new country would face when it selected its leaders. The hack politician, he warned, was the man to fear:

> Place before the eyes of such men, a post of *honour* that shall be at the same time a place of *profit,* and they will move heaven and earth to obtain it. . . . The struggles for them are the true sources of all those factions which are perpetually dividing the Nation, distracting its Councils, hurrying sometimes into fruitless & mischievous wars, and often compelling a submission to dishonorable terms of peace.[6]

Franklin shared this distaste for party politics with most of his contemporaries. They had experienced the shortcomings of party politics. Domestic Whigs and Tories had contended for power in the middle and northern colonies before the Revolution. The antics of James DeLancey's machine in New York left few of his victims with illusions about the ability of partymen to perform selfless public service.

As native-born Englishmen, they were aware of the immorality that molded the activities of the Whigs and Tories in Hogarthian England. Since many of them were scholars, they knew of the Machiavellian contortions of political parties in the Renaissance Italian city-states. They were repelled by what they saw and were determined their vision of the perfectable state would not be ruined by legalizing man's worst instincts.

Samuel Johnson spoke for many of them when a few years before the Revolution he described the mentality of English partymen: "Of all kinds of credulity, the most obstinate and wonderful is that of political zealots; of men, who, being numbered, they know not how or why, in any of the parties that divide a state, resign the use of their own eyes and ears, and resolve to believe nothing that does not favour those whom they profess to follow."[7]

Few took objection to Alexander Pope's definition of a political party: "Party . . . is but the madness of many for the gain of a few."[8]

So, taking these admonitions to heart, there assembled in Philadelphia in May 1787 this congress of political talent to begin deliberations over the new Constitution. They were convinced that no place would be found in it for that rogue institution, political parties.

Indeed, the first thought about the selection of the president was light-years away from the clubhouse and party politics. Pedantic Edmund Randolph, when he read off the Virginia Plan, the basic outline of the new government, stated in the seventh of the fifteen Virginia resolutions "that a National Executive be instituted; to be chosen by the National Legislature. . . ."[9]

The reasons for legislative appointment of the president were perhaps best explained by Roger Sherman, of Rhode Island, on June 1, 1787. He said he "considered the Executive magistracy as nothing more than an institution for carrying the will of the Legislature into effect, that the person or persons ought to be appointed by and accountable to the Legislature only, which was the depositary of the supreme will of the Society."[10]

These early democrats preferred that their government be under the direct control of an elected legislature. Their preference had been sharpened by their experience with English parliamentarianism; and it had been nurtured by their knowledge that the Continental Congress had successfully conducted the Revolution. Congress had exercised all executive as well as legislative functions of the beleaguered rebels. On the other hand, a strong chief magistrate too closely resembled the image of the monarch whose willful fist they had so recently thrown off.

It was only the impotence of the legislative-dominant Articles of Confederation government—which had been declining for six years prior to the Constitutional Convention—that coerced them into contemplating the creation of an executive department. Even then the Randolph plan envisioned a president who would be ineligible to serve a second term.[11]

Other delegates thought the only way to avoid tyranny would be to have a multiheaded executive department consisting of at least three coequal potential usurpers of the people's power; the three would counteract the idiosyncratic weaknesses in each other's character.

James Madison, the most influential of the delegates in terms of his impact on the final document, shared the common fear of a powerful chief executive. He advised them to construct a government "to protect the people against their rulers,"[12] which, along with the concept of a stable government, was the philosophical motivation of most members of the convention. But, no matter what the final powers and configuration of the presidency, the occupant of that office was not to be a product or pawn of party bosses.

Another reason for the delegates' antipathy to parties was explained by Richard Hofstadter, in his book *The Idea of a Party System.* Chapter two, entitled "A Constitution Against Parties," describes the attitude of Virginians, who lived in one of the states that did not have a party system, toward government organized and directed by party hierarchies:

"Sectional divisions there were, but before the Revolution they were not of grave consequence. Class differences there were also, and occasional personal rivalries, but they produced no parties, not even permanent factions. . . . A generation nurtured in this environment had no successful example of party government anywhere in its experience, but it had an example of a party-less government of a free and relatively benign character. . . ."[13]

As the troubled delegates debated in Philadelphia through the hot summer of 1787, they were confronted with the probability that their brief experiment with freedom would soon collapse; this was to be one last desperate attempt to order the affairs of state. Yet despite the intensity of their labors and their fear of the calamity that would result if they failed to construct a workable government, not one of them suggested that a solution to their problems could be found within the structure of party politics.

Liberty's safety and the stability of the state were not to depend on the gyrations of narrowly controlled party mechanisms. Rather it would rest on clearly defined checks built into the Constitution which would allow any branch of a tripartite government to forestall the power plays of its two competitors.

The writers of the Constitution envisioned the separation of powers as freedom's grand safeguard. Their document would balance one force against another, in this way protecting the citizen against the betrayal of trust inherent in the exercise of power. These were rational defenses against tyranny that were far more likely to achieve the compromises needed in a tranquil society than a dependence on the ability of contending parties to cancel out each other's predatory tendencies.

On September 17, 1787, they concluded their months of deliberations, and turned to the task of gaining the approval of the thirteen
nations which formed the Confederation. Most influential in this
matter were *The Federalist Papers,* a cogent plea for ratification,
written the following year by James Madison, John Jay, and Alexander Hamilton as a series of essays describing how the new government was to work. In *Federalist Papers* Nos. 10 and 50 Madison
reasoned powerfully against parties. At this decisive juncture, there
was no substantial sign of opposition to his viewpoint; if anything,
the perception held by leading political figures in the various states,
that the petitioners for ratification were firmly against the growth of
parties, contributed to its acceptance.

Ratification of the Constitution in 1788 changed no minds about
the need for political parties. Madison's fellow Virginian, Thomas
Jefferson, maintained an apparently unyielding skepticism about
them. On March 13, 1789, he wrote to Francis Hopkinson, "I am not a
Federalist, because I never submitted the whole system of my opinions
to the creed of any party of men whatever, in religion, in philosophy,
in politics or in anything else, where I was capable of thinking for
myself. Such an addiction is the last degradation of a free and moral
agent. If I could not go to heaven but with a party, I would not go
there at all."[14]

George Washington endorsed Jefferson's sentiments when he
wrote to Arthur Fenner, governor of the new state of Rhode Island,
June 4, 1790: "If we mean to support Liberty and Independence which
it has cost us so much blood and treasure to establish, we must drive
far away the demon of party spirit. . . ."[15]

In order to forestall the possibility of the growth of political parties,
the Convention had decided to create an Electoral College for the sole
purpose of selecting the chief executive. As its last substantive act, on
September 14, 1788, the Articles of Confederation Congress issued a
decree calling on the states to choose presidential Electors by January
7 of the following year.[16]

In actual practice the eleven states that took part in the 1789
presidential election selected their Electors with a great show of
inventiveness. They shared only one characteristic: none of them
allowed their Electors to wear party labels.

The designation of Electors was often left to state legislatures, whose members were likewise selected without any reference to party. In five states the Electors were chosen directly by the voters. In one of these, New Hampshire, if the voters could not haphazardly produce a majority, by whatever technique they could contrive, the choice was left to the legislature. Significantly, Massachusetts placed the *nominating* process in the hands of the voters. The voters proposed double the number of Electors needed, and the legislature picked the final slate.

In Connecticut, Georgia, and South Carolina, the legislatures selected without any reference to the voters' opinions. In New York, the legislature was supposed to pick Electors, but politics intervened and a deadlock developed so that none were chosen. New Jersey had the most unusual system. The governor and his council, without reference to the voters or the legislature, appointed the Electors.[17]

But regardless of how they were chosen on that January 7, 1789, the Electors were thought of as outstanding men, selected for their superior qualities to perform a vital mission. And these men with a mission were not to be disturbed by party-factionalized interventions in their deliberations, such as those sorry spectacles constantly performed by the Tories and Whigs in decadent old England.

There were to be no party squabbles to lead politicians into narrowly motivated internecine warfare, no deals for personal advantage. Instead the Electoral College would be a congregation of non-partymen, seeking only the most qualified man to be president. Having performed their solitary function, they would return to ordinary society, once again making their daily contributions to its labors. They would not profit from their decision beyond the profit all citizens would receive in a well-ordered community. Certainly they would not form a professional politician class whose financial destiny depended on their ability to control the selection of the president.

With constitutional ratification, the new electoral process went into operation on the first Wednesday in February 1789, when the Electors assembled in their state capitols. They each indicated a preference for two men, simultaneously choosing the president and vice-president. One month later, on Wednesday, March 4, their ballots were to be counted in the nation's capital, New York; lack of a quorum delayed the count by the first Congress until April 6.

Washington was finally inaugurated on April 30. There were no political parties involved in his selection. The members of the Electoral College did not consider themselves partymen; they were merely public-spirited citizens who had come together to perform a single service for their nation. The idealism that motivated most of them was shortly to be tested as men of different character saw an opportunity and would not let it pass.

2

The Low Point of
Party Influence

*The Fathers hoped to create not a system of party
government under a Constitution but rather a constitutional government that would check and control parties.
Although Federalists and Anti-Federalists differed over
many things, they do not seem to have differed over the
proposition that an effective constitution is one that
successfully counteracts the work of parties.*

Richard Hofstader[1]

During the first years of the Republic, before the development of
parties as we know them today, the nomination process set, in an
imperfect way, a democratic tone. Access to office was open to all
qualified voters, with no need to swear allegiance to leader or organization. Candidates most often nominated themselves, or bowed to the
wishes of their neighbors as expressed at town meetings and in a
variety of other gatherings: sometimes in an open field, or in a local
tavern.

Many states, cautiously advancing along an unilluminated road,
made no provision for nominating candidates: those interested in
running for office simply materialized before election day, thrust
forward in a variety of ways that does credit to man's imagination. In
the Boston papers of 1792, Professor Noble E. Cunningham, Jr.,
found listed there slates proposed for general consideration by "a
number of inhabitants of the county of Essex," or by "An Elector"
who modestly apologized, saying that "as it has become a custom to
nominate candidates for Federal Representatives, with and by the
advice of a number of gentlemen, I send you a list. . . ." There was also

a "coalition list" offered enthusiastically by "a large number of respectable merchants and mechanics."[2]

The candidate's name had to be presented to the voters on election day. In order to accomplish that in 1792, it required little more than the willingness of an aspirant to nominate himself by expressing a desire to run; it was then the function of the state governments to actually conduct the election. However, free choice in how candidates would be nominated quickly proved to be a fatal weakness. It became apparent that those candidates who did not run as isolated independents, but, rather, were able to attract the support of other members of the community (some of whom joined with them in drawing up a list of nominees for a spectrum of offices) were more likely to win. Still, the lists bore no party labels, and, in fact, partisanship was so lacking that the names of popular leaders tended to be used by each group of slate-makers.

The original impetus for American political parties came, as might have been expected, from rich merchants living in the cities along the coast and from the landed aristocracy. These individuals, a minority in any society, were most in need of a device for protecting their interests: they had more to lose, and, understandably, were anxious to develop political tools that might be of aid in safeguarding their position.

They decided to support the West Indies immigrant, Alexander Hamilton, in his plan to form the Federalist party. This did not take place, however, until well into Washington's first term in office, and it was not until halfway through the first decade of the nation's existence that two parties, with local organizations of varying efficiency, in only a handful of states, came into being. Even then, there were no mass meetings, no primaries, no conventions such as characterize modern parties.

In the first Congress, most members disagreed with each other as frequently as reasonably intelligent men always will, but their disputes were not complicated by the interjection of party intrigues. In the second and third Congresses a preponderance of participants still described themselves as independents.

In areas of New England and the Deep South local elites dominated the political process; they were the backbone of Hamilton's new party. There was never, however, a sustained, organized effort on the *national* level that would justify describing the Federalists as a political party in the sense of the two-party structure of today. The lack of rapid communication certainly held back such a development. More decisive, however, was the conviction of noble and ignoble alike that the new nation would expire convulsively if it followed the dictates of partymen.

In New York and Pennsylvania, the two states in which traces of local and statewide parties existed for over a hundred years prior to the Revolution, candidates for Congress were chosen in party nominating meetings, some on the local level, some statewide. But throughout the rest of the country candidates were nominated in nonpartisan caucuses, often assembled by an interested person or group through an invitation to the public in some newspaper, or by means of notices posted on tree trunks.

George Washington was the single most important reason for the failure of national parties to take root: Intellectually and emotionally he despised them. The most enduring strains in his character rebelled at the parochialism of parties: their inability to view the nation's interests as above their own. It was the unaffiliated yeoman and patriot who stood at his side at Valley Forge; there was no need, nor advantage to be gained by dividing them into factions. At the same time, he so completely dominated federal politics that it was inconceivable anyone would want to run against him. In the 1792 election the Electors searched their consciences for alternatives, but quickly concluded that Washington was incontrovertibly the best choice; this was a rare, but true, democratic consensus. Primarily concerned with winning his acquiescence to serve, the operators among them, who might have immediately been tempted to organize a party, found themselves with no room to maneuver.

As the election approached, Committees of Correspondence, such as had existed during the Revolution, sprang up throughout the states. Frequently they were creatures of the state legislatures, which, having been given a special place in the election process by the Constitution, were taking their responsibilities seriously. Correspondents selected by these committees wrote to their counterparts in the various states communicating their preference for Washington and seeking allies. Committees of Correspondence were one of the main political devices before the development of national parties and they continued to function into the first two decades of the nineteenth century.

At the same time, political clubs were being organized. Franklin's Society for Political Enquiries had been formed in Pennsylvania, in 1787, and the Sons of Tammany took their first feeble steps in New York in 1789. They were joined by pro-French Revolution "Democratic" societies in 1793 and 1794. These were local pressure groups, none of them directly associated with national figures.

This partyless government lasted for several years; however, by 1794 it had become apparent that the political life of the Republic, which its founders had originally conceived of as flowing naturally outside structured party lines, was being organized, in some states, along just such lines.

In that year, John Taylor, of Virginia, an early philosopher of democratic agrarianism, and a close friend of Jefferson, wrote about "a political appearance [parties], so baneful to the commonwealth. . . ." He could see nothing good in the device and rejected the thought that parties were inevitable in a democratic society. "The situation of the public good, in the hands of two parties nearly poised as to numbers, must be extremely perilous. Truth is a thing, not of divisibility into conflicting parts, but of unity. Hence both sides cannot be right. Every patriot deprecates a disunion. . . ."[3]

Such a "disunion" did not seem likely in 1794, for although Washington had determined not to run for a third term in 1796, he expressed his determination to only a limited number of intimates. As a result, activity for one or another candidate was discouraged until he finally announced his intentions.

So entwined had Washington become in the creation of the new nation that it seemed altogether natural, once he announced his retirement, that he should offer his fellow citizens some advice. On September 17, 1796, that advice was given in generous measure in his *Farewell Address*. School children know that on this occasion Washington warned his countrymen against "entangling alliances"; his influence was so powerful that this doctrine became the cornerstone of American foreign policy for almost one hundred and fifty years. Obscured by the impact of his central thesis is his blast, in that same document, against the development of political parties. "In contemplating the causes which may disturb our union," he warned, "it occurs as matter of serious concern that any ground should have been furnished for characterizing parties by geographical discriminations—Northern and Southern, Atlantic and Western—whence designing men may endeavor to excite a belief that there is a real difference of local interests and views. One of the expedients of party to acquire influence within particular districts is to misrepresent the opinions and aims of other districts. You can not shield yourselves too much against the jealousies and heartburnings which spring from these misrepresentations; they tend to render alien to each other those who ought to be bound together by fraternal affection. . . ."[4]

Washington had witnessed the growth of political factionalism during the mid-1790s. Hamilton (his favorite) and Jefferson were at each other's throats. This competition had progressed to the point where Jefferson and his friend Madison, both formerly implacable opponents of cabals, had joined to organize the Democratic Republic party in a few isolated areas where they had some influence. Clearly they viewed their reversal of position as a matter of political self-preservation. Hamilton was building the Federalist party with all the vigor he could muster. In this situation, Jefferson and Madison decided to compromise with their principles; the theory seemed to be that the devil must be opposed with his own weapons. Since few matters in life, and fewer in politics, are susceptible of only one solution, their choice of weapons was lamentable.

This was the way an agitated Washington chose to view the burgeoning, though still weak, party structures as he spoke to posterity:

> I have already intimated to you the danger of parties in the State, with particular reference to the founding of them on geographical discriminations. Let me now take a more comprehensive view, and warn you in most solemn manner against the baneful effects of the spirit of party generally.
>
> This spirit, unfortunately, is inseparable from our nature, having its root in the strongest passions of the human mind. It exists under different shapes in all governments, more or less stifled, controlled, or repressed; but in those of the popular form it is seen in its greatest rankness and is truly their worst enemy. . . .
>
> It serves always to distract the public councils and enfeeble the public administration. It agitates the community with ill-founded jealousies

and false alarms; kindles the animosity of one part against another; foments occasionally riot and insurrection. It opens the door to foreign influence and corruption, which find a facilitated access to the government itself through the channels of party passion.[5]

There was a fever in his words. The intensity of his expression is not usually associated with the cool, austere, almost detached image of Washington which is reflected in Stuart portraits. Yet this condemnation of political parties represented the opinion of the most mature Washington. It was addressed to his "Fellow-Citizens," not to party leaders who had helped him along the way, not to kingmakers who cloaked themselves in the guise of patriots only to advance their private interests. For him, the people, especially those who tilled the soil and owned property, were the new nation's source of strength, and its greatest source of weakness was the hack frequently found in party ranks, who sought power not out of a sense of duty, but out of a desire for plunder.

Washington's stern idealism, which led him to warn of the cankerous effects of party politics, had its greatest influence while he was alive. The election of 1796 was conducted, in large part, without party direction. Jefferson had stormed out of Washington's cabinet in 1793 and during the next three years remained in retirement at Monticello, while his congressional supporters, under the direction of Madison, strove to stir up sentiment for their hero.

Private citizens with influence in their own bailiwicks voiced their endorsements most frequently for John Adams or Jefferson. Maryland's *Federal Gazette and Baltimore Advertiser* reported that "Gabriel Duvall and Doctor Archer have pledged themselves to vote for Mr. Jefferson,"[6] should they be chosen as Electors. But in the very same paper, on October 20, 1796, a William Deakins, also wishing to become an Elector, informed the citizens of Prince George's and Montgomery counties of his total independence. He pledged himself only "to vote for that man, who to my judgment, after all the information I can obtain, shall appear best qualified." Furthermore, he would not commit himself to either candidate then being urged on the voters by congressional Federalists and Republicans. "I am not, nor will be made a party man."[7]

The new Jeffersonian party, which had sprung up to do battle with

Hamilton, was quickly dominated by the bold and violent, the passionate men described so graphically by Franklin and Washington. The strength of the party was centered in the state of Virginia and the cities of New York and Philadelphia, where—at least in those two cities—the sleazy element inherent in clubhouse politics became immediately apparent.

The leader of the new Tammany Democratic-Republicans was Aaron Burr, soon to show the intensity of his nature in the killing of Hamilton. Burr was a man consumed with ambition, guided by no scruple that would interfere with it. In 1806 he revealed the tone of his patriotism when he negotiated secretly, first with the British and then with the Spanish, in an attempt to set up a new kingdom in the Ohio Territory, with himself as its head, for no reason more important than that he might benefit from the act.

The public's traditional mistrust of political parties nevertheless kept the Democratic-Republicans in check. On the other hand, the Federalists showed little interest in reaching out for popular support; they were an elite of brains and money, too sure of themselves to seek support from leaseholders. These two neophyte political ventures were confined mostly to city government. The selection of men to fill national offices, senators and representatives, was still, as it was constitutionally meant to be, in the hands of members of the state legislatures.

After Washington's administration, the presidential selection process significantly changed; presidential nominees were chosen with greater frequency in caucuses formed in Congress. Solons of similar viewpoint would band together at nomination time, in two separate caucuses, and put forward the names of two men who they thought would honor the office. Although at first based on political orientation or preference for a particular candidate, these caucuses quickly became party apparatuses. Despite this, one of their two nominees—the men to whom they publicly drew attention—still had to be chosen as president by Electors; and, these Electors were nominated by the various state legislatures, and finally picked by the ordinary voter on election day.

By 1796, however, an additional subtle change had already occurred in the selection process. Many of the potential Electors had begun to announce their choice for president in advance of the vote by the state legislatures. In this way they might win a place on one of the legislative Electoral slates that would be presented to the voters in the November election. Taking their cue from the congressional caucuses, the aspiring Electors aligned themselves with one or the other of the caucuses' nominees. State legislative politicos had changed their view of the process; instead of seeking out independent men of character who could be depended on to pick a Washington from among the multitude, they now wanted to know whether the potential Electors, who sought a place on their province's slate, would vote for the congressional caucus nominee of whom they approved. Whatever the merits of the original concept of the Electoral College—and there are some who still persuasively argue for that concept—this weakening of independence spelled its moral destruction and rapidly reduced it to figurehead status.

The election of 1800, which pitted Republicans Jefferson and Burr against Federalists John Adams and C. C. Pinckney, was a fascinating campaign; it was one of the bitterest and, in terms of long-lasting results, one of the most momentous in the nation's history. It was well understood before the election that Jefferson was running for president, and that if they were successful Burr, his party confederate, was to be vice-president. But a quirk in the Constitution, which allowed them both to be recorded on the same Elector's list, resulted in a tied electoral vote for them, after they had defeated Adams and Pinckney. Had Burr been honorable (which is to say, if the sun would shine at midnight) the matter would have easily been resolved. Instead, Burr's willingness to betray his partner forced the deadlocked Electoral College results into the House of Representatives, where an epic clash of Machiavellian thrusts and counterthrusts took place. The crisis was finally ended when Hamilton reluctantly decided that between his two enemies he preferred what he considered Jefferson's radicalism to what he knew to be Burr's low character.

The Twelfth Amendment, which resulted from the Jefferson/Burr imbroglio, decreed that presidential and vice-presidential candidates were to be chosen by the Electors on separate "lists"; as a result, it would no longer be possible for two candidates running on the same list to end up with identical totals in a contest in which it had not previously been specified which of them was running for the presidency and who was to take second place.

It is interesting to note that in 1804, the first time a change was being made in the electoral process, the writers of that amendment were still not disposed to refer to parties. Yet parties had played their largest role in the election of 1800—which had led directly to the amendment. Instead of decreeing that separate *party* slates must be drawn up for presidential and vice-presidential nominations, the amendment significantly directed the Electors to draw up separate, amorphously labelled "lists." Their clear intention was not to legalize any party monopoly on the ability to nominate.

Ultimately the amendment itself—the only one of twenty-five changes in the Constitution to be caused by an election campaign— was of minor significance. It merely eliminated the possibility of an occasional dispute over who would be president and who would settle for the vice-presidency. Even in the absence of the amendment, the 1800 deadlock would have alerted all future members of the House to the potential for such a difficulty. It seems likely that informal techniques would have developed to forestall a similar lapse in the trustworthiness of another Burr. At worst, it would have been worked out as it was between Jefferson, Burr, and the Federalists, after some strenuous—but less than monumental—negotiating.

However, during the 1800 pre-election period a more portentous step was taken by Virginia Republicans. It was a step soon imitated by other states; it helped lay the foundation for disciplined political parties, and was a much more important result of that election than the almost trivial legalisms of the Twelfth Amendment. Jefferson's supporters passed a law requiring that Electors run on a general ticket. Individuals could no longer seek to become Electors on their own; they had to be part of a slate. This had the effect of concentrating power in the hands of the state's strongest party. It likewise eliminated any fear the organization might have of successful candidacies by independent Electors. Virginia Federalists legitimately insisted the law aimed "to exclude *one-third* at least of the citizens of Virginia from a vote for the President of the United States."[8]

Prior to that development, any citizen wishing to help choose the president was free to win the approval of a majority of his state legislators, and then play his role in the Electoral College. With Virginia's action a new filtering process was added to the selection machinery, a process that fundamentally altered the nature of decisions rendered by Electors. They previously could choose to run independent of either the Republican or Federalist organizations. The new restrictions were implemented in a Republican legislative caucus on January 21, 1800, at which those assembled picked a slate of twenty-one Electors.

The power to nominate Electors was being placed exclusively in the hands of those political activists willing to draw up and support a general slate—in effect, in the hands of political parties. Meanwhile the power to elect took on the bogus appearance of being democratized. In 1800, Virginia, Rhode Island, Maryland, North Carolina, and Kentucky provided that, in any contest where two competing party slates were drawn up by the state legislature, the successful slate of Electors would be finally chosen by the voters.[9]

This was to become the practice across the country. It was largely a sop to the innocent voter. For the power to *nominate* is as important as the capacity to elect. In fact, without the ability to influence the nomination the capacity to elect is a device for beguiling the naive. The present Soviet single slate of nominees—periodically presented to Communist voters—should illustrate this point.

James Madison placed it in perfect perspective at the Constitutional Convention on August 10, 1787, when he said:

> A Republic may be converted into an aristocracy or oligarchy as well by limiting the number capable of being elected, as the number authorized to elect.[10]

The election of 1800 proved the turning point at which the process of nomination was taken away from the people and concentrated in a small group. It was here, in the early days of the Republic, that the vital error was being committed. Instead of opening the nomination process to the voters, it was being restricted.

The men taking part in this antidemocratic maneuver had several rationalizations available to them, largely denied to present-day politicians: Federalists did not believe in democracy, and were arrogant in their aristocratic utterances. Noah Webster summed up their position:

"A republican government can be rendered durable in no other way than by excluding from election men who have so little property, education, or principle, that they were liable to yield their own opinions to the guidance of unprincipled leaders."[11] He wanted voting age to begin at forty-five. At the same time, opponents of democratic election in 1800 could persuasively argue that it was impossible to get all of the people together to take part in the nomination process. In that time of primitive transportation and communication, it seemed reasonable to some to narrow the initial process of nomination. Then the task of voters, largely isolated from each other, would not become impracticable at the ballot box.

Whatever the reason, the conforming tendencies of the new arrangement quickly became apparent. With one exception, every Federalist Elector voted for the May 8, 1800, Federalist Congressional Caucus nominees, Adams and Pinckney, while all Republican Electors voted for Jefferson and Burr.[12]

The voters in 1800, limited though they were in number by sex, slavery, and property requirements, had little to say about who was going to be president. That power lay primarily with the congressional caucuses and the state legislatures. The former unofficially nominated presidential candidates and the latter determined how members of the Electoral College were going to be chosen.

The election of 1804 was scarcely contested by the fragmented Federalist party. The Republicans held a congressional caucus on February 25 and nominated Jefferson by acclamation. The Federalists did not bother. Informally, various centers of Federalist strength, primarily in New England, agreed to support Charles Cotesworth Pinckney and Rufus King. They received only 14 Electoral votes.

Jefferson's party was now known universally as the Republicans. They had some semblance of cohesiveness, but national political organization was still unknown. Georgia, North Carolina, and South Carolina had no political parties, and the new frontier states of Kentucky and Tennessee had not progressed to the point where sophisticated thoughts about voting—much less party organizations—had intruded on the realities of everyday life.

The election of 1808 confirmed the power of the Republican Congressional Caucus as the instrument for selecting nominees. Vermont's Senator Bradley, who had been chairman of the 1804 Republican caucus, sent out a call to twenty-eight senators and one hundred and eighteen members of the House. He stepped on some toes when he also invited three Federalists. Nevertheless, approximately ninety-eighteen members of the House. He stepped on some toes when he also invited three Federalists. Nevertheless, approximately ninety-four legislators turned up and nominated James Madison and New York's George Clinton.

Since the Federalists held few congressional seats, and attendance at their Congressional Caucus was bound to be humiliatingly low, they created a new political institution: the *mixed legislative caucus*. Districts that did not have a Federalist congressman were invited by the Federalist state legislative caucus in Boston to send some representative of local Federalist sentiments to New York City in the third week of August. In this way, a respectable showing could be mustered.

This mixed caucus was one forerunner of the modern convention system. Local political leaders, as well as congressmen, had a hand in choosing the nominee. The Federalists were in the process of disintegration and were desperately seeking some contrivance which would bolster them in the country's disaffected Republican parishes. The mixed legislative caucus seemed to invite representation by those outside Congress. In reality, it had as much substance as most public relations gimmicks; the power to nominate the presidential candidate remained with a core of New England party leaders. There were eight states represented; only South Carolina and Maryland made the trip from Dixie; the West was notably absent.

The Federalists attending their caucus convention kept their deliberations secret, a move aimed, as much as anything, at hiding their weakness, and demonstrated the loose hold that party labels had on these early politicians by debating whether to give support to Republican George Clinton. In revulsion against the thought of supporting a Republican, although Clinton had been bidding for their favor, they renominated the 1804 losing ticket—Pinckney and King.[13]

Madison, backed enthusiastically by Jefferson, won easily; he received 122 of 175 potential Electoral votes.

John Adams, viewing the battle philosophically from retirement, wrote to Benjamin Rush, "Neither party will ever be able to pursue the true interest, honor, and dignity of the nation. I lament the narrow selfish spirit of the leaders of both parties, but can do no good to either. They are incorrigible."[14]

The approaching War of 1812 spelled potential economic disaster for the Federalist shipping interests of New England, since it could end trade between old and New England. The possibility revived signs of life in the moribund party. Businessmen in Atlantic ports were determined to find some candidate who would stop that war hawk, Madison. Since no one in their ranks could play that role, they began clandestinely working for New York Republican DeWitt Clinton. Clinton was the nephew of Madison's vice-president, but the elder Clinton was on his deathbed; it was time for a representative of the new generation.

In many respects, this was the first campaign *for a nomination* in American history. Before this the nominees were men of note, most of whom had been secretary of state or vice-president under the president they were to succeed; their prominence in the Revolution had added to the logic of their selection. In 1812 this stable ordering of political affairs faced a challenge. DeWitt Clinton was an "operator," in the state which had produced the prototype of political operators, Burr. He wanted to be president, and his ambition was his major qualification for the job. Working for his nomination was Martin Van Buren, then a freshman New York State senator, and the true founder of the American national party system.

In this first venture at opportunism, Van Buren had to devise an extraordinary strategy. The fact that Madison was the incumbent made his job difficult. Not only did Madison want a second term, he was the country's leading Republican, Jefferson's protégé and confidant; furthermore, he had been renominated at the May Republican Congressional Caucus.

Showing one of the qualities most necessary for a successful politician, Van Buren forged on with no display of queasiness. He was encouraged by the fact that the war, which broke out in June, was not going well. The Federalists were intent on reestablishing their now defunct business dealings with England. They wanted a "peace" candidate and if Republican Clinton was willing to serve their purpose, a deal might be arranged.

Committees of Correspondence circulated the good word about Clinton; and, as the Federalist delegates from eleven states assembled for a three-day meeting in September 1812, it was apparent he was making headway in the opposition camp. After a good deal of secret debate the Federalists decided not to nominate any candidate of their own, but to support Madison's philosophic bedfellow, DeWitt Clinton.

In New York the disposition of the Electoral vote was still decided in the legislature. Van Buren was faced with a problem. In the joint session, the Assembly and the Senate would vote on who was to get the state's bloc of Electors. However, the Republicans had a majority. Since Madison should have received the backing of his fellow Republicans, Van Buren's task was formidable. He could not allow Clinton to be placed in the posture of wooing the opposition Federalists merely to advance his own ambitions.

With liberal doses of flattery, promises, and threats—in short, wheeling and dealing on the lowest level—Van Buren managed to maneuver Madison's supporters into a position where they either voted for Clinton or abstained. In this manner, he delivered New York's huge electoral vote into Clinton's column without ever concerning himself over what the Republican voters of New York desired. It was a politician's vision of paradise.

The vision disappeared, however, when the Electoral College voted at year's end; Madison was reelected by a margin of 128 to 89. Interestingly, the contestants were self-proclaimed Republicans. The national two-party system was still not part of American life.

After Madison's reelection the tide turned dramatically in favor of the Federalists. The war was a disaster. The British occupied and burned Washington. The federal government was so ineffectual that each state began to function as though it were back in the era of the Revolution or the Confederation. On October 5, 1814, Massachusetts Governor Strong announced that the central government was nonexistent, and since Massachusetts was abandoned it would have to fend for itself.

The Massachusetts legislature, that day, sent out a call for a convention in Hartford, Connecticut, to meet on December 15; the subject was to be the possibility of setting up a new confederation in New England, abandoning the Union, and suing for peace with the British. Convinced the time was ripe for Federalist aristocrats to save the day, the merchants of New England prepared to disband the United States. They were confirmed in this miscalculation by the result of the November congressional elections. Only two of the section's forty-one newly elected congressmen were Republicans; faith in Madison, the war, and the Union were at an ebb in the Puritan provinces.

The delegates, mainly from Massachusetts, Connecticut, and Rhode Island, were indiscreet enough to assemble in Hartford. Their final report, on January 5, 1815, disappointed Federalist hotheads. Even so, its moderate tone did not protect the Federalist party from widespread accusations of treason; and, by the time the 1816 election rolled around, the British had been defeated, and a morbid gloom permanently clouded every Federalist brow. Madison and his Republican allies had kept America free and united; the Federalists were discredited; the Republican Congressional Caucus had only to announce its choice for the world to know who was going to be the next president. Their nominee was James Monroe, the inheritor of the Virginia dynasty, whose major opponent was another Southern Republican, William H. Crawford. With Jefferson's and Madison's endorsement, Monroe was the easy winner.

Monroe was fortunate to serve when he did. The country was at peace, its natural wealth so little disturbed by the exertions of "The Second American Revolution" that it recovered as naturally as trees recover their leaves after a severe winter. Jefferson's purchase of Louisiana was in process of being exploited. The great movement to the West had begun. In terms of politics, this was indeed the era of good feelings.

Monroe was in harmony with his time in that he was a confirmed opponent of political parties. Having witnessed the virtual disappearance of the Federalists, he was determined to campaign for "the gradual elimination of all political faction."[15]

He felt so strongly about this matter that he went on a tour of New England, where he spoke repeatedly of the need to destroy factions and create an "amalgamation." He envisioned the day when men would forget party and concern themselves only with what was good for the nation.

Martin Van Buren was the most extreme proponent of the opposite view. Years later, writing in retirement, he described the president's attitude. "Mr. Monroe, at the commencement of his second term, took the ground openly, and maintained it against all remonstrances, that no difference should be made by the Government in the distribution of its patronage and confidence on account of the political opinions and course of applicants."[16]

The venerable Van Buren looked back over the years and still wondered how Monroe could have been so mistaken; parties could not be maintained without the oil of patronage to lubricate their machines. Those who did not understand this were, at the very least, naive. John Quincy Adams was not dealt the same measure of generosity. Van Burean wrote of this exceptional statesman thusly: "He [Adams] therefore embraced with avidity and supported with zeal the project of Mr. Monroe to obliterate the inauspicious party distinctions of the past and to bury the recollection of their causes and effects in a sepulchre proposed by himself. . . ."[17]

Indeed, by 1820 it looked as if Monroe and Adams might have every prospect of presiding at the burial of party distinctions. The Federalists had given up the ghost, and Monroe, as the popular incumbent president, had no need for parties to nominate him, or for anything, beyond his agreement to serve, to convince the Electors that he should be reelected.

Senator Samuel Smith, nevertheless, made an effort to call a Republican Congressional Caucus for the purpose of nominating Monroe; his call was responded to with complete indifference. So few attended that no business was conducted, and no effort was made to convene another session. Instead the matter was left to the decision of the Electors, who were still being chosen in each state in varied fashion. In effect, this was a presidential election in which political parties had no role.

Monroe won in the Electoral College without opposition. A New Hampshire Elector voted against him on principle, since he felt George Washington should remain the only president elected unanimously.

Thus by 1820 a new system for selecting presidents had evolved. The most important element in that system was not the individual voters, but rather the state legislatures. In some states the legislatures kept the power to choose Electors completely in their hands, meeting in legislative caucus every four years to determine who those Electors would be. In other states, the legislatures had created a bogus system of popular selection of Electors: The voters were encouraged to think that their ballot box deliberations on election day in November were

decisive in picking their state's Electors. In reality, professional political activists in the state, many of them sitting in the legislature, had
organized general slates committed to a man who, they thought,
would advance their parochial interests. They had succeeded, as Madison warned, in limiting the number capable of being elected.

With the exception of DeWitt Clinton, the presidential candidates
were only peripherally involved in the maneuvering. They certainly
wanted to be president, but in each case they had earned the right to
think they were the logical choice.

The politician's rapacious nature was largely held in check during
the first quarter-century of the nation's existence. The electorate was
relatively small, estimates being that not more than 6 percent of the
adult population was eligible to vote. The select nature of that group
created a commonality of view on many important subjects and kept
the problem of minority representation, with its potential field day for
political operators, at a minimum.

There were few jobs in the national government, and few contracts
to be apportioned, which meant the lightning rod of greed was not
there to attract that natural force at work in each potential politician.
In addition, blood had so recently been shed in the creation of the
nation that thoughts of tacking together factional apparatuses, which
would enable their manipulators to squeeze out some personal advantage, were considered unpatriotic. One had to be a particularly ripe
sinner to think in terms of excluding the voter from the electoral
process, which is a fairly accurate, if somewhat unorthodox, description of the basic purpose of political parties.

At the same time, the growth of parties was discouraged by the high
caliber of the potential presidents. Washington, Adams, Jefferson,
Madison, and Monroe thought of themselves as patriots, national
leaders, bearers of the torch of liberty that they had jointly lighted
during the Revolution. They were frequently above faction, and
attacks made by them, or on them, tended to be on issues.

It is significant that the greatest of our presidents came almost
uniformly from this group. The first four were *philosopher/kings,* in
the true meaning of Plato's term. They were authors, inventors,
political geniuses, men of conviction and dedication.

They were not uniformly successful. They were, however, above corruption and their failures were seldom of the spirit. It is difficult to point to any significant action taken by them solely from party consideration. And so, when they failed, it was most often failure due to the imperfectability of man's reason, and their inability to control circumstance.

A new era was about to dawn in this political Eden.

3

Posts of Honor, Places of Profit

The danger of parties to free governments arises from the impossibility of controlling them by the restraints of political law; because being constituted upon selfish views . . . no division of power, no responsibility, no periodical change of leaders, no limitation of "thus far you may go and no further," stops their career. . . . They are universally disposed to persecute, plunder, oppress and kill . . . and under the title of patriots, are, like fanaticks under the title of saints, ready to perpetrate any crimes to gratify their interest or prejudice.

John Taylor of Virginia[1]

As Monroe's administration was coming to an end, a tremendous dispute arose over who would be his successor.

There were at least four major contenders, all of them Republicans. John Quincy Adams, who had managed to live down his earlier membership in his father's party, was clearly the best qualified; he had been an outstanding secretary of state in Monroe's administration.[2] Henry Clay, first to become a perennial candidate for the presidency, was beginning his disappointing quest. William Crawford, who had suffered a major stroke during the campaign, revealed the quality of his desires by fighting it out from his sick bed until the last vote was counted. (His friends issued reports that the paralyzed former senator was merely indisposed.) Finally, the hero of New Orleans, Andrew Jackson, then a senator from Tennessee, was the least serious of the contenders.

Left to tradition, the matter would have been settled in the congres-

sional caucus; Republican congressmen would have gathered some-
time early in 1824 and negotiated their way to a ticket. Clay, longtime
Speaker of the House, felt he would have had an advantage in such a
setting. Crawford, who had been a major candidate since at least 1816,
when he lost out in the caucus to Monroe, was equally confident. The
question suddenly became: Should the caucus be used at all? Was it
the correct nominating instrument at this moment in history?

In any matter involving a potential conflict between viewpoints,
just when it seems that an agreement is about to be achieved, a slight
shift in perception persuades the majority there is a need for a con-
tinuation of the argument. So it was in 1824. The old method—
nominations by congressional caucus—was no longer fashionable; it
would no longer serve; its enemies saw all its weaknesses, and its
friends hung back from its defense in embarrassment over their possible error. The idea of leaving the nomination of the president to a
caucus, no matter how well qualified the members of that gathering
were, became repugnant in that rambunctious democratic society; it
smacked of inequality, at the very least.

Meetings were held throughout the nation to protest the arrogation
of power by Congress. What right, orators demanded, did congressmen have to interject themselves between the people and their presidents? There was no reference in the Constitution to a congressional
caucus. The protestors insisted the caucus had reduced the Constitution to a meaningless piece of paper; it was, they claimed, as though a
band of powerful men had taken advantage of their position to seize
the state.

Indisputably, the Constitution placed the power to select presidents
in the hands of the Electoral College. The members of that college
were to be picked within each state, and there was no suggestion at the
Constitutional Convention that the Electors should accept congressional advice. Even more distant was the possibility that the Electors'
ability to select would be limited to those names put forward in
Washington by an extralegal gathering of congressional leaders.

Resolutions passed in Ohio in 1823 reflected the mood of the
country. "The time has now arrived when the machinations of the *few*
to dictate to the *many*, however indirectly applied, will be met with
becoming firmness, by a people jealous of their rights. . . . The only
unexceptional source from which nominations can proceed is the

people themselves. To them belongs the right of choosing; and they alone can with propriety take any previous steps."[3]

The people, according to these democratic theorists, were to meet in public gatherings, at local conventions, at mass meetings, and express their preference. Word of their action would then be communicated to others of similar sentiments in other states. In this manner, citizens would inform to the various legislatures whom they preferred as Electors.

The absence of a caucus in 1820 helped undermine the institution in 1824. At Crawford's insistence, a call, nevertheless, went out. As the February 24 meeting approached it became clear that only Crawford favored the gathering; he had the strongest organization. The modesty of this distinction is revealed by the fact that invitations had been sent to 216 congressmen, but only 68 attended. Crawford received their almost unanimous vote; however, the vote carried no authority. It actually had a negative impact, since it showed the limits of his strength even within his supposed citadel. The caucus was now discredited.

Within days a debate over the caucus system had begun in the Senate. There were blasts against the "new, extraordinary, self-created central power, stronger than that of the Constitution."[4]

Two themes run through the denunciations: The congressional caucus was taking over a power granted to the states; and it was undemocratic. "It is an encroachment on the sovereignty of the people," one critic said, "the more alarming inasmuch as it is exercised in the corrupt atmosphere of executive patronage and influence. Make me President, and I will make you a Minister, or Secretary, or, at all events, I will provide you with a good berth. . . ."[5]

The debate went on for three days. When it was finished "King Caucus" was dead, but what would replace it was only dimly foreseen. Its shape began to take form during the campaign of 1824. Each candidate had to woo the Electors, who in six states were still selected exclusively by the legislature.

New York was the largest of these states; at the same time, it was the most politically organized and most corruptly managed. Martin Van Buren, who had been elected to the Senate in 1821, was the leader. Cautious, manipulative Van Buren had more than a decade of experience in statewide political organization. In 1822, determined to widen his horizons, he travelled South. His purpose was to reestablish the old Republican alliance between the New York and Virginia machines; he wanted a return to the grand old days of Burr and Madison.

Van Buren had originally committed himself to South Carolina's John Calhoun, but his travels convinced him Georgia's Crawford was the stronger candidate, and so he switched his allegiance. At the same time, he let it be known that he was determined to revive the congressional caucus. In effect, he committed the politician's unpardonable sin: He placed his money on two losing horses; he was backing the wrong candidate and the wrong institution. He even lost New York, where after a battle in the legislature with DeWitt Clinton and his People's party, a majority of the state's Electors lined up behind Adams.

In the meanwhile, other states were embroiled in more democratic contests. There were large gatherings of men who voted their commitment to one or another candidate; informal conclaves of legislators met outside the capitol chambers to discuss their preference; finally, there were county and state conventions, composed entirely of delegates elected from localities.

This was, perhaps, the most chaotic election in American history. As the months passed, the individual contests for places in the Electoral College proceeded at a hobbled pace. Each state voted at a time most convenient to its taste. It slowly became apparent that none of the leading contenders was fashioning a majority. When the Electoral College met, Jackson received 99 votes, Adams 84, with the remaining Electors preferring first Crawford, and lastly Clay; Jackson had not achieved a majority; the presidential election was once more to be decided, as in 1800, in the House of Representatives. Since there were twenty-four states, each possessing, in this crucial matter, only one vote, the fate of the candidates depended on the House leaders who could produce the votes of thirteen states.

Clay, with the lowest Electoral count, was eliminated even before the matter was presented to the House, since the Constitution specified that in such a deadlock only the names of the top three candidates could be considered. In January 1825, one month before the House assembled, Clay threw his weight behind Adams. Daniel Webster, then the last representative of the old New England Federalists, also struck a bargain with Adams: Should Adams be elected with Webster's support, he would lift the ban against appointment of Federalists, which had been in force since the Hartford convention.

Although Adams was the best-qualified candidate and his victory should have brought forth a sigh of relief from each patriot, just the opposite occurred. Jackson, who had started with so few expectations, finished by agreeing with his managers that he had been swindled out of the presidency. Indisputably, in the eighteen states where Electors were chosen by popular vote, he had accumulated 155,872 ballots. His opponents' totals were: Adams, 105,321; Clay, 46,587; Crawford, 44,282.

Pausing long enough only to vote against Clay's nomination as secretary of state, Jackson resigned from the Senate and returned to his Tennessee home to lick his wounds and plan retribution.

A passion for the wounded warrior arose in the country. Van Buren, who was tied to the sick, defeated Crawford, was now convinced Jackson was the rising star. New York's serpentine politics, however, would not allow him to act on this knowledge. Jackson, always loyal to his supporters, considered DeWitt Clinton his leader in the Empire State and did little to encourage Van Buren, whose wirepulling propensities were well recognized by his contemporaries.[6] It took Van Buren years of hard work and maneuvering to overcome Jackson's suspicions.

His first stratagem was to represent himself as the leader of the forces opposed to President Adams. He took every opportunity to publicly castigate the Adams-Clay cabal. He also cultivated his friend, John Calhoun, whom he saw as a possible intermediary with Jackson.

By June 1826, Calhoun, depressed over his own presidential prospects, had aligned himself with Jackson. The main thought of this dour, opinionated, philosophical Southerner was that aging Jackson would be lucky to survive four years in office.[7] He could postpone his hopes for that long, if, as Jackson's vice-president, it became apparent to all that he would be his successor.

Van Buren expressed approval of Calhoun's approach and began holding conferences with him and other Jackson men, smiling broadly and waiting anxiously for some gesture. On January 13, 1827, in an attempt to win Jackson's favor, he wrote a letter to newspaper editor Thomas Ritchie, member of the Richmond Junto. The Junto was a group of Virginians who considered themselves old-fashioned

Jeffersonians, not yet completely in the camp of Jackson. In his letter Van Buren called for an alliance of "planters of the South and the plain Republicans of the North," all of which would be arranged at a national convention.

Jackson was now, at least, privately passing assurance to him and Ritchie that he was even more for decentralization and local responsibility than Jefferson had been; it was enough encouragement to drive Van Buren on to greater efforts. As was so often true of the New Yorker, he was gambling out of desperation.

Jackson, however, still maintained his tie with Clinton. "The Old Ditchdigger" had finally completed the Erie Canal, a work begun in 1816, which was responsible for the development of New York City as the port of the West. He had once again captured the governorship and was blocking Van Buren's hopes at every turn.

Things began to look up for Van Buren in February 1827, when he was reelected to the Senate. The freedom that such a success brings to a politician is experienced by no other practitioner of that craft in America: For several years, at the beginning of his six-year term, he may relax, or cultivate other interests, while his constituents (in this case the legislators of New York) are in no position to affect his tenure. The framers of the Constitution provided this safe berth deliberately, hoping it would inspire independence of action and reflective thought. Occasionally it has.

Within six months Van Buren was sending out feelers to Jackson in the hope that a final reconciliation might be effected. In September 1827, Jackson let Van Buren know he still considered Clinton his New York friend. Nevertheless, that winter Van Buren took the lead, in Congress, in forming a Jackson majority caucus. He worked indefatigably on Jackson's behalf organizing Committees of Correspondence throughout the nation.[8] At this point, fate intervened to strengthen his hand. On February 11, 1828, Clinton died, removing from Van Buren's path the last obstacle to a partnership with Jackson.

Van Buren had several factors working in his favor beyond the indisputable popularity of his war hero. Perhaps they can all be summed up in Nathaniel Macon's statement that the politicians of the 1820s had become primarily motivated by "love of a snug office."[9]

Van Buren was willing to extend himself in pursuit of their passion. He understood that a new climate had developed in America.

Government jobs, which had always been the goal of a handful of political activists, had been relatively scarce during the first three decades of the country's history. During that time these plunderers had been edged away from the patronage trough by elitists with ties to the Revolution. Now that these relics were dying off, and the number of jobs was expanding with the expanding country, new, undreamed-of opportunities for boodle were presented to charming schemers like Van Buren. But before the boodle could be divvied up, it was essential to elect a pliant president.

To accomplish this, Van Buren and his clique mounted a vicious attack on Adams, whom he pictured as a haughty aristocrat, scornful of popular opinion. He maintained that when Adams had been elected by the House of Representatives the will of the people had been subverted.

M. Ostrogorski, in his classic *Democracy and the Party System in the United States,* described the effect of Van Buren's campaign: "These charges aroused in honest and simple souls a profound indignation, a regular exasperation against the enemies of the people. These enemies were all the men of intelligence, of culture, of wealth, of social refinement."[10]

And opposing these effete snobs was a man of genuine substance: a war hero, a backwoods egalitarian, a dedicated Jeffersonian whose personal integrity was never successfully challenged. "Old Hickory" clubs sprang up all over the country; parades were held to advertise his virtues. As the 1828 election approached, his supporters were so enthusiastic, so well organized, and so uniform in their opinion, that there was no need, or thought, of a nominating caucus.

Adams' problem was not as easily solved. For four years, despite his natural ability,[11] he had been so ruthlessly attacked, and so effectively hamstrung in Congress, that his performance as president had been disappointing. Nevertheless, when the Massachusetts legislature voted to endorse him in February 1828, several other state legislatures and conventions followed suit.

Predictably, Kentuckian Clay once again fancied himself in the White House. He was attractive, irresponsible, a born plunger, but at the same time a thrilling orator with a beautifully musical voice—a beloved figure in his day, but very little trusted.[12]

Adams, who spent the remainder of his long life sitting in constructive judgment of his contemporaries in the Congress, considered Clay with disdain. "His school has been the world, and in that he is a proficient. His morals, public and private, are loose, but he has all the virtues indispensable to a popular man."[13] Adams was the candidate of New England and the old Federalist strongholds, and men such as Clay and Jackson clearly aroused his patrician prejudices.

Jackson, however, was looking for support in other, less discriminating quarters; and he found it. He won decisively; the popular vote was: Jackson 647,231, Adams 509,097. In the Electoral College Jackson's margin was even greater, 178 to 83.[14]

Jackson's victory had been accomplished without the help of any national party; no such group existed. A national committee representing the interests of each candidate had been set up in the capital to write broadsides and correspond with local committees throughout the country. These committees, however, were not united under one party name. On election day the voters wrote the name of the man they favored on a slip and dropped their ballot into a box. And, in fact, the election results were most often printed merely with the names of the candidates.

The nation had elected its seventh president without the aid of national political parties, and there seemed to be no demonstrable need for any. Presidents were being nominated and elected without them. Events had shaped the electoral process in an intriguing fashion. By 1828 Adams and Jackson were the logical candidates. As a result, those interested in politics throughout the country had raised their voices on behalf of one or the other.

But a subtle change had again occurred. Whereas the Electors of the first five presidents had largely dispersed to their local communities after accomplishing their lofty objective, Jackson's supporters quickly revealed they had an additional, debased objective. They descended upon Washington to claim their reward, and found in their charismatic leader a man willing to appease their appetites.[15]

This philosophy was described by Van Buren's chief ally in New York State, Senator William L. Marcy. In a response to Clay's 1833 allegation that Van Buren had introduced New York's spoils system into national politics, he frankly conceded the justice of Clay's accusation:

"It may be, sir, that the politicians of New York are not so fastidious as some gentlemen are, as to disclosing the principles on which they act. They boldly *preach* what they *practice*. When they are contending for *victory*," he told the senatorial audience, "they avow their intention of enjoying the fruits of it. If they are defeated, they expect to retire from office. If they are successful, they claim, as a matter of right, the advantages of success. They see nothing wrong in the rule that to the VICTOR belongs the spoils of the ENEMY."[16]

Van Buren had an opportunity to press this battlefield view of politics into practice. In a burst of gratitude, Jackson no sooner reached Washington, on February 11, 1829, than he appointed him secretary of state, a warning to Vice-President Calhoun that his old wirepulling ally was now his rival for the presidency.

Van Buren moved to capitalize on his advantage. A lonely Jackson had lost his wife the previous year. In addition to being desolate, he was bitter. He believed her death had been hastened by the cruelty of snobs who had advertised their contempt for her backwoods manners. The new secretary of state, likewise a widower, became the president's companion, accompanying him on daily horseback rides. During periods of inactivity they found the subject of appointments a congenial topic. Jackson, always a fierce contender, could not be magnanimous in victory; instead he was unforgiving and unrelenting. He wanted his enemies punished! Van Buren's spoilsman's approach to politics fit in perfectly with this cast of mind. For, once a Jackson enemy was dispatched, his place could be taken by a Van Buren crony.

Jackson announced in his first presidential message that "the rotation [of civil servants, appointed by previous administrations, out of their jobs] constituted a first principle in the Republican creed."[17] In his first eighteen months as president, Jackson replaced 919 of approximately 10,000 federal officeholders.

This discharge of men merely because they did not share his opinion of himself may seem a minor form of vanity. In reality it was the basis for caudillo politics and a fundamental threat to democratic society.[18]

It was during Jackson's administration that the level of political morality, which had been so high for the first years of the Republic, began to sink. His role in that decline should be reappraised. The inclination on the part of liberal historians has been to misread his impact. The label "Jacksonian democracy" has tended to conceal the destructive aspects of some of the General's democratically proclaimed, but basically undemocratic, programs.

It is true that during the span of his prominence property qualifications for voting were largely eliminated. However, the widening of the franchise had been going on from the moment the country was founded. By 1812, six states had eliminated property qualifications for voting. One has only to compare the popular vote in 1824 (350,062) with that in 1828 (1,156,328)[19] to detect the strong movement toward universal, white, manhood suffrage, even before Jackson was inaugurated.

Although General Jackson was reputed to be a genuine democrat, he was a slaveholder. Rationalizations may be found for this in terms of the mores of that pre-emancipation era; the fact nevertheless remains that Jackson and his supporters did not find it difficult to live with slavery and had no intention of working for its abolition.

In his *Age of Jackson* Professor Schlesinger offers another explanation for the General's approach to what many Americans, even then, considered a moral issue—human slavery. "The Jacksonians in the thirties were bitterly critical of abolitionists. The outcry against slavery, they felt, distracted attention from the vital economic questions of Bank and currency, while at the same time it menaced the Southern alliance so necessary for the success of the reform program."[20]

Jackson's opponent was not similarly reticent about opposing that evil. As early as 1820 John Quincy Adams decried slavery as "the great and foul stain upon the North American Union."[21]

Part of the weakness in Jackson's viewpoint was his partiality for states' rights. It was a weakness which he inherited from Jefferson and passed on to generations of conservative legalists. It was easier to defend slavery if you attributed some extraordinary value to state governments. For Jackson, the decentralization concept was vital: if Southern states wanted to continue their "particular institution" then his own defense of states' rights placed that issue beyond discussion.

All of this was tied to his Jeffersonian commitment to a strict constitutional interpretation. If the Constitution did not specifically grant a power to the federal government, then it could not be exercised by his administration. One shudders to think of how modern government would have functioned should Jackson's dedication to this totem have continued in the ascendancy. It would have been impossible to regulate railroads, telephones, or power companies, since there was no reference to them in the Constitution.

The concept of "the evil of government" underlay much of Jackson's thinking. The average man had to protect himself against the encroachments of a government too easily controlled by aristocrats of wealth and power. While proselytizing for the farmer and the skilled worker against the corruptness of the banker and the boss, his proposals worked against the best interests of his friends as well as against his enemies.

He was unyielding in his opposition to industrialization, which held out the promise for a better life. His hatred for the Bank of the United States, which Federalist Alexander Hamilton had created, and a generalized hatred for all banks, led him to an absurd position on paper money. This primitive prejudice complicated America's politics for one hundred years, frequently threatened the destruction of commerce, and often resulted in depressions.

An expanding country, sorely in need of credit, found in Jackson's misunderstanding of economics a threat to its development. His opposition to paper money meant that trade had to be slowed down until enough metal could be dug up to physically enable business agreements to be concluded. The symbolic nature of money, true even for hard, tangible gold, had eluded him.

His determination to destroy the central bank—instead of molding a national bank into a more effective commercial instrument, which at the same time would be more concerned with the financial needs of the poor and the middle class—could make sense only to a wilderness child brought up to sleep on his assets. His decision to withdraw United States deposits from Nicholas Biddle's Bank and distribute it to "pet" banks around the country weakened the fiscal integrity of the government and was the direct cause of the Panic of 1837, to that time America's most serious economic crisis.

Yet that great molder of the party system, Martin Van Buren, looking back at his hero's life from the vantage point of the late 1850s, concluded that his fight against the Bank was the most lasting monument to his wisdom, and the major justification for the existence of the Democratic party. In his *Inquiry Into the Origin and Course of Political Parties in the United States,* Van Buren rhapsodized over a policy which now, at best, seems wrongheaded, and which was, even

as the aging Democrat wrote, helping to bring on the cataclysm of the
Civil War:

"Who can call to mind without amazement the extent to which the
impression was fastened on the public judgment that a national bank
was of vital necessity to the healthful action of the Federal Government . . . and now see that all this was sheer delusion . . . without
applauding the true conservatism and patriotic spirit of the Democratic party during a forty years' struggle to expel from our system so
dangerous an abuse, or without rejoicing that that great object was
finally achieved and blessing the memory of the brave old man to
whom the achievement is mainly to be credited."[22]

Jackson's extraordinary success as a candidate further reenforced
the political doctrine so often followed after his time by bankrupt
parties: Even the most disreputable political organization could win
with a military hero. Within the space of four years, bumbling,
doddering William Henry Harrison, the "hero" of Tippecanoe, was
being used to dazzle the electorate. Taylor, Frémont, McClellan,
Admiral Dewey, Leonard Wood, MacArthur, and Eisenhower were
just down the road, easily convinced by Jackson's example that practicing to storm a hill and kill men was sufficient preparation for
guiding their nation's destiny.

Weakening the concept of the honorable service-presidency was
Jackson's devastating view of the new political morality. His subscription to the dictum "To the victor belong the spoils" endorsed a
philosophy of government completely abhorrent to the nation's
founders; they did not view election to office as a mandate to plunder.

Few actual jobs were involved, and Jackson's notion of patronage
was not what it was to become under the refined sophistication of
subsequent practitioners. He had nevertheless breached the fragile
wall of benign motivation, which had partially sheltered the people
from the powers available to their anointed leaders. Civil servants
were no longer entitled to their jobs simply because of satisfactory
performance; they now had to "know someone." Jackson's appeal
was essentially to the lowest possible denominator. He weakened the
concept of service for social benefit and replaced it with the more
traditional allure of the *quid pro quo:* "I'll scratch your back if you'll
scratch mine."

The elderly Franklin had uttered a warning which might better have been taken to heart by Jackson. "I am apprehensive therefore... that the Government of these States, may in future times, end in a Monarchy. But this Catastrophe I think may be long delayed, if in our proposed system we do not sow the seeds of contention, faction & tumult, by making our posts of honor, places of profit."[23]

Andrew Jackson, determined as his six predecessors to serve honorably, changed the direction of American politics. During his administration national posts of honor became opportunities for profit. In the process he laid the foundation for the construction of national political parties, since the only encouragement needed by local hacks to raise their sights above the ward level, where city clubhouse organizations had been turning over stones for many years, was a glittering federal prize offered by a grateful president. General Jackson understood that the troops are encouraged by a share of the plunder. No president before his time so boldly defended that raw technique for apportioning important jobs in the federal government, and, in the process developing a loyal, if inadequate, corps of mercenaries.

Merit and ability were no longer as important as ambition and gall. The reach must exceed the grasp. The vehicle which transported this greed from fantasy to reality was the party system. With its deals, secret agreements, payoffs, and relatively unexceptional leaders, it was the perfect instrument to maximize the corrupt impulses present in most men. Instead of seeking political checks on man's worst traits, Jackson, by holding out the prospects of profit, was stimulating the excesses of depravity which had not yet made their appearance but were soon to become the hallmark of national political parties.

4

National Parties Appear on the Horizon

If we wish to preserve what we are accustomed to call liberty, the first necessity is to clear our minds of cant, to look at the modern party system as it is and above all, accept the fact that it is new, that it must be studied in its own terms, not in terms of nostalgia for the past.

D. W. Brogan[1]

Andrew Jackson, bolstered by the Iago talents of Martin Van Buren, was the founder of the modern national Democratic party. With some difficulty, that party can be traced back to Jefferson. Democrats are regularly reminded of this genesis by political bosses at Jefferson-Jackson Day dinners, where their main hope seems to be that their captive guests will not notice the change in the quality of leadership, or, at least, will be too polite to comment.

The party of Jefferson and Jackson has always advertised itself as the people's party. Its leaders have aimed at associating it in the public's mind with the aspirations of the least affluent citizens. Although after the 1830s this was a fundamental fraud, primarily a public relations gimmick, there was enough truth in this claim to allow the leaders of that party to repeat it *ad nauseam*.

The astute Alexis de Tocqueville, in his classical study of the 1830s, *Democracy in America,* supported this class theory of the New World's party politics.

"The deeper we penetrate into the inmost thought of these parties," the French visitor said, "the more we perceive that the object of the one (the Federalists' party) is to limit and that of the other (the Republicans) to extend the authority of the people. I do not assert that the

43

ostensible purpose or even the secret aim of American parties is to promote the rule of aristocracy or democracy in the country; but I affirm that aristocratic or democratic passions may easily be detected at the bottom of all parties, and that, although they escape a superficial observation, they are the main point and soul of every faction in the United States.''[2]

The distinction was clearer at that point than it was almost ever to be again. Since then, in a situation where the average citizen was given a choice between believing either that the Democrats or the Federalists/Whigs/Republicans represented his interests, most of the time it was far easier to be deceived by men claiming to be democrats.

The Federalists, who by the 1830s were increasingly being called Whigs, clearly always represented the powerful, the moneyed, and the pretentious. A workingman needed an ox-like mind to consider them his friends.

On the other hand, the early national leaders of Jefferson's and Jackson's party were always asserting their lack of responsibility for improving the average person's life. They wanted his vote, but they urged him to seek redress for his problems in his local community. In effect, this was a formula for inaction. The local community, as in the case of any fragmented governmental unit, was under the control of the local magnate. The largest landowner was in alliance with his fellow squires. Or the one man who owned a factory was in alliance with merchants and landlords. They were always in a position to overwhelm the isolated, ignorant laborer. To tell this unfortunate he must fend for himself in that den of wolves, because there was a Jeffersonian principle about the best government being the one which governs least, was to condemn him to perpetual anguish in that anarchistic state in which man had always lived.

In any society there are conflicting interests. The just society is the one in which those interests are fairly balanced to the benefit of the largest number, while at the same time minorities are not abused. Such a thought had not gained the currency it now has, during the party-forming period of the 1830s. Many people thought, in Calvinist style, that each man got what he was destined to get. Others, without need to rationalize their greed, simply took as much as they could seize. It was unfortunate that national political parties were being organized during such a period of laissez-faire morality; for it is that fundamental note of irresponsible callousness which became the hallmark of the two-party system. In fact, such a period of moral indifference was doubtless essential for the development of a party system, since the atmosphere of purer times would not have nourished such a creature.

Van Buren commented on this characteristic of his creation. He spoke of "the inducement, always so strong with political parties, to avail themselves of every opportunity that presents or seems to present itself to *'commend the poison chalice'* to the lips of their opponents— a temptation they find it hard to resist, however much their own hands or consciences may have to be soiled in the operation."[3]

With the ruin of the congressional caucus in 1824, it was necessary to devise a method of replacing it as a presidential-nominating instrument. Some method of picking candidates was essential. How could a mass of voters, isolated as they were from each other, possibly select a president unless some technique was devised to narrow their choice to manageable proportions?

The state legislative caucuses might have provided the answer. For decades they had been nominating candidates for the Senate and for statewide offices. By 1828, in many states, they had taken on the additional responsibility of selecting a list of presidential Electors, pledged to a candidate of their choice, Adams or Jackson.

However, the legislative caucus had changed under the democratizing pressures of the 1820s. As in the case of the congressional caucus, the pure legislative caucus (composed exclusively of elected members of the legislature) had met with general disapproval and had largely disappeared. Voters from districts which had not sent a legislator of their persuasion to the state capitol resented the idea that only those voters from districts which had were represented at the party caucus. More important, clubhouse leaders who had not elected their candidate did not appreciate the fact that they had no representative in the legislative caucus.

To meet their objection, a new institution was developed. It was a modification of the mixed legislative caucus, in reality a state convention system. Those districts in which voters had not elected a representative of their persuasion were able to hold a local convention which would choose a delegate to the state legislative caucus/convention. This was nomination in the old fashion, with a slight new wrinkle: It had the appearance of a more democratic institution than the legislative caucus.

Local politicians quickly discovered, however, that most voters were not interested in county and state conventions, which left these centers of power completely in their hands.[4] The old propertied elite, which had held control over the franchise for much of the first thirty years of the Republic, and always found time to take its political role seriously, had been overwhelmed by the sheer number of newly enfranchised city voters. Most of them were too occupied with making a living to concern themselves with politics. This group was more easily led by the clubhouse manipulator than the self-made, self-confident property owner, whose monopoly on the vote had previously been a deterrent to the sleazy operator.

The nominating technique used in the 1828 election was chaotic but seems to have sufficed. Although it was disoriented and rambling, Adams and Jackson finally *were* thrust into a confrontation by its inexorable process. Voters on election day understood, as they approached the ballot box, that they were to deposit their votes for the advocates of either Jackson or Adams. The Electors chosen by rival legislative caucus/conventions were adherents of either of those two contenders. Most often voters approached the ballot box with lists of Electors who supported their hero. These lists were published in newspapers, or distributed on handbills. As was to be expected, men of energy were ready to take advantage of this amorphous tangle and try to fashion it for their own use.

The Anti-Masons, a party which had formed in the backwoods of New York in 1826, dedicated to the proposition that the world must be freed from the menace of the fraternal order of Masons, inadvertently pointed the way to a new nominating technique.

In September 1831, they met in Baltimore in the first important national convention.[5] The Federalists had surreptitiously conducted something like a convention/conference in 1808 and 1812, when their representation in Congress was so low that any attempt to caucus would have left the chamber almost empty. The Anti-Masons, although a somewhat outlandish clique, demonstrated that a convention could attract the attention of the nation.

A boisterous public gathering conveyed the idea that a large number of people were delivering a democratic judgment as to who should be the party nominee. This was a more refreshing image than that possessed by the congressional caucus. The congressional gathering consisted of men of *influence,* who looked down their noses at the people. The gathering in Baltimore was an assemblage of the people.

Henry Clay, once again ready for the grind, prepared to challenge Jackson. Determined to make his best effort, he organized the National Republican party as the vehicle for his ambitions. As the year 1831 rolled along, various state legislative caucuses and public gatherings passed resolutions proposing him as their candidate.

When the Maryland legislature urged the National Republicans to hold a convention in Baltimore, fashioned after the one held by the Anti-Masons, Clay found the idea attractive. He was going to need every innovation conceivable to defeat the popular incumbent.

A call was sent out for a convention to be held from December 12 to December 16.[6] Delegates were chosen on the basis of state congressional representation; those states with larger populations had the larger delegations. One hundred and fifty-six delegates from eighteen states and the District of Columbia attended. This was the first major party convention.

Clay was unanimously nominated. The convention set up campaign committees in each state, although six Southern states had not bothered to send delegates to Baltimore and the effort for Clay within those states was minimal. In New England Committees of Correspondence sprang up in almost every county.

At the same time, Jackson's men were maneuvering to again frustrate Clay. In March 1830, Jacksonians in Pennsylvania caucused and proposed his name for a second term. In effect this was a request, from an informal group, that he run. The next month a caucus of his supporters in Albany endorsed Pennsylvania's initiative. New Hampshire followed in June. During the winter, legislative caucuses in Alabama and Illinois got on Jackson's bandwagon.

On January 22, 1831, eleven months before the National Republican's convention, Jackson had announced that if called upon he would run. A second Pennsylvania caucus responded to the hint and Jackson, acting out his role in the scenario, issued a letter of acceptance.[7]

The one remaining question for Jackson was how to rid himself of his vice-president, John C. Calhoun. There had been a dramatic confrontation between the two on the South Carolina nullification issue, at an April 13, 1830, Jefferson birthday party. Calhoun proposed a toast suggesting Carolina's right to secede from the Union, which enraged Jackson and ended any possibility of reconciliation.

Even more condemning to Jackson was the evidence, leaked to him by Calhoun's enemy, the still-paralyzed, vengeful Crawford, about the Carolinian's attitude toward Jackson during his 1818 Florida foray.

At that time, Jackson, at the head of a military force, had pursued a number of marauding Seminole Indians into Spanish Florida. Along the way he had seized the Spanish forts at Pensacola and St. Marks, pausing only to hang two British citizens who (he concluded) had furnished supplies to the Indians.[8]

The Spanish government was then absorbed in abortive attempts to quell rebellions in its South American colonies. Although Jackson's raid into Florida was unauthorized, it convinced the distracted Spanish that they could not resist the aggressive instincts of the United States to fill out its Southeastern border. This led to American acquisition of Florida the following year. Nevertheless, Jackson's bold action met with less than universal approval. Monroe's cabinet, in which Crawford served as Treasury Secretary, had secretly debated censuring him. Calhoun had gone further, demanding his arrest and trial.

Jackson never forgave those who deserted him on this issue. It seemed clear to him that in this case anyone who could object to the killing of a few Indians and a couple of friends of George III, while being oversensitive to his invasion of a country with whom the United States was at peace, must be acting solely out of hostility to him. But until 1830 Calhoun's betrayal had not been exposed. An exchange of letters between the two on the subject of the Florida expedition left Jackson convinced that the flinty Calhoun must be expunged from the ticket and replaced by his good friend, the loyal Van Buren.

In pursuit of this patriotic objective, Jackson arranged to have the New Hampshire legislative caucus issue a call for a convention in Baltimore in May 1832. It was six months after Clay's confederates had once again demonstrated the convenience and manipulative possibilities of such a national gathering. By the time the convention assembled, the new party was commonly referred to as the Democratic-Republicans, a method of differentiating it from Clay's National Republicans.

Each state was entitled to as many delegates as it had Electors. The sole purpose of the first Democratic demiconvention was to dump Calhoun. Jackson would have been the Democratic presidential candidate even if no convention were held. It was, in reality, a vice-presidential convention. Van Buren's nomination was accomplished without much difficulty; Jacksonians rallied to him by a margin of 208-75.[9]

Jackson contributed another antidemocratic tradition to American political life at this convention. His managers demanded two rules which narrowed the possibilities of future unbossed conventions.

First, the "unit rule" was adopted: In any state where a majority of the voters had cast their ballots for one faction of the party, all of the delegates in that state were pledged to that candidate. This tended to wipe out insurgency movements. It almost eliminated the possibility that a candidate unpopular with the party leaders might accumulate votes from states in which he had not won a majority, and then overwhelm the choice of the leaders with a huge vote in a handful of states.

The second rule was aimed at the same objective: Two-thirds of the delegates' votes were required for nomination. In this way Van Buren and his coterie of Jackson supporters insured against the possibility that a combination of minority candidates might join together and agree on an anti-Van Buren candidate who might paste together a majority, narrow though it might be.

This papier-mâché convention concluded with the nomination of Van Buren. The delegates departed, not even bothering to take the time to adopt a platform. The president of the convention was authorized to appoint a correspondence committee for each state. With this gesture toward unified organization, national political action took a back seat to action by local activists. This was a period of genuine decentralization—brought about by distance and primitive communications.

Clay's effort to employ a national convention as an instrument with which to defeat Jackson revealed its basic defect as a political tool. It had been widely used during the 1820s on the precinct, district, county, and state levels, partly in an attempt to involve greater numbers of voters in the nominating process. Clay's purpose was different, and at the same time, less sincere. He was merely looking for a publicity technique which would impart to his struggle against

Jackson a levelling quality he obviously needed against the president's tested appeal among the masses. All Jackson had to do to counteract this sham was to stage a sham of equal size.

There was little that aspiring, hardworking, self-advertising Clay could do to advance himself when his opponent was as overwhelmingly popular as Jackson. He had to stuff the ballot boxes or accommodate himself to defeat. Once again Clay was forced to make that accommodation. The popular vote—and all but South Carolina now chose their Electors by popular vote—was 687,502 for Jackson, 530,189 for Clay,[10] and a few thousand for the Anti-Mason candidate, William Wirt who took Vermont's seven electoral votes.

Immediately after the election, the National Republican party, having so poorly served its master, collapsed. Jeffersonianism, states' rights, egalitarianism, a balanced budget, hard money, and the people's party reigned supreme.

De Tocqueville spoke of the political situation as he observed it precisely at that time. "At the present day the more affluent classes of society have no influence in political affairs; and wealth, far from conferring a right, is rather a cause of unpopularity than a means of attaining power. The rich abandon the lists, through unwillingness to contend, and frequently to contend in vain, against the poorer classes of their fellow citizens. As they cannot occupy in public a position equivalent to what they hold in private life, they abandon the former and give themselves up to the latter."[11]

It was becoming clear to the old Federalist gentry that the government of the United States would always belong to their inferiors, unless they developed some strategy for convincing the multitude that it was best to leave their destiny in the hands of their betters.

The first step in that direction, although it did not look promising, lay in the building of a new political party, the Whigs.

The South Carolinian defenders of nullification had called themselves Whigs as early as 1832. By 1834 the name had become widely used to designate the opponents of Jackson. They were unable, however, to decide on one candidate to oppose Jackson's choice in the 1836 election, Van Buren.

As the election approached it became apparent the Whigs had no focus to their campaign. As a result of numerous meetings, several candidates were in the field whose appeal did not extend beyond their section of the country. Clay quickly let it be known he was not available. On the other hand, Daniel Webster was ready and Calhoun was willing.

In the South, Tennessee's Senator Hugh L. White, a disaffected Jacksonite, had his candidacy launched in December 1834 by a majority vote of the Tennessee congressional delegation. The legislature of Alabama lent strength to his campaign when it nominated him.

By 1835 it had become evident that the Whigs, although winning occasional contests for governorships and a good number of congressional seats, were not in any sense a national party. They were so disorganized that a call for a national convention was not issued.

An attempt was made to unite around the aging figure of General William Henry Harrison. Harrison had left his mark on American history twenty-five years earlier, when he had fought an indecisive battle against Chief Tecumseh near the Tippecanoe River in the Indiana Territory. When Harrison rode off the battlefield, he was filled with doubts about its outcome, and was surprised to learn later that Tecumseh's warriors were in retreat. Nevertheless, myths of invincibility may grow from small seeds, and Harrison's reputation as a frontier hero grew as witnesses to the battle died off.

A Pennsylvania newspaper first suggested Harrison might be able to defeat Van Buren. He was, after all, a genuine hero, whereas "the wire-puller" from New York was only the protégé of a hero. The bandwagon started rolling with a Pennsylvania convention of Whigs and Anti-Masonites in December, 1835. When, in 1836, Ohio supporters held a similar convention, Clay publicly endorsed Harrison.

Webster tried to head off the Harrison boom by proffering him the second position on a ticket headed by himself. When his most generous offer was rejected, a Massachusetts convention nominated him and New York's Francis Granger.

The field was swarming with Whig candidates. They agreed the most promising strategy was to forgo any attempts at unifying behind anyone. Each of them would run with the expectation that their combined efforts would prevent Van Buren from accumulating a majority in the Electoral College. Once again the election would be focus to their campaign. As a result of numerous meetings, several forced into the House, where they would, at their leisure, decide on which one of them was to be the next president.

The Whig's strategy was born out of desperation. As Jackson's second term was coming to an end, his reputation and influence were at their height. With his help, Van Buren seemed an unbeatable candidate.

Working against this certainty was the fact that Van Buren was basically an unattractive person with none of the attributes, except guile, possessed by successful politicians. He was an arranger, a wheeler-dealer, who aroused in others no emotion more rapidly than suspicion.

In order to head off the possibility that some glittering personality might ride out of the sunrise and sweep the Democrats into his insurgent camp, Van Buren decided to hold a national convention, similar to the one held by the Anti-Masonites and National Republicans four years earlier. Such a convention would be under the tight control of Jackson's lieutenants, and, therefore, Van Buren would emerge from it stamped with the party's imprimatur. It would be difficult for any glamorous party rebel to challenge him for support among Democratic voters after such an official council had crowned him as its designated candidate.

Party leaders in New Jersey cleared the way; they issued a call for a national convention. Van Buren's New York cohorts quickly held a legislative caucus and endorsed Jersey's suggestion. A convention was convened in Baltimore in May 1835, over a year and a half before the election. It was the first time the Democrats had used a national convention to pick a presidential candidate. It was their second consecutive convention assembled solely for the benefit of Martin Van Buren.

Credentials for six hundred delegates were issued. Over half of that total were for gentlemen from Maryland, an exaggerated example of papering the house.[12] Van Buren was nominated without difficulty.

His election was more in doubt. Despite the splintered nature of his opposition, he managed to win only thirty thousand more votes than their combined total. Although Van Buren was running with Jackson's blessing at a time of general prosperity, approximately 1,494,000 people had scattered their votes over the field.

Politicians learned a lesson from this election: an unpopular man could be nominated by a small group at a national convention. Furthermore, running as the standard-bearer of a national party, he took on a strength which he did not personally possess. Although an unpopular, suspect figure had never before won the presidency, Van Buren and his spoilsmen had demonstrated that, with organization, such a victory was possible.

The defeated Whigs had made a deadly error: They had chosen to leave the field open for all contenders. Given the grand opportunity to win against a colorless manipulator, each had gone his own way, independently finding disappointment at the end of his path.

That some sort of nominating apparatus was needed to activate the quadrennial national referendum seemed logical to many. Yet the country was no longer sympathetic to the concept of elite selection implicit in the original Electoral College. Although nomination by newspaper, mass meeting, legislative caucus, mixed local and state conventions, and consensus (which had assumed the nominating power of the congressional caucus) seemed to work, there was something so variegated about it that it gave the appearance of being too disordered, too vague. A concerted attack on it was destined to succeed.

The only question was whether some legal structure could be given to democratic nominating procedures before the politicians fashioned an extralegal procedure more suited to their disreputable purposes. Was it going to be possible to move from the relatively anarchistic nominating process of rural America into a fair, efficient, honest, system suitable for an emerging industrial nation?

5

The Political Party Coup

> *We must never expect to find in a dogma the explanation of the system which it props up. That explanation must be sought for in history. The dogma records but does not explain a supremacy. Therefore, when we hear some one appeal to democratic principle for a justification in suppressing the individual, we have to reflect how firmly must this custom be established, upon what a strong basis of interest must it rest, that it has power so to pervert the ideas of democracy.*
>
> John Jay Chapman[1]

The men organizing the new political structure were determined that it must be responsive only to them. For the first years after the Revolution, power had been held by the rural landed aristocracy and urban property owners. During the 1820s it had seemed to be passing over to a white, male, democratic consensus, but those most interested in politics had detected a flaw in this process which made it easy for them to seize control.

By the 1830s the city voter, now the most numerous of the country's voters, was ignorant and distracted; he hated the immigrants from Ireland and Germany who were making it more difficult to get jobs; he was grimly prejudiced against newly arrived Catholics who he thought took orders only from the Italian pope. Down on his luck, he had the vote, but no time for politics.

The value of the franchise was depreciating even as it was becoming available to more people. The individual voter saw the significance of his ballot fade as multitudes of other voters began to share his formerly more exclusive privilege. The rootless city worker was more interested in moving west to a promising life than bothering his head about exercising his political rights.

On the other hand, the Western farmer was too far out of touch to exercise any political influence. Faced with the need to keep his wife and himself from losing their balance in the loneliness of the prairies and with the ultimate necessity of supplying his family with enough food to sustain it, he left politics to those who had time to waste.

Many wealthy and industrious Americans simultaneously lost interest in running for office. This was a vibrant time to be engaged in commerce. The country was opening up. The opportunities for the active and the acquisitive seemed limitless.[2] Adding to their disenchantment was the obvious low esteem with which the average man viewed the status of the rich: disrespect was rampant, distrust was universal. What reason did a sophisticated gentleman, trained to order around his inferiors, have to bow to their wishes, or court their approval?

There was, of course, an element of frustration in this snobbish reaction; Jackson had really driven them out of politics. He had been a ruthless foe, who had pursued them as though they were heathen Indians slinking in the swamps.

In addition, most of them found party politics unsuitable to their disposition and tended to agree with Tocqueville's evaluation of the corruptible nature of democratic government: "In aristocratic governments, those who are placed at the head of affairs are rich men, who are desirous only of power. In democracies, statesmen are poor and have their fortunes to make. The consequence is that in aristocratic states the rulers are rarely accessible to corruption and have little craving for money, while the reverse is the case in democratic nations."[3]

The aristocrats of the 1830s associated themselves with the disparaging attitude the delegates to the Constitutional Convention had displayed toward parties. They saw them as a source of evil and division. This was a view that was to change shortly, but at this time, so close to the establishment of the Republic, the warnings of Washington and Franklin were still vividly recalled.

Jackson had rejected these attitudes years earlier, since he was associated with causes supported by the majority of voters. Why should he repudiate an institution that would allow this majority to organize itself into an irresistible force? He was so embittered toward his personal enemies, and so brilliant in his organizational ability, that he grasped the opportunity to create party machinery, thereby mustering the force needed to overwhelm his opponents. His popularity and determination were instrumental in reversing the traditional Revolutionary abhorrence of political parties.

As soon as he took office, he laid the groundwork for a unified modern national party, which is to say he described the operating mechanism of party patronage. In his first annual message to Congress, on December 8, 1829, he raised the practice of rewarding his political cronies to the level of a democratic dogma. "The duties of all public officers are, or at least admit of being made, so plain and simple that men of intelligence may readily qualify themselves for their performance. . . .

"No individual wrong is . . . done by removal, since neither appointment to nor continuance in office is a matter of right . . . and although individual distress may be sometimes produced, it would, by promoting that rotation which constitutes a leading principle in the republican creed, give healthful action to the system. . . ."[4]

During the eight years of his administration, the American government was despoiled and debased. Petty moilers, who had failed at everything in their localities, saw in Jackson's philosophy a second chance. If all the old General required was loyalty, then they would copiously supply it. Loyalty, after all, is a fairly primitive virtue; members of a street gang are perhaps the most loyal individuals on the face of the earth. In government service, some commitment to ethical standards and a reasonable display of ability must accompany loyalty to a leader. Only then will that personal loyalty be of value to the community.

Jackson did not seem to understand that distinction. As a result, the government was packed with his self-seeking supporters, ready to prove their allegiance in every campaign. Since their jobs depended on the party's success at the polls, the successful performance of their official jobs became a secondary consideration. Much of their time, while theoretically at their desks, was devoted to building the party. As election day approached, efforts on behalf of the taxpayers ceased, as their efforts for the party increased. As a result, a disreputable breed of politicians proliferated.

For a variety of reasons, this kind of individual suited Jackson; his background made him sympathetic to earthy types, while his advanced years and bitterness over real and imagined slights numbed him to the failings of men ready to swear fidelity.

Van Buren, however, had none of these excuses. When he was sworn in as president (March 4, 1837), he understood one fact above all others: He would not be reciting the oath of office if it were not for the party. What Jackson had done partly because of misguided philosophy and pain, Van Buren did mostly because of self-interest.

The simplistic thinking which led Jackson to admire the loyal spoilsman also led him to veto laws that would have aided in the building of road and canal systems linking the West to the East. It had likewise led him to block the development of a rational banking system. He and Van Buren were not enlightened enough to create an efficient monetary system motivated by public service rather than private avarice. They sensed that something was wrong with the newly developing centralized bank, but his response had been to try to get along, as much as possible, without any but the simplest, most localized banking mechanism.

The penalty for this sure prescription for disaster was suffered by Van Buren. Two months after he took office, the economy collapsed. For the next four years the country struggled along in a depression. Prepared superbly for the veiled maneuverings in smoke-filled rooms, Van Buren proved incapable of developing a plan for ending the crisis.

All he could propose was to hold the line against a national bank and paper money, and maintain the Jeffersonian/Jackson line that everything would straighten out if only the government did nothing.

The Whigs profited enormously from this wrongheadedness. In the elections of 1838-39 they almost succeeded in taking control of the House. They were so encouraged by the signs of victory that an absolute panic for it set in.

Clay once again determined to win the nomination. But how was it to be done? The congressional caucus was dead and the Whigs had never held a national convention. Clearly, this was the time to try one.

Clay had seen Jackson twice use a national convention to advance the interests of the unpopular Van Buren. He had confidence in his ability to convene an equally tractable group of state politicians and have them perform an identical ritual. It was a confidence reenforced by his experience in organizing the National Republican convention at the beginning of this Jacksonian decade.

To further his objective, he held a series of caucuses with his congressional supporters during the 1837-38 session. On May 15, 1838, these meetings led to the issuance of a call for a convention in Harrisburg, Pennsylvania, for November 1839. This was Clay territory, an important consideration in those days of poor transportation where many of those in attendance were sure to be local politicians.

But Clay did not have an open field; the ineptness of Van Buren wafted the smell of victory into the nostrils of several prominent Whigs. Even Democrat Calhoun, flirting with Whiggery, was waiting patiently for sympathetic Whigs, who knew his merits, to fall in behind him. Among Clay's other challengers were Daniel Webster, friend of any businessman, who was convinced his time had come; General Winfield Scott, lionized for his skirmishes against the British on the Canadian border in July 1814, who now sought promotion to commander-in-chief; finally, General Harrison, who felt his strong 1838 demonstration of voter appeal entitled him to the nomination.

Clay faced all of them, determined this time that a unified party should present its candidate to the voters, and that the candidate should be himself. The early decision to stage a convention gave Whig organizations throughout the country an opportunity to hold state conventions; delegates to these conventions were picked by county conventions, whose delegates had been selected by local caucuses. Clay emerged from this convoluted process with a distinct advantage, but not with the margin which would have insured his control.[5]

This Whig convention in the heartland of Pennsylvania became the prototype of all future two-party nominating conventions.

It was the first one completely under the domination of *state* political leaders. Although Clay sought to use it for his purposes, as Jackson had used the Democratic conventions, he eventually came to realize he had created a monster with a will of its own.

Two political bosses emerged from this epochal convention; they were Thaddeus Stevens of Pennsylvania and Thurlow Weed of New York. Their dispositions predisposed them to acting out the role of powers behind the throne; however, they had conflicting motivations.

Clubfooted, criminal lawyer Stevens was a man of convictions and an overpowering ability to impress those convictions on men of lesser mettle. He had been an Anti-Masonite at the 1831 Baltimore convention, convinced that that fraternal order was conspiring to take over the government. But his enduring passion concerned his opposition to slavery. He hated injustice, was fiercely idealistic, a gambler and womanizer who never married: he insisted that his code of honor would allow him to sleep with any woman except a virgin. He eventually became the congressional leader of the Radical Republicans after the Civil War and led an impeachment move against Andrew Johnson, primarily because the beleaguered president did not share his determination to punish the defeated South.

Stevens found Clay unsuitable in respect to both of these tenets of his philosophy; he was a Mason and a slaveholder. In this regard Stevens was not a pristine forerunner of future party bosses; he was too *engaged,* too committed to issues. He was essentially an aberrant figure in party politics, a type seldom to be seen in the sweaty backrooms where expediency ruled.

Thurlow Weed was a more recognizable political type. Boss Tweed, Tom Pendergast, Jake Arvey, Carmine DeSapio, Jim Farley, and others of their breed would have found him a congenial companion. It was not entirely accidental that he emerged from the sewer of New York politics, the same sewer in which Burr and Van Buren had nourished themselves. It took decades for politicians in other sections of the country to sink to the level achieved by New York practitioners of that profession in the Republic's earliest years.

Weed, a printer by trade, whose robust, aggressive nature soon made him the owner of the Albany *Evening Journal,* was a man of practical, contentious disposition. He signalled the tone of his personality in an exchange with the editor of a rival paper, the *Argus,* calling him "Martin Van Buren's pimp." Without any apparent fear that he might be sued for libel, the vilified one responded that Weed was a "rapist."[6]

Weed opposed Clay for the simplest of reasons: he did not think he could win. Weed's vision of the model political campaign was not one of a testing of ideas, where men spoke from their hearts about their most enduring aspirations; it was not a search for a superior man who would provide the country with capable leadership. He thought of campaigns as contests where two contending forces fought for victory, which was then translated into jobs to reward those thousands of soldiers who had worked on behalf of the organization. It was Weed's view of the matter that was to prevail in his time and thereafter.

He viewed Clay as an independent man, accomplished in his own right, a man hardly likely to take orders from those who put him in office, a man intent on dominating the new party; in short, a man unsuitable for Weed's purposes.[7]

He preferred some nonentity, who would shine only when a publicity spotlight was turned on him and would disturb no one with well-defined opinions. He was not interested in a candidate whose visage was scarred by innumerable previous battles. Therefore, his candidate was boneheaded General Winfield Scott.

To achieve his aim, he played the game as roughly as it was ever to be played. Clay had been taking the cure for his liver at Saratoga Springs, while he waited for nearby Albany politicians to pay court to him. Instead he received a visit from Weed. It was a bad time for Clay to seek the nomination, the string-puller suggested. For the first time in a presidential campaign the abolitionists were effectively raising a protest against slavery, and he must allow time to cool that incendiary issue; he must step aside and set his eyes on 1844 when Weed would be in his camp. Clay packed his bags and went in search of more sympathetic company.

Weed then set in motion what has come to be known as the "triangular correspondence," no doubt because of its crooked-line approach to its objective. He stirred up his confederates in three parts of the state to write to politicians sympathetic to Clay, urging them to double their efforts for Clay since, in their own districts, little could be done to salvage the cause of the oft-defeated Kentuckian. Deceived in this manner by Clay's seeming supporters, many of those leaning toward Clay, but not wanting to tie their fortunes to a loser, changed their minds. Weed was able to take a delegation to Harrisburg ostensibly committed to Scott, but—more fundamentally—obedient to his direction.

Weed then worked on Webster. He suggested to his managers that since it was hardly likely Webster would be the candidate, it would be more to his interests to fall in with Weed's anti-Clay stratagem. In return for this, Weed pledged to Webster a commanding interest in the Whig administration. Webster, always receptive to a proposition, whether sealed with hard cash or symbols of prestige, withdrew. He was to become secretary of state in the new Whig government.

The delegates assembled in Harrisburg were probably unaware of the historical significance of their activity; they were totally involved in the events of the moment. Nevertheless, they were setting the pattern of future American presidential politics. The mark of that pattern was manipulation at quadrennial national party conventions, by a handful of powerful men, of the mass of distracted delegates. These delegates never understood the grand strategy. They handed up their votes at the correct time, consoled by the knowledge that their jobs would be secure if they behaved themselves. Most of them were officeholders who recognized in their enemies their potential successors.

Weed was instrumental in having the convention adopt a rule that a consulting committee be appointed consisting of three representatives from each state. The committee would meet to exchange views. This ploy closed out most of the delegates even more effectively from direct contact with strategic discussions. After these consultations, the three delegates from each state returned to their companions, who had been amusing themselves with liquor and good company. They gained their attention long enough to vote on their recommendations for either Clay, Scott, or Harrison.

On the first ballot, Clay led his opponents with 103 votes, Harrison had 94, and Scott's rear guard numbered 57, including, most prominently, Weed's muddled militia.

Relentless Stevens now employed a device resorted to frequently in subsequent conventions. He had in his possession a letter written by Scott, which expressed sentiments against slavery. It was never meant for wide circulation. In writing it, Scott's only sincere intention was to win over Stevens and some other antislavery delegates.

Since Stevens' opposition to slavery was genuine, it might be thought he would be most sympathetic to a man willing to take a stand at his side. Stevens, however, was not only an opponent of slavery. He was a politician supporting Harrison.

Of greatest concern to Stevens was the fact that the slave state of Virginia was one of the few in Scott's column. Abolitionist Stevens wanted that slave state on his side! In service of this passion he saw to it that Scott's letter was placed in the hands of the Virginia delegates. The results were predictable. Virginia, opposed from the first to Clay, swung into Harrison's column, and the struggle was over.

Not a moment's thought was given to writing a platform; a statement of principles was bound to offend one or another of the members of this polyglot crew. Besides, the leaders of the party knew what *they* stood for.

Trickery, deceit, and opportunism had won the day. Something extremely important had happened to national politics. The man wanted by the majority of Whig voters was shoved aside. In his place was a doddering relic of battles thirty years in the past—so inadequate that to mention him in the same breath with Washington, Adams, Jefferson, Madison, Monroe, Quincy Adams, or even the spirited Jackson, was to joke.

Daniel Webster, nursing his chronic disappointment over losing his chance to be president, paused on February 16, 1840, to evaluate the impact of parties in a letter to his close political ally, Edward Everett of Massachusetts: "We shall have had bad times, whoever may be in or out. The people have been cajoled and humbugged. All parties have played off so many poor popular contrivances against each other, that I am afraid the public mind has become in a lamentable degree warped from correct principles."[8]

Meanwhile the Democrats were confirming that a new political era had dawned. As it had before, the New Hampshire state convention issued a call for the third national Democratic party convention. It was to meet at the Musical Hall in Baltimore, May 4, 1840, six months after the well-financed Whig gathering.

As in the case of the previous Democratic conventions, Martin Van Buren was the chief beneficiary of its activity; he was renominated by acclamation. His vice-president, Richard M. Johnson, who was married to a mulatto, and therefore an anathema to the Calhoun wing of the party, was not renominated.

In an endeavor to dictate the philosophy of the party, Calhoun insisted on having the convention issue a statement of principles, in effect the first party platform.[9] The nine sections of this pioneer document were largely a restatement of positions taken by Jefferson and Jackson: Democrats were against strong government, no federal money would be spent on building roads, the hated national bank was condemned, rigid economy was espoused, and the protective tariff, which made imported manufactured goods so expensive for the agricultural South, was opposed.

But closest to Calhoun's heart was the plank supporting states' rights; the federal government was enjoined to stay out of "state" matters, such as slavery. Van Buren, always most concerned with winning elections rather than making any other point, was in the process of gaining Calhoun's support for his nomination. If this support could be gained only by turning over the future direction of the party to Southern slaveholders, well, so be it; the platform included most prominently, a blast against abolitionists.

The Whigs moved into the campaign confidently; Van Buren's fumbling leadership gave them the issues, and their affluent backers provided more than adequate financing. This was the first campaign in which vast treasuries were collected and spent.

As part of this flaunting of funds, the Young Men's Whig Convention was bankrolled. It assembled in Baltimore, while the Democrats were in session, for the sole purpose of raining on Van Buren's parade. This was the earliest large scale use of "dirty tricks" to confuse opponents and win elections by surreptitious tactics. Harrison's young men made noise, ridiculed their elders in the Musical Hall, attempted to delay meetings, and in numerous ways set the tone of the filthiest, silliest, and most terrifying presidential campaign yet seen in America.

Since the Whigs could not appeal to working-class voters on primarily economic issues, although these were the issues of greatest concern to them, the bosses of the new party determined to appeal to them on the basis of nonsense, beguiling sound, and captivating color. In this pre-Madison Avenue era, the Whig managers showed an instinctive understanding of image-making, sloganizing, and form over substance.

Horace Greeley, then a young Whig publicist being subsidized by Thurlow Weed, ground out vituperative attacks on Van Buren,[10] picturing him drinking champagne out of crystal goblets in a gaudily decorated White House, while his whiskers reeked of French cologne.

The Democrats were confused and convinced of only one thing: they were probably going to lose. The country was still in an economic doldrum; unemployment was high; their candidate had no power to enchant. Aside from the fact that he was an incumbent, which in this case was an additional liability, Van Buren could hope for victory only if enough confused voters somehow identified him with Jefferson and Jackson.

Sensing defeat early, the Democratic newspapers began to swing wildly. The *Baltimore Republican,* desperate for a telling sally, remarked that Harrison, then sixty-eight, rather than being ready for the White House was ripe for a pension. Furthermore, the *Republican* was sure Harrison would prefer to spend the rest of his time on earth in his log cabin drinking hard cider.

Within days Whig papers were reprinting and elaborating on the sneer. Certainly Harrison was at home in a log cabin, proclaimed Whig editors (many of whom had never been in one), but so were many ordinary Americans. Whig drum-beaters declared that this insult against log cabin dwellers was an insult against all humble Americans. The only way to wipe it out was to vote for Harrison.

The log cabin became the symbol of Whig aspirations. Greeley named his campaign paper after it. Replicas of log cabins were built in town squares across the country, with a coonskin nailed to the door and the latchstring out. Inside, more often than not, was a keg of cider, frequently spiked with whiskey. After a while the revellers would fill the night air with shouting and singing.

> Let Van from his coolers of silver drink wine,
> And lounge on his cushioned settee.
> Our man on his buckeye bench can recline,
> Content with hard cider is he,
> The iron-armed soldier, the true-
> > hearted soldier,
> The gallant old soldier of Tippecanoe![11]

Little log cabins were built and carried in processions. Women wore pins and men badges engraved in the image of Harrison's favorite abode.

Rather than issue a list of their dogmas, the Whigs printed a songbook. The most popular number had a catchy chorus, without a single thought in it except victory; it could be heard in alleyways and taverns across America until election day.

> Tippecanoe and Tyler too:—
> Tippecanoe and Tyler too.
> And with them we'll beat little Van, Van, Van,
> Oh! Van is a used-up man.[12]

A high point in the pageantry came on May 29 and 30, when Harrison, and a bevy of his brewed-up followers, camped out on the Tippecanoe battlefield pursuing Tecumseh's ghost. The obscenity of that gesture was the hallmark of a campaign where not an idea was allowed to intrude.

This was the first party-controlled campaign in American history and clearly the most debased and vicious. After torrents of senseless oratory, hundreds of cavalcades, entertainments, and boozeries, the proof was in that, given the support of an avariciously motivated party organization, enough gold to build Kublai Khan's palace, and the right press agent, an ignorant, decaying relic of worse days could be elected president of the United States.

Harrison's popular margin was fairly narrow: 1,275,017 against 1,128,700. Despite this, he accumulated 234 electoral votes, [13] almost four times Van Buren's total. The Electoral College was clearly not functioning logically: One man, one vote was a doctrine whose day had not yet dawned.

No sooner had the results been announced than a horde of spoilsmen descended on Washington. The capital was inundated with Whigs, seeking to feather their nests, whose campaign chant had only so recently been "Away with the spoilers!"

So great was the crush that the hostelries of Washington were inadequate for the task; clamorous petitioners found sanctuary in the hallways of the White House. There they bedded down on cold floors in the expectation they would be able to settle their accounts with the president as soon as the first rays of dawn poked him from his bed.

Simplicity being his most pronounced characteristic, he would not stand on formalities. Those who sought his presence had only to line up at the door to the Oval Office and wait their turn. The gang which had started "the rotation" was being rotated.

The American government was at one of its historical low points; it was being ruled by a party led by contentious rivals, Clay, Webster, and for a short period, Calhoun. That distracted party, representing the interests of the new rulers of industry, but determined by all means to disguise its prejudices, had elected a pliable soldier, remembered now only as the man who served in that office for the shortest period of time.

Within a month of delivering the Inaugural Address, stitched together for him by Webster, Harrison[14] spoke to his last boodler and galloped off to his celestial Tippecanoe. In such a place his enemies could be easily identified by the colored feathers in their hair.

With his death, the party found itself in the hands of Harrison's vice-president, John Tyler; it quickly discovered the new president's most notable quality was intractability. All Weed's, Stevens', and Webster's scheming had been set aside by divine providence. Tyler had been chosen by them for the vice-presidential nomination only after the position had been offered to three others, none of whom considered himself fool enough to settle for what he deemed so unpromising a prospect. A Jacksonian Democrat whose thin skin was easily pricked, Tyler had come over to the Whigs not out of commitment, but with calculation. Since this was the mortar that bound most men to the party, his opportunism went unnoticed.

Once sworn in, Tyler—a man of ordinary intellect and tunnel vision—determined to clear out those so recently appointed by Harrison. The "party guillotine" was sharpened; the purge of the civil service was swift and bloody. This was followed by open warfare with Clay, who had inaugurated himself as phantom president when Harrison took his oath and now found himself just another Whig in the eyes of the stubborn apostate Democrat sitting in the White House.

When Clay's national-bank bill was vetoed by Tyler with a resounding Jefferson/Jackson denunciation, the Kentuckian signalled for a mass resignation of the cabinet. It was a signal obeyed by all except Webster, who did not want to appear to take orders from his only peer. Within days a caucus was assembled and Clay read Tyler (to whom he referred as "His Accidency")[15] out of the party. Unable to be a kingmaker, Clay had determined to be a regicide.

The Democrats recovered swiftly from their 1840 defeat. The Whigs had demonstrated an incapacity to rule. So obvious was Tyler's failure that an abortive move had been made to impeach him—the first such action against a president.

Van Buren, slavering for retribution, waited confidently for the nomination in 1844. He had, however, underestimated the opposition of other state bosses. His stand against the annexation of Texas had alienated Southern leaders, who wanted the former Mexican territory to enter the Union as a slave state. The master opportunist had allowed himself finally to be defeated on an issue.

His enemies joined, as the convention opened, to pass a rule that the presidential nomination could only be won with a two-thirds total. This had been the same device used by Van Buren to secure the vice-presidential nomination in 1832, but it was the first time the Democrats were to use it in a presidential contest. The motivation was identical both times: to shut the door against a candidate unacceptable to the bosses; then it had been used for Van Buren, now it was employed against him.

On the first ballot he received 151 out of 266 votes. However, the second ballot mournfully trumpeted his eventual defeat; despite his most strenuous exertions, he lost ground. Still he hung on until the seventh ballot, his bitterness growing with each desertion.

James K. Polk, who had been Speaker of the House, and on nobody's list for president, was then placed before the convention. He received only 44 votes, but before the next ballot his supporters buttonholed each delegate. Their man was the perfect candidate, they argued; few people knew him; he was a noncontroversial individual who would offend none, and, no doubt, would be susceptible to suggestions made by those nominating him.

The delegates were convinced, and Polk was nominated. As its last act the convention created a 15-member national committee to bring "an immediate and full organization of the party throughout the Union." It was to function only until election day. Robert J. Walker was the first Democratic national chairman. As head of the National Committee he ran a campaign marked by fraud, especially in New York and Louisiana, where false registration and multiple voting were common.

In this manner, and for these reasons, the next president of the United States was chosen. Historians have labelled him the first "dark horse." In a setting where race-track terminology was increasingly apt, his managers had used the convention to edge out the favorite, Van Buren. Walker had then boxed out Tyler, once again a Democrat, who wanted to run so badly he then arranged his own convention; lack of party support, however, forced the president out of the race.

Polk had once again demonstrated to party bosses that the organization, not the candidate, was all-important. This nonentity had beaten the great Clay, once again the Whig's candidate. It was the day of the party; it did not matter whom the party bosses nominated, only who controlled the organization.

Voters had come to think of themselves as members of a party. It was comforting to be a something: a Democrat or a Whig. The unaffiliated, standing by themselves, had to suffer with the knowledge that they were faceless in a mass of pilgrims without a destination.

It was a comfort—if only a minor one—to accept an identity neatly packaged and so reasonably priced. Party bosses in each of the states were busy giving that reassuring sense of identity to newly arrived immigrants and the rootless failures of older native stock. To be a Democrat and drink the boss's whisky on election day was to be part of the new American adventure.

In reality, the voter, whatever his background, was being permanently shut out of the political process. The creation of tightly organized national parties, controlled by a distant group of anonymous men, who used the new national conventions as their marketplace, spelled the end of the movement toward democracy which had sprouted in the 1820s.

Calhoun had understood the nature of this bloodless political revolution. His suspicion of national conventions had been aroused in 1832, when the first Democratic convention had been called by Jackson specifically to eliminate him as vice-president. In 1844, as his name was about to be presented to the Democratic convention, he published a letter explaining why he would not allow himself to be nominated in that fashion.

"I, acting with General Jackson and most of the leaders of the party at that time," he wrote about the period before national conventions, "contributed to put it [the Congressional Caucus] down. . . . Far, however, was it from my intention in aiding to put that down, to substitute in its place what I regard as a hundred times more objectionable in every point of view. Indeed, if there must be an inter-mediate body between the people and the election, unknown to the Constitution, it may be well questioned whether a better than the old plan of a Congressional caucus can be devised."[16]

The leaders of the party did not find national conventions objectionable from any point of view. They were an ideal instrument, at once giving the appearance of being the ultimate democratic tool, while actually shaped so as to fit perfectly into political palms.

The outspoken abolitionist senator from Missouri, Thomas Hart Benton, at the height of his powers but soon to lose his seat to a proslavery opponent, described the condition of democratic elections in the new era of national conventions:

"The people have no more control over the selection of the man who is to be the President than the subjects of kings have over the birth of the child who is to be their ruler."[17]

The political party system had taken control of the government. By the mid-1840s it had achieved an absolute monopoly of power. It had become a mechanism, on the national level, solely for nominating and electing malleable presidents, and on the state and local level a device for selecting officeholders and distributing patronage. It was not concerned with national objectives, how the government was to be run between elections, or even the quality of the candidates it selected.

Within fifty years of the founding of the Republic, political parties had achieved the status so feared by Ben Franklin; they had become devices for manipulation of government by the "bold and the violent."

6

The Bold and the Violent

We have a country to serve as well as a party to obey.

James K. Polk, in his *Diary*, December 12, 1848[1]

Parties breed a contempt for truth and the public weal; frequently partymen think and act corruptly. Nevertheless the dogma expressed so succinctly in that essential typing exercise, "Now is the time for all good men to come to the aid of their party," holds for the faithful.

This cliché substantially explains why so many Republican politicos came to the defense of Nixon, Mitchell, Stans, and Kleindienst long after most honest citizens were demanding their commitment to the nearest federal prison.

Party conformity is worst in those politicians of the simplest minds and the lowest morality; it is as though, lacking the ability to detect right from wrong, they have elevated party regularity to a higher moral plane than honesty.

The model for this behavior was established between 1830 and the Civil War. Tocqueville spoke sardonically of this period: "I have often heard the probity of public officers questioned: still more frequently have I heard their success attributed to low intrigues and immoral practices. . . . To pillage the public purse and to sell the favors of the state are arts that the meanest villain can understand and hope to practice in his turn."[2]

This tradition of parasitical behavior developed during that party-building era; it resulted in the aversion the public has ever since had toward politicians and the low esteem in which their line of work is generally held.

Tocqueville analyzed part of its sorry genesis. "In a democracy private citizens see a man of their own rank in life who rises from that obscure position in a few years to riches and power; the spectacle excites their surprise and their envy, and they are led to inquire how the person who was yesterday their equal is today their ruler.... They are therefore led, and often rightly, to impute his success mainly to some of his vices; and an odious connection is thus formed between the ideas of turpitude and power, unworthiness and success, utility and dishonor."[3]

During the 1840s it took no special perception to detect the dishonor of politicians. This was a moment for politicians—unfortunately otherwise occupied—to join with the army of issue-oriented citizens fighting to eliminate child abuse, exploitation of workers, inhumanity to the insane, and a hundred other causes then crowding to the surface of a chaotically developing society. Instead, all the pressure for reform came from outside the party system. The abolitionists, the temperance advocates, penal reformers, all of them did their work in isolation from the Weeds and the Websters. Political parties represented the reformer's enemy; allies were to be found in every other camp.

Instead of working for constructive solutions to current problems, the leaders of political parties devoted themselves to the corruption of democratic institutions. It was precisely at this point in the 1840s that parties took the power to select the president out of the hands of the people's representatives and deposited it in the hands of the kingmakers who ran the state organizations.

The device invented for this revolutionary change was the national convention. Prior to 1840 none of the major presidential nominees had been habitually selected by conventions of herding politicians. It took Martin Van Buren to recognize the exquisite possibilities of the new apparatus. Think of it: Political parties represented the only nationwide group ready to mobilize for the election-day ceremonials. What better idea could there be for the operator than to make it almost impossible for anyone not sponsored by a party to have the opportunity of presenting himself to the voters?

If only the state branches of the party could organize themselves, no matter how temporarily, once every four years, to agree on a man who was pliable to their will and homogenized enough to appeal to a majority, they could have the power to determine who would be the country's ruler; and then the final irony, they would be his ruler. All they had to do was to stop committing their state slate of Electors to a candidate before the leaders of the national convention signalled who that candidate should be.

And so, a crucial decision in American political life was made, with little subsequent realization of how dramatically the system had changed. A few leaders, in each major party, had usurped the power to nominate the only two men who were going to be on the quadrennial ballots.

They saw no need to eliminate the Electoral College since, in almost robot fashion the Electors legitimized the results of party-managed mock elections. It could never again, however, pretend to be that assembly of public spirited citizens envisioned by the men who created it.

Likewise shouldered aside were the people's representatives in the state legislatures and Congress. After the 1840s the president of the United States was selected by those least qualified by ability, temperament, and moral rectitude to take part in that awful responsibility.

James Bryce, the perceptive British observer of the American scene before 1900, wrote in *The American Commonwealth,* "The men I have met in America, whose recollections went back to the fourth decade of this century, agreed in saying that there was in those days a more violent and unscrupulous party spirit. . . . Great corporations had scarcely arisen; yet corruption was neither uncommon nor fatal to a politician's reputation."[4]

Although the source of the corruption has varied from time to time, occasionally coming from so many conduits that pinpointing its origin was not easy, its existence was never in doubt; the germinating parties of the 1840s were run by a tireless group of misfits and degenerates.

They were not necessarily the Clays, the Websters, and the Calhouns. They did not ordinarily stand at stage center, delivering public utterances and running for offices. The real leaders of government were ward, county, and state power merchants, who were not offended by the fact their names were to be unheralded in history books.

For these men, politics was not a public service but a method of earning a living. They were usually uninterested in vying for office, often having contempt for the surface appeal possessed by the front men they manipulated. They worked best in the shadows of the backroom.

With great foresight, Elbridge Gerry, Madison's vice-president, described the character of these future kingmakers at the time he was a delegate to the Constitutional Convention. "Men of indigence, ignorance & baseness, spare no pains, however dirty, to carry their point against men who are superior to the artifices practised."[5] Yet these lumps of "indigence, ignorance & baseness" were the decisive factors in the new political system.

James Knox Polk would have no part of them. Upon taking office in March, 1845, he announced that he did not consider himself the party leader, wanted to have nothing to do with the party that had placed him in office, and would not again put himself in the hands of politicians by seeking reelection.[6]

Tyler, wanting more than anything to continue in the White House, had been at their mercy during the previous four years; he had spent those four years scheming of ways to win them over or destroy them. Polk, a man of frail physical resources, but grim determination (his diary is filled with references to his weariness), was concerned only with his ambitious program for national expansion; California and Oregon must become part of the Union. Nothing must stand in the way of that program, not the Mexicans, not the British, least of all, his own ambitions for reelection. He would be a one-term president, but he *would* be president!

Appointment to his cabinet was conditioned on a pledge to abstain from political activity; in fact, each cabinet member, no matter how forcefully his tongue was stuck in his cheek, had to sign a statement disavowing his presidential aspirations.[7] Van Buren's suggestions were ignored, as were Calhoun's. The men at the head of the departments were to be administrators and functionaries; they had a role to perform that had nothing to do with politics. Polk felt he and his appointees were in charge of running a country, of seeing to it that the destiny of millions was protected; he viewed that as an awesome responsibility, a responsibility that few subsequent presidents have taken as seriously.

His administration was largely occupied with the conduct of the Mexican War, which he provoked and managed with relish. The

Democratic party languished, deserted by the president it had selected. Since the national party depended on leadership from the White House to pull it together for its periodic assault on the presidency, Polk's hostility condemned the Democratic organization to rudderless drifting between 1845 and 1849.

Further complicating matters for the Democrats was the newly preeminent position of the South in party affairs. With the adoption, in 1844, of the two-thirds rule for the presidential nomination, philosophic direction of the party passed over to slavery's advocates.

Northern politicians wanted power; they wanted a winning candidate who would distribute jobs to their corporals and sergeants. Southern politicians wanted to buttress slavery against the tide rising for emancipation. Southerners, although no longer a majority at Democratic conventions, always controlled more than a third of the votes. They now had a veto over the nominee. From 1844 until the debacle in the 1860 Charleston secessionist convention, they successfully traded off the presidential nomination for party endorsement of their position. The moral depravity of Northern party politicians was seldom to reach so low a point; faced with the choice between opposing an institution condemned by their social, moral, and religious code, and the sentiments of their constituents, they sold out for a party advantage.

When the Democratic convention assembled at Baltimore's Universalist Church on May 22, 1848, party prospects seemed dim. Van Buren was aging and still angry over his brutal treatment in 1844. Because of a challenge from the conservative "Hunker" wing of the New York organization, inspired by the federal officeholders appointed by Polk who were not beholden to Van Buren, the former president had been denied the honor of leading the largest delegation to the convention. New York sent two sets of delegates but an attempt at compromise which would have seated both delegations, each with half of the state's vote, enraged Van Buren anew. He led his "barnburners" out into the night, there to illuminate the gloom with the incandescence of their fervor.

The party was an easy victim for Southern realism; it was divided by Van Buren's animus and the ordinary personal ambitions of minor hacks: Michigan's Lewis Cass, Van Buren's nemesis in 1844, Levi Woodbury of New Hampshire, and James Buchanan, a member of the cabinet who would not live up to his pledge to abandon politics for public service, all scrambled after the nomination.

On the question of whether new states would have slavery, Cass took a position acceptable to the South. The Western businessman came out for popular sovereignty; each new state was to decide its status at the time of entry. Having paid the price, Cass entered the convention so sure of nomination he supported the 1844 two-thirds rule.

The second man on the Cass ticket was General William O. Butler, a Kentuckian who had made a name for himself in the late war. The Democrats saw either of two generals as their opponent, and attempted to counter Whig "glamour" with a bit of their own.

Although the 1848 convention failed to nominate a winning candidate, it was an organizational victory for party bosses. As its last act the Democrats voted to set up a permanent party structure. A central national committee was created, consisting of one delegate from each state. Significantly, the delegates were not chosen by an open vote of party members. Rather, they were to be selected by a vote taken by each state delegation at the convention.

Since the control of the party was to reside in that national committee, the method of selecting it was of paramount importance. The national committee thereafter issued the call for each quadrennial convention; it determined where the convention would gather and, when there were disagreements about credentials, who would be permitted to attend. More than one presidential nomination—most significantly, Eisenhower's in 1952—was determined by a national committee's decision on which delegates were to be certified.

This committee, the only durable structure in the party above the state organizations, was to be handpicked by state bosses. Another obstacle had been placed in the path of voters.

When the Whigs met in the Chinese Museum in Philadelphia one week later, on June 7, they had every reason to be happy. Thurlow Weed, as early as 1846, had determined General Zachary Taylor was the right man to permanently sidetrack four-time-loser Clay's unquenchable presidential ambitions. Weed saw the former as an obvious winner.

Taylor, known affectionately as Old Rough and Ready (a sobriquet chosen by his friends to remind the masses of Old Hickory), was being poorly treated by Polk. Therefore, after his February 1847 victory on the slopes of Buena Vista, the thin-skinner Taylor was ready to seek vengeance. He viewed himself as the victim of presidential jealousy, and was determined to vindicate his honor.

Taylor sought the limelight and, although a stranger to civilian politics, was not a man easily advised. He had no party affiliation, and when he proclaimed his availability, said he would accept the nominations of any and all parties. The flattery of his friends had convinced him that he was the most popular man in America, the obvious choice as the next president. It was as though popularity determined suitability, a yardstick which would have made Elvis Presley and Frank Sinatra presidents in their time.

Since the leaders of Whiggery were determined the nominee would either be one general or another, Taylor was challenged only by Winfield Scott. Taylor's victory was never in doubt; not only had he won the more bloody battles, but he had the better nickname. In a contest of diminutives between Old Rough and Ready and Old Fuss and Feathers, the outcome was preordained.

By 1848 slavery was an issue of overriding importance. Legions of Northerners objected to the noxious institution and were girding themselves for the struggle to end it. Since the Democrats were more than ever under the control of slavery's proponents, surely the Whigs should have been the party of the abolitionists. That, however, was not to be. The Whigs nominated General Taylor, a Southern slave-holder, whose appeal was expected to be strong in that Democratic stronghold. At the same time, his backers insisted that his military reputation would attract those same Northerners whose love of the sounding bugle had led them to support *Tippecanoe* in '40 and "Fifty-four forty, or fight" in '44.

The moral bankruptcy of the Whigs and the Democrats led to the formation of one of the nation's more important "single issue" parties; the Free Soilers, dedicated to the eradication of slavery. Its ideological predecessor, the Liberty party, had been organized in New York in December 1839, but its presidential candidates won few votes in 1840 and 1844. Given another chance, in this era of uncertainty over whether California and the Mexican territory would enter the Union as slave states, the Liberty abolitionists found common cause with disaffected New England Whigs and the terribly disgruntled Martin

Van Buren. He led his vengeance-seeking "barnburner" supporters into the new Free Soil Party and won its presidential nomination.

Rather than deal with the issue which they espoused, the Whigs and the Democrats labelled the Free Soilers renegades and apostates and in this manner avoided dealing with them at all. Van Buren won only the pleasure of siphoning off enough votes from Cass in New York to throw the state to Taylor, delivering its crucial thirty-six electoral votes, and the election, to the general.

It is interesting to note that between the years 1828 and 1848 Van Buren played a prime role in determining the winner of each presidential election. He was an extraordinarily influential figure in the molding of American political institutions. His contribution to hard-line, national machine politics makes him one of the handful of important figures in American history. His will still has a role to play in the selection of every president; in the election of our worst presidents, it has been decisive. His son, known popularly as "Prince John" a New York politician and lawyer, sounded the family credo when he originated that piece of standard party wisdom, advising members of the Empire State machine to "vote early and often."[8]

No sooner did "Old Zach" move into the White House than he cleaned out the Polk gang. Included in that sweeping of the stables was a Salem custom-house employee, Nathaniel Hawthorne, who thereupon wrote *The Scarlet Letter*. Likewise detached from a payroll (of a newspaper that had supported the losing candidate) was Walt Whitman, who then wrote *Leaves of Grass*. Some irreverent wits have insisted these were the only accomplishments of Taylor's administration.

Emerson suggested why Taylor could not be expected to achieve on any higher level; in the poem prefacing his *Essay on Politics*, in which he attacked political parties, he wrote:

> Fear, Craft and Avarice,
> Cannot rear a State,
> Out of dust to build
> What is more than dust . . .[9]

Taylor died on July 9, 1850 and was succeeded by Millard Fillmore, a New York politician, whose vice-presidential candidacy was used by the Whigs in the 1848 election to tempt some disaffected Van Buren-ites. Taylor had outlived Calhoun by little more than three months, presiding over the Union during the last convulsive congressional attempt to compromise with slavery.

The Mexican War, with its prizes of deserts and mountains, had stoked the fire over slavery to a searing heat and had accelerated the South's move toward secession. As his last major act, Calhoun had attempted to open all the new territories to slavery. On January 27, 1850, Clay proposed a compromise aimed at achieving the same balancing of positions his Missouri Compromise had achieved thirty years earlier: California was to enter the Union as a free state, the slave trade was to be outlawed in the nation's capital, and in return, a stronger fugitive-slave act would be enacted. Webster joined his voice to that of Clay and Calhoun, and after months of debate the com-promise was passed.

It left the Whigs and Democrats in an impossible position, since it was based on the assumption that a compromise could be made with slavery. The Democrats, now trembling at the constant threats of Southern politicos to leave the party, crossed their fingers and praised the triumvirate for their statesmanship. The Whigs, mortally wounded by their attempt to be everything to every man, took this last blow from Clay and Webster and prepared to expire.

Faced with an issue of overriding social, ethical, and political significance, the two parties proved for members in that generation what they have confirmed for members of every generation willing to look facts squarely in the face; they were a contrivance for the personal advantage of a handful of men.

The transcendentalist preacher, Theodore Parker, speaking to his Boston congregation on October 31, 1852, only a week after Webster's death, lashed out at these first great national-party leaders, but saved his most stinging comment for the fallen Massachusetts giant: "No great ideas, no great organizations, will bind him to the coming age. Ere long, men will ask for historic proof to verify the reputation of his power. . . . Boston now mourns for him! She is too late in her weeping. A Senator of the United States, he was pensioned by the manufactur-ers of Boston. . . . His later speeches smell of bribes."[10]

Parker was a New England type who is the joy of honest men; courageous, eloquent, filled with love for humanity, he involved his logical mind and energetic body in every major matter of conscience in his day. For him moral issues were as important concerns as they were irritating inconveniences for Webster. In his famous address on "The Nebraska Question," he unleashed his righteous outrage on national parties:

"There is . . . no vital difference between the Whig party and the Democratic party; no difference in moral principle. The Whig inaugurates the desire to get money. . . . One is not higher and the other lower; they are just alike. . . . A Democrat is but a Whig on time; a Whig is a Democrat arrived at maturity; his time has come. A Democrat is a young Whig who will legislate for money as soon as he has got it; the Whig is an old Democrat who once hurrahed for the majority. . . . The young man, poor, obscure, and covetous, in 1812 was a Democrat, went a-privateering against England; rich, and accordingly 'one of our eminent citizens,' in 1851 he was a Whig, and went a-kidnapping against [fugitive slaves]."[11]

The presidential election of 1852 sounded the death knell for the Whigs; intent on agreeing with the Democrats that the divisions caused by slavery had been ended by the sophistry of Webster and Clay, they nominated Old Fuss and Feathers: there was to be no argument over anything. As professionals they were going to field their most attractive symbol and then sit back and hope the day would be won by their most durable ally, the voter's gullibility.

To counter the brass-button polish and blast of General Scott the Democrats nominated Franklin Pierce, a politician from New Hampshire, almost as unknown in his day as he is in ours.

The choice of Pierce illustrates a basic precept of party bosses: When the party is fairly certain of victory, the leaders prefer to nominate colorless candidates; such men are easier to handle and less likely to propose ideas that might upset the voters. Occasionally this preferred path of action cannot be followed; some overwhelmingly popular figure may sweep aside their plans. The theory is worshipped within the operator's den, however, and is followed frequently enough to make it an iron law of politics.

The Democratic sachems were sure that they could nominate anyone, even Franklin Pierce, and beat the Whig warrior, since Van Buren's "barnburners" had spent four years wandering in the wilderness and had found the experience chilling; the lack of patronage had the usual effect it produces on politicians, a debilitating morosity which could only be cured by victory.

Convinced they had sacrificed too much when they followed Van Buren into the Free Soil camp, they reverted to type, giving the Democrats every obvious reason to consider New York's electoral votes as good as won.

At the same time the Whigs were being deserted by thousands of Southern Unionists, who four years earlier had campaigned for the party and the Union. The growing strength of emancipation sentiment among Northern Whigs hurt their sensibilities. It burst forth at every national meeting no matter how hard the leaders tried to suppress it. Unionist support was rapidly disappearing in the South, as the polarization of the two sections became more pronounced, and toleration of dissent became as unfashionable as it usually is in times of stress. The South was becoming "solid" for the Democrats.

General Winfield Scott paraded about the country trying to marshal his phalanx. Pierce the unknown, smiling much and talking little, vindicated the wisdom of the party leaders; Scott won only four states.

The Democratic party had reached the height of its organizational effectiveness and the depth of its moral degradation; it was no longer the party of Jackson and the people, the party of Northern and Western democracy. It was the tool of mercenaries in Northern clubhouses, willing to do the bidding of Southern slave masters so that a patronage reward could be exacted.

Those scholars who defend the national party system, as it developed after 1840, stress its superiority as a unified structure for the selection of political leaders over the previous multifaceted arrangement. Ignored in this apologia is the fact that the efficiency of this institution was aimed almost exclusively at fattening the wallets of those who controlled it.

If indeed the original method of selecting the leaders of the state had proved to be too disorganized, too anarchic for the new day, then the move should have been from anarchy to a superior organization. What emerged instead was certainly more organized, but unfortunately for most citizens, who were only the victims of this efficiency, it was organized venality.

7

The Birth of the Republican Party

[Politicians are] a set of men who have interests aside from the interests of the people, and who, to say the most of them, are, taken as a mass, at least one long step removed from honest men.

Abraham Lincoln, in a speech to the
Illinois legislature, January, 1837[1]

The Republican party was born in the 1850s out of national frustration over the inability of the Democrats and Whigs to come to grips with the slavery issue; it was a moment when emotional idealism had come to a boil and nothing could cool it short of justice.

Perhaps the single most influential event in its birth process was Democrat Stephen A. Douglas's decision to bring the Territory of Nebraska into the Union. Douglas's motivation was sullied; he was deeply involved in western land speculation. Although officially representing Illinois interests in the Senate, he was more grimly defending his own. He had invested heavily in acreage which he envisioned as the eastern terminus for the proposed transcontinental railroad; however, three routes had been proposed for that monumental project, southern, central, and northern. The North's most influential Democrat, five feet of swaggering verbal virtuosity, whose mentality was obtuse to moral issues, was determined that the central route through Nebraska must be chosen, so that his gleaming new city might rise at its eastern terminus.

In order to make this the most attractive alternative, it was necessary to populate the area and confer statehood on it. In January 1854 he introduced a bill to establish the Territory of Nebraska. It was the first step in the process of carving states out of the great plains. The South, fearful that these new states would bar slavery, had previously blocked similar legislation. To make it more palatable to its staunchest opponents, he proposed that the people of Kansas and Nebraska determine whether their state permit slavery. His assumption was that Kansas would become slave and Nebraska free: Something for everyone—a politician's dream.

The only difficulty with his declaration for "popular sovereignty" was that all of the Nebraska territory lay north of latitude 36°30′, and under Clay's Missouri Compromise, was perpetually banned to slavery; any tampering with that compromise was bound to inflame Northerners.

Jefferson Davis, who saw in Douglas's popular sovereignty an opportunity to take the banner of slavery into the western territories, became Douglas's leader in the South. Davis's influence was so great with Franklin Pierce that the president's major effort became to solidify the Democrats behind Douglas's scheme. These three statesmen, apparently, did not comprehend, or were indifferent to, the likely result of the mischief they were stirring up.

Davis, blinded by his proslavery sentiments, was abandoning the real interests of the South; he was willing to give up the southern routing of the transcontinental railroad, which would have bound the markets of the South together. In exchange he wanted an opportunity to make slavery legal in an area where its natural chances for survival were nonexistent. Pierce saw this as an opportunity to unite the Northern wing of the Democratic party, momentarily mesmerized by the "little giant," and the Southern wing, shortly to follow Davis down the path of insurrection. Douglas rationalized his greed mellifluously in the idiom of patriotism. Although disaster was barely beyond their noses, these three saw only a profit.

The debate lasted for three months, each day bitterer than the last. Through it all Pierce cajoled the Democratic party, as though there were little more at stake than the vindication of his leadership. With minor exceptions, Northern Democrats fell in line.

With the passage of the Kansas-Nebraska Act on May 25, 1854, and the introduction of slavery into Kansas, the birth of the Republican party became inevitable. Charles Sumner, Abolitionist senator from Massachusetts, was undaunted by the large majority in favor of the "Crime against Kansas"; he viewed it as an essential step in the direction of emancipation. He pointed out that "it annuls all past compromises with slavery, and makes all future compromises impossible. Thus it puts freedom and slavery face to face, and bids them grapple. Who can doubt the result?"[2]

In little more than a month opponents of slavery were assembling in Jackson, Michigan, to form a new antislavery party. The meeting on July 6, 1854, was one of a number of such party-forming gatherings held almost concurrently; this one was distinguished by the fact that it selected the party's name. Its single-minded idealists felt that the party of Jefferson was no longer entitled to identify itself by his label, as it still did occasionally, since it had abandoned his republican vision.

During the next two years the party slowly gathered strength, finding its greatest nourishment in the Northwest. Working against it was simple inertia—the main glue, along with greed, that holds together the present-day two-party system. In addition, the Free Soil party occupied much the same antislavery ground and saw little need for an intrusion by the Republicans into its territory.

Finally, a new party appeared, simultaneously wooing the footloose; it was the notorious American party, better known as the "Know-Nothings."

The earliest organizational trace of the Know-Nothing party was the secret "Order of the Star-Spangled Banner." It was a New York based group composed of native-born Protestants rigid in their terror of being overwhelmed by foreigners.

While in the grip of that terror they were tantalized by the conviction that their annihilation could be avoided with the performance of covert rituals. They were taught identifying grips, passwords, signs of safety and distress, and were informed of meetings on heart-shaped paper, which was red if there was some danger involved. Candidates were nominated at private, unannounced meetings; an unyielding discipline tied the members to pledges of secrecy. When the uninitiated inquired as to what transpired at these ceremonials, the response was invariably, "I know nothing." Common usage quickly, and with surprising appropriateness, labelled this group of troglodytes "Know-Nothings."

By 1854 these Know-Nothings had developed a fierce polemic against the horde of immigrants flooding into Northern cities. They were not only strangers, a normal cause for suspicion, but they were poor scroungers, seeking the jobs of children of earlier immigrants, depressing the wage scale, crowding already burgeoning cities, and jabbering away in Babylonian gibberish.

Furthermore, the Know-Nothings believed they saw these foreigners being used by city politicians to destroy democratic institutions. Even such a rational man as Bryce could comment thirty-five years later, "From the immigrants neither national patriotism nor a sense of civic duty can as yet be expected; the pity is that they have been allowed civic power."[3]

In 1854 the American party, as they preferred to be called, carried the state of Massachusetts and almost won in New York. The movement had struck a popular note. As rulers of the old Bay Colony, they proceeded to cater to simplistic appetites; no Catholic school or nunnery was safe from the inquisitorial mind of Calvin's descendants.

By the summer of 1855 there was no doubt that the new major faction would be the American "Know-Nothing" Party; the Whigs had withered and the Republicans were obviously going to remain a Western sectional amalgam. The apogee of the movement came during that summer, as the first national convention assembled to nominate a ticket for the 1856 presidential election. Joyous delegates came from every section of the Union. At last true patriots were going to have their say. The best people, inspired by the most poisonous sentiments, were going to set things right.

However, things went wrong immediately. Ex-President Millard Fillmore was nominated for president, which might have been a deathblow had not a superior device for self-destruction materialized. The Southerners, Protestant to a man, and, as a result, a major reservoir for Know-Nothing membership, had a voting advantage on the convention floor. They used this advantage to pass a series of proslavery resolutions.

Hatred of immigrants united all bigots in the party, but love of slavery appealed only to Southern bigots. Within moments of the passage of the first platform plank, calling for the extension of slavery into the territories and vigorous enforcement of fugitive-slave-recovery laws, the Northern disenchanted were on their way in search of another party. In a period of time no longer than it takes to call a press conference, there was a Northern American Party. Its leaders began negotiating with Western Republicans, whose party was now invigorated, shortly after what might have otherwise been a stillborn birth, by an infusion of Know-Nothing, antiurban zeal.

It is possible to view political parties as a technique of aggressive men to sublimate their desire to seize the government by force. Such a theory is suggested by V. O. Key.[4] In American politics that theory receives its most illuminating support in the inspiration, growth, and demise of the Know-Nothings. Active, even fanatic men gravitated to it; they saw their opponents as the personification of evil, and barely contained their urge to do battle in defense of their vision. Had the conflict over slavery not disbanded them, the violence associated with their electioneering might have precipitated civil war: Instead it was allowed to ripen among the Southern clans for another five years.

As the early months of 1856 passed, the antagonism between Northern Republicans and Southern Democrats intensified; Kansas was bleeding, gangs of proslavery toughs murdered Northern emigrant families trying to settle in the promised land.

Charles Sumner rose in the Senate May 19, and delivered a speech about "border ruffians." In the process, he could not restrain himself from making some remarks about South Carolina's Senator Butler. Butler's partisans found these remarks tasteless. Three days later Preston Brooks, Butler's enraged relative, walked onto the floor of the Senate, and, as Stephen Douglas placidly looked on, caned Sumner into insensibility. Sumner, who remained in the Senate as an Abolitionist for many years, never recovered physically or psychologically. Brook's bravery was recognized by that special code of Southern chivalry, which allowed its guardians to defend murder, rape, and assorted violence against blacks. He was feted throughout Dixie and accumulated a stock of souvenir canes donated by admirers.

In this atmosphere of frenzied disorder, on June 17, 1856, the Republican party convened its first convention in Philadelphia's Musical Fund Hall. Only four slave states had even partial representation: Delaware, Maryland, Virginia, and Kentucky. Many of the one thousand delegates from the North and the West visualized themselves as earnest carriers of the truth; to most of them slavery was an aberration in a democratic society with which decent men could not compromise. The South had its party, Thaddeus Stevens exhorted; it was time for the North to create its own; failure to do so would encourage the advocates of slavery to press that noxious institution into the territories. Many of the delegates spoke of a doomsday when

Jefferson Davis would be insisting on resumption of the African slave trade, which had been outlawed since 1807, and even the legalization of slavery in the North.

Many of the earliest theoretical Republicans, those speculating about the possible creation of a party, were not politicians in the sense that Van Buren or Clay would have defined that word. They were often men of principle, as philosophers of parties frequently are, and often pure in motive. The largest number were taken up with a cause, or rather, two causes: Their platform stated that it was "both the right and the imperative duty of Congress to prohibit in the Territories those twin relics of barbarism—Polygamy and Slavery."[5]

The South had been so aggressive in pushing the cause of slavery that Northerners—with the exception of William Lloyd Garrison and his Abolitionist friends, who were pointedly absent from this convention—were not yet ready to insist that slavery be wiped out. Instead they were setting up tentative positions against the advance of Southern claims, which they sensed knew no final bounds. Slavery was to be outlawed only in the new territories.

John C. Frémont, explorer of California, husband of Senator Benton's sparkling daughter, Jenny, swept the delegates into his camp. The slogans of the new party were "Free soil, free speech, and Frémont," and "Jenny's bent-on freedom". With these snappy chants on their lips they entered the campaign against Democrat James Buchanan, who had edged out President Pierce and Stephen Douglas, both too closely identified with Kansas knavery.

Many Northern Whigs joined the Republican cause with a sigh of relief; at last the compromises were over. The Northern branch of the American party held a convention and endorsed Frémont but nominated its own vice-president. This threatened Republican victory in the Electoral College; it took a summer of hard bargaining, and bribery by Thurlow Weed, to convince those refugees from know-nothingism to line up behind the full Republican ticket. Weed was Frémont's chief supporter, convinced his man could win the key state of Pennsylvania if only the convention would nominate the corruptible boss of the state, Simon Cameron as its vice-presidential candidate. His thesis was never tested since the convention nominated the incorruptible William L. Dayton.[6]

Almost from the first, the Republicans were heavily supported by the financial community. Perceiving an opportunity to capture control of a potentially powerful group, business interests in Boston, New York, and Philadelphia took a leading hand in organizing the National Committee. They raised a campaign treasury of several hundred thousand dollars. The national chairman was New York's Edwin D. Morgan, one of the wealthiest men in America.[7] This was to be no amateur party, set up on impulse, or likely to disappear at the first sign of difficulty. Its most influential founders conceived of it as the new conservative party of the business community; it was the legitimate successor to the Federalists and the Whigs.

Morgan organized meetings of businessmen at which large sums of money were donated. Agents were dispatched to solicit "contingency gifts," which would be collected only if Frémont won. Gifts of that sort were not contingent on the fact that the donor sympathized with Frémont's objectives, but rather that once in the White House, the latter would be in a position to deliver on some contingency *quid pro quo*. Newspapers, always a target for party bribery during presidential elections, were subsidized, and carved out editorial positions agreeable to their new paymasters.

The Democrats made a parallel effort to raise a war chest, relying largely on the generosity of New York banker August Belmont. America was beginning to develop its industrial plant: corporations were multiplying, and fortunes such as Belmont's were being established; and money to protect these powerful interests was being made available to political parties in greater quantities.

From the time of William Henry Harrison, lavish use of funds during campaigns had become the accepted practice. As the quality of the candidates went down, the amount of money spent to convince voters they were Titans rose. However, the new industrial revolution was making its impact on the North and it was this Republican campaign of 1856 that marked the introduction of professional enterprise in the raising of campaign funds.

The results were promising: The Republicans, who had never presented a candidate, persuaded 1,335,264 people to cast their votes for Frémont; Fillmore's Know-Nothing and moribund Whig supporters managed to capture 874,534 ballots; Democrat Buchanan amassed 1,838,169 votes, and was elected.[8]

Within two days of Buchanan's inauguration the Supreme Court handed down the infamous Dred Scott decision. To the applause of the Democratic South, Chief Justice Taney, Jackson's old friend, led the Court into declaring that slaves were property and like any other property could not be taken from their owners no matter what laws were passed by trouble-making Northern states. Stung by this lash, the Republicans began to gird themselves for the 1860 electoral battle.

Abraham Lincoln was to be the nemesis of slavery and the disoriented Democrats. He had served one term in Congress during the Mexican War, but first drew attention to himself on October 16, 1854, with a speech in Peoria; until that moment he was indistinguishable from other Whig politicians. Aside from an unusual reputation for honesty, an exaggerated tendency to speak the truth, a contemplativeness almost universally absent from the average politician's makeup, and a sense of humor that received its widest scope in anecdote, there was little reason to think this tall, awkward native of Illinois with his relatively unattractive face, would be a man for the ages.

Still far from an Abolitionist at the time of the Peoria speech, the injustice associated with Douglas's attempt to introduce slavery into Kansas touched his humanist instincts and led him to an advocacy of gradual emancipation.

He took an extremely active role in Frémont's 1856 campaign, making over ninety prepared speeches. Within two years he was challenging Douglas for his Senate seat. The most dynamic Democrat since Jackson was facing a man whose qualities were only beginning to be suspected.

During the summer and autumn of 1858 the nation's attention was focused on the two greatest speakers of their time. They took part in a series of seven debates in which the issues of the 1860 presidential election were laid out.

By the time of his Quincy speech on October 13 (the sixth in their series) Lincoln was clearly the voice of crusading Republicanism. "The Republican party think it [slavery] wrong—we think it is a moral, a social, and a political wrong. We think it is a wrong not confining itself merely to the persons of the States where it exists, but that it is a wrong in its tendency, to say the least, that extends itself to the existence of the whole nation. Because we think it wrong, we propose a course of policy that shall deal with it as a wrong. We deal with it as with any other wrong, insofar as we can prevent its growing any larger, and so deal with it that in the run of time there may be some promise of an end to it."[9]

Douglas was entangled in land and political dealings that clouded whatever judgment he might have had on this issue. He reacted in the manner of any partyman intent on personal gain at any expense. "If each state will only agree to mind its own business, and let its neighbors alone," he advised callously, ". . . this republic can exist forever divided into free and slave states. . . ."[10]

Douglas's reputation, and his incumbency and organization, won the senate seat for him in '58, but the real battle was for the presidency two years later, and in that struggle Douglas was overtaken by events.

Douglas went into the Democratic convention in Charleston, on April 23, 1860, with a substantial lead, convinced that if only he could hold the party together, he would be president. Buchanan, whose pro-South stance had lost him the support of the Northern wing of the party, preferred his vice-president, Kentucky's John C. Breckinridge. The president was captivated by thoughts of America's Manifest Destiny; he dreamt of an expanding nation deterred by no race of men and finally halted only by the oceans. He wanted to annex Cuba, which would serve as a new source of slaves; Breckinridge unreservedly backed this aggressive stance.

As the Democrats assembled in Charleston, they knew their task was going to be difficult; South Carolina was determined to secede from the Union; most of the other Southern states were equally determined to have slavery endorsed in the territories or secede from the party. Alabama's William L. Yancey spelled out the South's terms: The party must support the proposition "that slavery was right."[11]

Northern Democratic politicians had come to the convention with a compromise which told everything that had to be known about them. Unable to endorse Yancey's honest bigotry, they were, nevertheless, willing to enable his philosophy to make its way in the territories—if only he would be satisfied with face-saving platform language. They passed a resolution proposing to "leave slavery in the territories to the Supreme Court."[12]

Since the Dred Scott decision had left no doubt as to how the Court would rule on such a matter, it was clear Northern Democratic bosses had once again found it preferable to win, rather than do right. Control of the customshouses from Boston to Baltimore, jobs in the post offices of the North, and patronage totalling millions depended on their willingness to accept the humiliation of an amoral compromise with slavery, and on the South's willingness to accept the morally defective Douglas.

The compromise was never consummated. Southern leaders had painted themselves into a rhetorical corner: "Southern rights" had become more significant for them than human rights, and they viewed Douglas as a dubious champion in that cause. Their suspicion of Douglas stemmed not from their judgment of his character, but from their doubts about his ability to deliver. They had supported him on the issue of popular sovereignty in '54, assured by the Little Giant that Kansas would be theirs; yet, barely six years later, Kansas was in the hands of John Brown's brethren.

Eight Southern delegations bolted from the Democratic convention, making it statistically impossible for Douglas to win the nomination, since the two-thirds rule for presidential designation was still in force. After fifty-seven deadlocked ballots, the Charleston convention adjourned on May 3, after Douglas took the Democratic road show to Baltimore, where, on June 18, he found the requisite number of docile delegates to designate him the Democratic nominee.

Determined on a confrontation, Southern Charleston secessionist Democrats convened in Baltimore on June 28 and nominated John C. Breckinridge. This was not to be a me-too election, such as the two-party system had generally produced. The fragmented Democrats alone were presenting alternatives to the electorate: Those who wanted the slave hatcheries of Cuba to be under the American flag, and human bondage to be extended to every corner of the Union, could vote for Breckinridge. Those who were willing to let the Supreme Court make up their minds could vote for Douglas. Those Southerner Democrats who did not like Douglas, but wanted to remain in the Union regardless of the election's outcome, could vote for Tennessee's Senator John Bell. He was nominated by a new party, called the National Constitutional Union. Bell's brothers believed in "no political principle other than the Constitution of the country, the union of the states, and the enforcement of the laws."[13]

The real choice was between three somewhat similar philosophies which added up to an endorsement of slavery or a willingness to live with it, and the position of the antislavery Republican party.

The Republicans had assembled in Chicago on May 16. It was two weeks after the collapse of the Charleston convention, which foreboded the likely defeat of the Democrats. It was also a little less than six weeks before the secessionist Democrats met in Baltimore to nominate Breckinridge, which confirmed the likelihood of the Republican victory.

The Republican platform, issued May 18, 1860, showed the steadying hand of professionalism in control; although slavery in the territories was condemned, slavery in the South was countenanced. John Brown was denounced, along with the Missouri border ruffians whom he had fought. Their victory in the 1858 congressional elections had convinced Republican kingmakers they were soon to elect their first president, and as in the case of the special knowledge imparted to Adam as he bit into the apple, the effect was corrupting.

The party was moving to the right, accommodating itself to the precepts of its most influential members. The protective tariff (for which Northern industrial interests had always yearned) and the Whig's plank on internal improvements became tenets of the new Republicanism. For some it was of greater long-range importance although for most it was not of equal weight with the slavery issue. The Republican party was no longer wedded to one issue, and was therefore not likely to fall apart as soon as that issue was resolved. It was a permanent party, run by organization men, employing all the murky political tactics developed over the previous thirty years.

Lincoln was nominated on the third ballot—a savvy political choice. Thurlow Weed's New York henchman William H. Seward was the most renowned member of the party, but was considered to be too outspoken against slavery. He was too controversial. Ohio's governor Salmon Chase, whose antagonism to slavery went back to 1840 and the Liberty party, offered token opposition.

It would be comforting to think Lincoln's sterling qualities had singled him out for leadership; however, our hindsight understanding of his greatness was not shared by the politicians who chose him. They were attracted by his benign, humorous manner and humble log-cabin background, so reminiscent of Jackson and Harrison; but they were most concerned about finding a winner.

The country's political structure, by 1860, closely imitated the free enterprise system. For men like Weed, success meant winning elections, and in the pursuit of their prizes they were prepared to act with the same delicacy then being displayed by the robber barons of industry who were newly roaming across the American landscape.

As in the case of the successful entrepreneur, the techniques used by the triumphant politicians were not likely to be examined. So why bother being fastidious? Victory excused every excess.

Lincoln's election brought on the war that Southern leaders had boasted of wanting for decades; it was the war that Jefferson saw coming in the 1820s and that John Quincy Adams felt was inevitable. Yet the vote had been indecisive: Lincoln tallied 1,866,452; Douglas 1,375,157; Breckinridge 847,953, and Bell 589,581.[14] The popular vote of Lincoln's opponents far outweighed his. If the Democrats had not split, they would have had little difficulty winning, thereby avoiding the savagery of the next four years.

At the same time the total vote was 4,468,069, less than 50 percent of those eligible to vote out of a population of approximately 32,000,000. Although the destiny of the nation was to be decided by the outcome of this election, parties had proved to be shockingly inadequate as instruments for getting the voters to the polls.

Finally, Lincoln received 180 votes in the Electoral College, although Douglas, not far behind in the popular vote, was endorsed by only 12 Electors; Breckinridge, who had little more than half the number of votes received by Douglas, tallied 72 electoral votes. A number of them were from South Carolina, where no popular vote was taken and the plantation aristocracy still registered its opinion by regal fiat of the state legislature.

Lincoln won all the Northern states except New Jersey, but received scarcely a vote below the Mason-Dixon line. The North had chosen a man of principle—representing a party that in its infancy had attracted some men of principle—to lead it in search of a solution to the greatest ethical question of the day.

Yet the solution was not to be found in the radius of party politics. A national party, almost for the first time motivated partly by biblical injunctions about justice and mercy, was precipitating a carnage of blood. The old corrupt parties had always been able to find a workable compromise, one that was unsatisfactory only to those victims too weak to protest. But this matter was to be settled on the battlefield, where Democrats fought Republicans with Gatling guns. Justice, bowing to force, won because it had more troops.

8

The Death of the
Republican Party

A more lovely knot of politicians would be hard to find. Self-important, humorless, itching for power, and scornful of ethical scruple, they sold their wares at their own valuation and paraded behind a front of crusading zeal. Unmerciful in their pressure upon Lincoln, they used the stratagems of patronage, party trickery and propaganda to impose their pattern upon all phases of the war effort.

James G. Randall[1]

The Civil War was simultaneously a Republican party triumph and one of the root causes of its eventual failure. Its only political enemy was the Democratic party, which expressed a multitude of rationalizations and disavowals, but allowed itself to be identified with the insurrection. Massive numbers of enrolled Southern party members were in rebellion against the government. Republicans were in that position so longed for by professional politicians; their party was identified with the welfare and safety of the nation, while their opponents were legitimately labelled traitors.

There was a resulting arrogance about the behavior of the Republican party during the Civil War. It was in sharp contrast to Lincoln's humility. Shots were being fired just beyond the Potomac, but a professional clubhouse type like Simon Cameron (the secretary of war) was conducting himself as though Union troops were fighting to enrich him and safeguard his control of the corrupt Pennsylvania party machine. His fortune had been established on the basis of state printing contracts his newspaper (the *Harrisburg* [Pa.] *Republican*) received in return for political support. He was also alleged to have defrauded the Winnebago Indians in 1838 while serving on a commission to settle their Wisconsin land claims; in recognition of his exploits during this foray he came to be called "The Great Winnebago Chief."[2]

By 1860 he was the dictator of Pennsylvania politics, and Lincoln's determination to unify the Northern states behind the war effort had led to his cabinet appointment. Habits of a lifetime, however, are seldom changed by elevation to high office, although myth has it that men are ennobled by such an experience. Cameron viewed his great office as a great opportunity with which the war should not interfere. In his capacity as secretary of war he authorized the purchase of defective guns for the Army at premium prices; then, when Army inspectors noted their defects, he ordered them sold to the public at the price such worthless goods should command. Strangely enough, he was soon directing Army agents to purchase the same blemished second-hand merchandise, again for top dollar; thereupon splitting the profit with his relative, who had acted as middleman—the only factor explaining his apparently irrational behavior. By 1862 even Lincoln's patience was exhausted; he was forced to remove him in response to public outcry.

Cameron stands as proof that although criminals in the private sector may rot in jail, criminals in government, once exposed, often prosper. Lincoln, in the midst of the war, felt compelled to paper over this scandal by certifying Pennsylvania's boss as minister to the Czar's court; the theory seemed to be that in such a setting his presence would not offend.

Exile, however, did not appeal to Cameron, and within the year he was back home unsuccessfully trying to gain a new senatorial appointment from the Pennsylvania legislature.[3] As the war proceeded, political power gravitated toward such Republicans, but their party background did not prepare them for the demands of that responsibility. Lincoln stood as the main restraint to their appetites.

The election of 1864 came at the height of the war, and partymen, revealing the shallowness of their dedication to democracy, began talking about simply extending the president's tenure for the duration of the conflict. He would not hear of it: "We cannot have free government without elections; and if the rebellion could force us to forego or postpone a national election, it might fairly claim to have already conquered and ruined us."[4]

A party convention was assembled in Baltimore, June 7, consisting of Republicans and Democrats who supported the war; it was labelled the National Union. Lincoln was renominated, although Salmon Chase, his secretary of the treasury, thought of himself, and was considered by party professionals, as a compromise candidate if Lincoln could be induced to withdraw.

Andrew Johnson, occupation governor of Tennessee, and a war Democrat, was chosen as Lincoln's running mate. He had one major credential. At the start of the war, when all other Southern senators had decided to legislate for Jefferson Davis, he had remained at his Washington desk. He was also a tailor of considerable talent, having practiced that vocation from his youth until mid-adulthood, when the profits seemed greater in politics. He had been an illiterate country yeoman until his wife taught him to read in the early years of his marriage. But he avoided reading any works of philosophy, literature, or history then popular at the colleges catering to those he viewed as snobbish aristocrats. He seems to have approached reading as an accountant approaches statistics: It was a device for more efficiently recording business transactions. He was to the last a slaveholder, uninterested in emancipation, supporting the Northern cause merely because he thought it was illegal for any state to leave the Union. His simple mind imbued that legalism with more power than the sentiment that man should not make a chattel of his brother. Lincoln had hoped Johnson would have special appeal to border-state Democrats.

Lincoln's party opponents were men who had been trained to place their aspirations before all. During the summer their personal ambitions led the president to the conclusion that it was impossible to win reelection. The war was dragging on with no sign of victory, new quotas for the inequitable and unpopular draft were soon going to be issued, and Horace Greeley, the most influential publicist of the day, was using his *New York Tribune* to accuse Lincoln of inept leadership.

At the same time Thaddeus Stevens, Charles Sumner, and the Radical Republican Congressional majority were intent on punishing the South, and they had come to view Lincoln as the chief opponent of the draconian measures they were proposing. His July 4 pocket veto of the Wade-Davis Bill—their measure to subjugate and cleanse the rebels—confirmed their worst fears. By August 18 Greeley and the Radicals were circulating a petition calling for a new Republican convention to cancel Lincoln's nomination! On August 23 a discouraged Lincoln wrote about the effect of this political sniping. "This morning, as for some days past, it seems exceedingly probable that this administration will not be reelected."[5]

Six days later, the Democrats, meeting in their Chicago convention, demonstrated how thoroughly they misunderstood the temperament of Northern voters. Drawing attention to their traditional alliance with Southern causes, they adopted a resolution whose implementation could help only to rescue Lee's armies. "After four years of failure to restore the Union by the experiment of war . . . justice, humanity, liberty, and the public welfare demand that immediate efforts be made for a cessation of hostilities. . . ."[6]

General George McClellan, gamecock of the Northern armies, was nominated by these "Peace Democrats," who were hopeful of resuscitating their party with an injection of militaristic charisma. McClellan, backed by "Copperheads" within the party who sympathized with Southern democracy—which was not able, because of circumstances, to attend the Chicago ceremonials—pressed home in his speeches the theme that Lincoln was needlessly prolonging the war.

Sherman's capture of Atlanta on September 1 made the Democrat's defeatism seem preposterous. As military victories piled one on the other during October, even the Radical Republicans felt impelled to make a show of enthusiasm for Lincoln: His victory margin in the Electoral College was 212-21.

By the beginning of February 1865, however, Lincoln's attempts to draw the South into peace negotiations had so enraged the majority of his party that Thaddeus Stevens felt free to say "that if the country were to vote over again for President of the United States, Benjamin F. Butler, and not Abraham Lincoln, would be their choice."[7]

Lincoln's death on April 14, 1865, eliminated the restraining influence of his honest leadership. Since Vice-President Andrew Johnson was a Democrat from the South who favored Lincoln's policy of leniency to those of his brothers who had swerved from the path, his directions to Republican professionals were hardly likely to command any kind of respectful attention. In addition, a few weeks earlier, at the inauguration, he had taken the oath in an obviously drunken state and had suffered the indignity of being pulled away from the lectern after a fifteen minute tirade; a scandal from which his reputation never recovered.

Suddenly, there was no major focus of power within the all-powerful party. Lincoln might have kept the overly ambitious, the corrupt, the opinionated, the vendetta-seekers in line, although this is by no means a confident speculation; without him, each potential Caesar was encouraged to cross some Rubicon.

As the party's future seemed assured, parasitical elements, which had always competed with the idealists who had founded the party, began to take over.

While the Radical Republicans were calling for Johnson's impeachment, control of the party had passed to America's richest men; the party of idealism had become the tool of those men who owned the country's banks and industrial plants. Let Stevens and Sumner scream; the men who understood what was important were busy with tariff, banking, and railroad legislation. Even while the war was on, they had succeeded in raising the tariff, passing a monopolistic private national bank bill, and authorizing grandiose giveaways of public lands to developers of the transcontinental railroad.

Now the true purpose of the Republican party, worked for diligently even as its congressional leaders were proclaiming their aim was to emancipate the slaves, emerged. It was to make sure no governmental shackles were placed on business. This was the most volatile period of industrial development, massively stimulated by the war effort; it was the moment when American economic policies were being defined. The leaders of this new class of industrial magnates were determined no fetters should be placed on their freedom to exploit. The Republican party was suited to their needs.

Thaddeus Stevens, the embodiment of puritanical vindictiveness, who became the virtual dictator of the country during the Johnson administration, managed the readmission of the Democratic South into the Union so as to insure Republican dominance forever. He proclaimed the rebellious states "ought never to be recognized as capable of acting in the Union, or of being counted as valid states, until the Constitution shall have been so amended . . . as to secure perpetual ascendance to the party of the Union."[8]

This somber leader of the Joint Committee of Fifteen, the group that guided congressional reconstruction, was determined the Republican party would take as its prize of war the permanent possession of the government. His hatred of Southern gentry was combined with his understanding that if the Confederacy were readmitted to the Union with its 1860 status unaltered, the Northern and Southern wings of the Democratic party would soon again be in control. Of what value was four years of bloodletting if Southern slavocracy was allowed to gain by election what it had lost in battle?

Stevens concluded the only possible way to avoid such a disaster was to readmit the rebellious states under conditions that insured their domination by the Republican party. Since Southern whites were unlikely to abandon the Democrats, it was imperative no Southerner be allowed to sit in Congress until the former slaves participated in elections, from which their former masters would be excluded.

This view was not part of Lincoln's plan for reconstruction, nor was it Johnson's; however, Johnson was in a position to do little more than object. As in the case of Tyler in 1841, he was not a member of the party that had nominated him; and, having split with a large number of Democrats on the war issue, he had no substantial support in either party.

Stevens felt free to tell the members of the House that Johnson was an "alien enemy, a citizen of a foreign state."[9] His strongest senatorial supporter, Charles Sumner, declared, "Jefferson Davis is in the casement at Fortress Monroe, but Andrew Johnson is doing his work. . . . Next to Jefferson Davis stands Andrew Johnson as [the Republic's] worst enemy."[10]

The congressional election of 1866 highlighted the political dilemma left by the war. A group calling itself the National Union met in convention and pledged its support to Johnson; it was composed of moderates from both parties. They decided, however, not to form a party or take part in any campaign that year. This decision had the practical effect of depriving Johnson of an opportunity to elect a Congress of his persuasion. In most districts the voters had only two choices: They could either vote for the Radical Republican or they could endorse the Copperhead Democrat.

Making the choice inevitable for most voters was the Republican strategy. The men who would have pilloried Lincoln, had John Wilkes Booth not done their work, made a point of avoiding any discussion of economic issues. These were, as always, the issues of paramount importance to the average voter; instead, they insisted on waving "the bloody shirt of rebellion" in the faces of their chagrined rivals. Republicans were the defenders of "freedom and democracy," while their adversaries were advocates of "slavery and oppression"; worse yet, they were traitors, they had killed Northern boys intent on upholding the principles of the Declaration of Independence. There was scarcely a Northern voter (almost the only kind of voter whose ballot was going to be counted in 1866) who had not lost a relative in combat; as a result, the shellshocked electorate was extremely vulnerable to that sort of emotional appeal. The Republicans made "patriotism" the issue, and continued to run on it for the better part of the next quarter of a century.

The immediate impact was to give the Radical Republicans a clear two-thirds margin in both houses. As long as carpetbag advisors and military occupation made sure that defeated Southern whites lived accordingly to the new rules, the Union was safely in the hands of Stevens and his Republican friends.

Since one of the few things keeping the avaricious tendencies of the professional partymen even vaguely in line was the element of competition from the opposing party, the elimination of this slight deterrent had a degenerative effect. Without the fear of political opposition, there was no need to provide decent candidates, or even candidates who projected the image of decency; all Republican office-seekers need do was wave that bloody shirt and speak of the fallen dead. The Democrats were too demoralized to effectively make the point that the party of Lincoln was now the party of wealth and monopoly.

The height of this frenzy was reached in February and March of 1868, as Stevens and Sumner led their cadre into an abortive effort to impeach Johnson* when he discharged Secretary of War Edwin Stanton.

*See author's *The Impeachment of Richard Nixon* (New York, Berkley/Putnam, 1973), pp. 18-29.

Had Ulysses Grant, hero-ultimate of the raging battlefields, stood behind his commander-in-chief when the Radical Republicans directed Grant to allow the reinstatement of the Machiavellian Stanton, and Johnson ordered Grant to bar Stanton from his office, the matter might never have come to a head; Grant's prestige in February 1868 was as high as Johnson's was low, and the Republican party was already eyeing him as its presidential nominee. Johnson had less than a year left to his stormy administration when impeachment charges were finally filed against him. If Grant had obeyed his president's orders, the confusion in Radical Republican ranks would have probably provided the Tennessee tailor with enough time to escape into retirement and an obscurity that history no longer allows him.

Instead, Grant timidly turned the Department of War back to Stanton and waited to see what fate had in store. This weak, self-seeking maneuver was more characteristic of Grant than his contemporaries were willing to admit; Grant had been a flawed character from the start. After graduating from West Point in 1843, he was assigned to the infantry; the excitement of the Mexican War wore off quickly and he became bored with Army life; he drank himself into alcoholism and in 1854 was cashiered from a service where heavy drinking was not a novelty and seldom viewed as a disgrace.

During the civilian years before the war he failed as a farmer, real estate agent, St. Louis customhouse timeserver, and was finally forced to ask his brother for a job in his Galena, Illinois, leather shop;[11] each year he sank lower socially and financially.

The war, which destroyed so much, rescued him. Had he been readmitted to the regular army he would have probably spent four years drilling recruits; however, his application to be recommissioned did not even receive the courtesy of a response; and instead, in June 1861, he was appointed colonel of the Illinois Volunteers. After two months in that ragtail outfit he was made brigadier-general, a surprise to no one more than himself.

Grant's success as a Union general, occasionally marked by spectacular failures such as his complete detachment from his troops at Shiloh, is similar in quality to the success of other military geniuses with which history is replete: Head of a superior force, always backed by an overwhelming mass of armaments, his straight-line mentality was suited for the simple job required of him.

This critical view of his talents was not shared by Northern voters. The nominating convention met within days after Johnson's acquittal, and the Radical Republicans saw nothing more clearly than Grant's popularity; he was the unanimous choice on the first ballot. Schuyler Colfax, Speaker of the House since 1863, whose most constructive attribute was neatly described by his popular diminutive, "Smiling," but whose corrupt nature was as yet known only to those who were bribing him, received the same kind of overwhelming endorsement for the second spot on the ticket.

The platform revealed that Whiggery had captured the party; the political slogan may have been "Crush the South," but the economic philosophy was "All for the businessman." Most delegates assumed the greatest good government could perform was to encourage private interests; they thought the supreme duty of the state was to help its most energetic citizens make money. The only legitimate reason for congressional activity was to create an atmosphere in which businessmen, the royalty of the American realm—guided by the profit motive—could harvest the riches of the newly tamed continent.

The president and Congress were in a position to apportion a multitude of favors: there were western lands to give away and subsidies for building railroads; fortunes were to be made if the tariff was raised to protect this or that industry; gigantic government contracts were available to make some lucky enterprisers rich.

Before adjourning the delegates pledged to pay back the government's war debts in gold. Since those to whom the government owed the debt were substantially bankers who had originally lent the Treasury cheap paper money, this decision meant that bank bondholders were going to make a killing. At the same time the farmer would have to repay his war-incurred greenback debts with deflated, scarcer, hard money. He had borrowed cheap paper money from those patriotic Republican bankers, but the Republican convention was determined he, too, would pay it back with costly gold.

Several weeks later the Democrats met in New York City; their main purpose was to end Reconstruction and turn the problem of the freed slave back to the tender mercies of Southern politicians. The loss of the war was conceded, but the mind of man was resourceful enough to invent new, perhaps legal, forms of slavery. Southern states were already passing "Black Codes," which authorized the arrest of unemployed freedmen, quickly labelled "vagrants," who were then placed in the hands of their former masters to work off bogus court fines.

The Democrats made every attempt to exploit the economic issue, which was showing signs of developing potency; farmers, who had bought land and machinery to expand production during the war and, as a result, increased their indebtedness, were having difficulty meeting payments. What made matters worse was rising productive capacity—mustered out soldiers were returning to their farms and more land was being planted in an attempt to pay off previously incurred debts. The "paradox of values" was in deadly operation. Just as the struggling farmer needed a helping hand from inflation, he was being ground under by hard money, to the accompaniment of suggestions from bankers that he work harder; yet, every additional bushel of grain he produced drove prices lower.

The Democratic platform condemned Republican "corruption and extravagances." By 1868 political spoilsmanship was so scandalously apparent—its practitioners seldom took the trouble to disguise their tactics—that even the Democrats felt free to comment. They demanded the war debts be paid off in greenbacks instead of gold; they called for a modification of the banking, tariff, and railroad legislation passed by a wartime Congress, which so favored promoters, bond swindlers, and an assortment of fly-by-night cheats.

Although Andrew Johnson wanted the Democratic nomination, too many Copperhead intransigents were present, still driven by bitter memories of the Charleston convention, to allow their most conspicuous apostate that honor within his former abode.

Salmon Chase who was, near the end of the war, appointed as Chief Justice of the Supreme Court by Lincoln, in an endeavor to relieve himself of an embarrassment, was still pursuing the presidency. Having been rebuffed by the Republicans, partly because of his role as presiding judge of the Senate during Johnson's impeachment trial, he turned to the Democrats. A determined drive by his supporters, well financed, and organized with a slickness possessed only by professionals whose questions about spoils have been satisfactorily answered, came up short of the mark.

In his place, on July 9 the vulnerable Democrats nominated, after twenty-two ballots, the former governor of New York, Horatio Seymour. They had acted in typical party fashion, nominating an enfeebled and ineffectual man; the quality of their choice was indicated by the fact that although the party platform was committed to paper money, Seymour was publicly defending the virtues of hard money.

The results were closer than might have been expected. Although Grant won twenty-six out of thirty-four states in the Electoral College, that victory was based on special factors: Three Southern states were controlled by carpetbag governments and pacified by armies of occupation, thus insuring the Republican nature of the returns. Finally, his popular margin of 306,000 out of a total vote of 5,715,000 was the result of 700,000 votes cast by blacks.[12] Their continued access to the polls was so much in doubt, in the restive South, that the vote revealed the Republican party's hope of permanently becoming a national organization was an illusion.

The best chance the Republicans had to break out of their sectional trap was that Grant would prove to be a sterling civilian leader. Then future generations of Americans might decide Lincoln's party was the natural political home for all men who wanted good government. What they got instead was an administration that displayed its corruptness in larger-than-life dimensions, an administration that gave politics and politicians an enduring and disreputable name.

Grant was the perfect product of party politics as it had been practiced in the decadent atmosphere of the post-Jackson era. In his essay on the hero of the Gilded Age, Vernon Parrington described the leader of conscienceless Republicanism:

"He was dazzled by wealth and power, and after years of bitter poverty he sat down in the lap of luxury with huge content. He took what the gods sent, and if houses and fast horses and wines and cigars were showered upon him he accepted them as a child would accept gifts from a fairy godmother. . . . He was never happier than when enjoying the luxury of Jay Cooke's mansion in Philadelphia. . . . As he grew fat and stodgy the vulgar side of his plebeian nature was thrown into sharper relief. He accepted gifts with both hands. . . . The hands of his closest advisers were dirty; yet he stubbornly refused to hear the whispers or see the dirt. In judging men and policies he was no more than a child. . . .

"In what must pass for his political views Grant was as naively uninformed as a Wyoming cowboy. Utterly wanting in knowledge of political principles, he was a fit leader for the organized mob that called itself the Republican party, whose chief objective was the raiding of the treasure-box of which it was the responsible guardian."[13]

It was the proper moment for Americans to pause and ask, how did such a man become the leader of his country? What does the presence of a Grant in the White House tell us about our method of selecting a president?

The price of organized corruption kept mounting, and was paid in rising unemployment, plundered government treasuries, and a dispirited sense of civic virtue. By September 1869, less than a year after he took office, it had become clear that an anile Grant would avert his eyes from the wrongdoings of any enterpriser seeking a profit.

Jay Gould and Jim Fisk, as representative of their period as were John Dillinger and Dutch Schultz of theirs, determined to corner the gold market. They took advantage of the reliance the uninformed put in that sanctified metal; natives of the South Pacific put the same faith in clam valves, and the ancient Chinese developed a similar fetish for stones with square holes gouged out of their center.

Since the price of gold fluctuated, depending on how many innocents were seized by a taste for it at any given moment, Gould and Fisk were determined to buy low, hold on until the demand for their monopolized inventory became overwhelming, and then sell at the highest possible price. The scheme could work only if the Treasury, the largest single owner of gold, could be induced to refrain from selling when the skyrocketing price would have normally drawn it into the marketplace.

Making all of this possible were the thieves surrounding Grant in the Oval Office—particularly his brother-in-law Abel Rathbone Corbin, a paid lobbyist for Gould and "Jubilee Jim" Fisk.[14] Some of the president's closest associates, many of them clustered around the secretary of the Treasury, were conniving to aid the swindlers. They convinced Grant he should announce in his inaugural address that government obligations would be paid in gold. This was all the encouragement the gold twins needed. By September 24, 1869, the "Black Friday" when Gould and Fisk were almost in control of the gold market, cries of anguish from those being bankrupted by these two Midases had finally reached even Grant's ears. At that point he ordered the treasurer to dump four millions in government gold onto the open market, and the Gould-Fisk corner on the universe collapsed.

Henry Adams, the scion of two presidents, took a scornful look at Grant's performance. After commenting that the General's apparently simple mind "was more disconcerting than the complexity of a Talleyrand,"[15] he went on to evaluate the nature of his incompetence. "The worst scandals of the 18th century were relatively harmless by the side of this which smirched executive, judiciary, banks, corporate systems, professions, and people, all the great active forces of society."[16]

Probably the greatest corruption of this administration was associated with the development of the railroads. The wealth of the continent could not be tapped until a convenient method of transportation had been developed; railroads were obviously the answer. The government should have been the builder of such a national enterprise; it was the only agency capable of legitimately mobilizing the needed capital. Since it was also the owner of most of the land through which the transportation network would be built, and the only entity in possession of an army to enforce law and order in the wilds through which the belching locomotives were to chug, its responsibility to shepherd the endeavor seemed self-evident.

Despite the obviousness of this choice, only mavericks like Thomas Benton gave the idea serious thought; instead, it was simply a matter of determining which rapacious promoter would get his foot in the door first. Since none of them had the money to sponsor this enormous project, it was clear the man with the best political connections, the greatest accumulation of guile, and the least scruples was likely to bring the hammer smashing down on the golden spike.

Poor Stephen Douglas had died before the passage of the Pacific Railway Act on July 1, 1862, but he would have approved. Two corporations were authorized to build the central line: The Union Pacific was to start at Council Bluffs, Iowa, and race westward; the Central Pacific took off from Sacramento, California, and galloped to the east. Since Congress gave away alternate blocks of land on each side of the right-of-way to a depth of ten miles, and authorized building loans of $16,000 to $48,000, depending on the difficulty of the terrain, the most energetic crew would end up with the largest pot;

but even for the laggards, there was enough bounty to justify the effort. This was especially true because the back-breaking effort was being made by Chinese coolies and Irish roustabouts, not the schemers, whose most strenuous exertions were made at social gatherings for partymen.

A second railway act was passed July 2, 1864, and seems to have been based on the concept that the first one had not been sufficiently generous; it doubled the land grants and relegated the government to second mortgagee. During the next four years Leland Stanford and Collis Huntington, the two directors of the Central Pacific, amassed twenty-four million acres along their right-of-way, almost the size of the state of Indiana.[17]

Meanwhile, the Union Pacific hustlers were finding an even larger rathole down which to pour taxpayer's money. Not satisfied with the government's twenty million acres and munificent loans, they developed a plan to defraud private investors. The swindle was simple, but so audacious that only men convinced they had the rulers of the country in their pocket would have chanced the effort.

The promoters of the Union Pacific knew the quickest, gaudiest profits could be made on construction costs and stock manipulation. Why wait on the possibility that rails laid out in the wilderness, where only occasional nomads ventured, would be able to generate enough traffic to make the trip worth the fuel? The sensible thing was to skim off the cream while Congress was keeping the bucket full.

The coterie of cheats who controlled the Union Pacific set up what appeared to be a completely autonomous company, named the Crédit Mobilier, whose sole function was to supply construction materials for the grand effort; the trick was to set prices for the supplies at such an exorbitant level that the Union Pacific, in order to pay its bills, would be drained of all its monetary resources. Those who had invested in the railway company were defrauded, while the thieves who controlled the Crédit Mobilier, and habitually dined with congressmen and cabinet officers, were bathed in gold. During one dismal year, while the Union Pacific's desperate financial condition led to talk of bankruptcy, the board of directors of the Crédit Mobilier were rewarding their select stockholders with a dividend of 348 percent.[18]

Among these happy stockholders were the most influential politicians of the day; it had been necessary to insure the neglect of their duty to investigate the con game, in order for it to succeed. Therefore, piles of Crédit Mobilier stock certificates were stacked on the desks of any congressman willing to avert his gaze: the more influential, the larger the pile.

When the *New York Sun* finally began to expose the story in December 1867, the only thought was that the newspaper must be acting irresponsibly. The charges were too sensational; most newspaper editors refused to believe them.

During the first three years of the Grant administration, as scandal piled upon scandal, and Congress was finally shamed into launching a special committee to investigate charges against its own members, apologists in the press were not in short supply. On January 22, 1872, the following bit of unintentional humor appeared on the front page of *The New York Times:* ". . . the truth is that for the past three years reform has been practically, positively, and persistently pushed in every department of the General Government."

The *Times* then went on to attack those unpleasant persons who were accusing Grant of corruption. Perhaps the editors of the *Times* were somewhat peeved at the thought that their rival, the *Sun*, was first on the scene with this story, and that Horace Greeley, another rival in the crowded New York newspaper field, was leading the outcry against Grant. Its persistent belief in his purity, however, stirs conjecture—at this great distance—about its motivation. "It is capable of abundant proof by impartial investigation . . ." the *Times* continued, ". . . that every department of Government, from the day of the inauguration of President Grant to the present, has been earnestly at work in the reformation of abuses, in rooting out corrupt officials."

But for those who were impatient, the *Times* had an explanation about why cleansing the body politic took so long. "And if they have not been able to correct all the abuses that exist, it is simply because the system of public affairs bequeathed to this Administration by its predecessors has covered so much that needs reform that it has been morally and physically impossible to grapple with every existing evil in less than three years."

The *Times* also had an explanation for the greater corruption in government under Grant: ". . . the embezzlements and defalcations of the present day are not only not the result of a decline of official integrity, *but they are the direct result of the fact that the Government is holding its subordinates to a stricter accountability than ever before.*"

For the doubters on the subscription list, the *Times* had final proof: "The number of suits begun; the number of indictments rendered; the number of convictions obtained, which are all matters of record, conclusively establish this fact."[19]

Others drew different conclusions after reading the record. On May 31, 1872, Charles Sumner, breathing fire, got up on the Senate floor and delivered a four-hour speech denouncing Grant. Still, and only for a short time longer, the party loyalist Sumner labelled his speech "Republicanism vs. Grantism." In the speech, which started out with only a few members in their seats and concluded with a jammed gallery, Sumner compared Grant to Caesar, George III, and "many of the most infamous characters in history."[20] He accused him of taking and giving bribes, an impeachable offense; scary talk from the leader of the Johnson impeachment drive. Neglect of duty was his smallest charge. "Grant," he insisted dramatically, "will be pronounced by future historians, first in war, first in nepotism, and first in gift taking."[21]

Iowa's Senator James W. Grimes, whose vote against Johnson's impeachment had cost him his career, gave his unvarnished opinion of Grant's party. "It looks at this distance as though the Republican party were going to the dogs. . . . Like all parties that have an undisturbed power for a long time, it has become corrupt, and I believe that it is today the [most] corrupt and debauched political party that has ever existed."[22]

Grimes' opinion of the party's moral state was confirmed by the actions of its leaders when the Crédit Mobilier scandal began to surface. Massachusetts' Oakes Ames, who was the conspiracy's paymaster in Congress, finally began to tell all; since Congress was the source of all the company's revenue, Ames explained, it had been vital to maintain its good will; even a less than determined investigation would have exposed the Crédit Mobilier hoax: it was, therefore, necessary to constantly placate the congressional gods with suitable offerings.

"I have found," Ames explained candidly as to why he had given railway stocks to so many of his congressional colleagues, "that there is no difficulty in getting a man to look after his own property."[23]

Ames' story, told before an uncomfortable Special Congressional Investigating Committee, was sensational: he confessed paying Vice-President Schuyler Colfax $1,200 as dividends on Crédit Mobilier stock he held for him in his account. Colfax wanted to know in cross-examination whether Ames had paid him the money while he was presiding in the Senate, or merely on the floor of Congress. Colfax's memory was defective on a number of matters, but Ames' flawless records were there to act as an irrefutable reminder.

Ames implicated scores of congressmen. Perhaps an exchange between himself and Pennsylvania Republican William ("Pig Iron") Kelley, known for his devotion to the protective tariff, will give the flavor of those tainted times.

Ames had accused Kelley of being a stockholder since June 1868. Kelley rose to question his benefactor: "How soon can you deliver my ten shares of Crédit Mobilier stock and dividends?" he queried.

As an uproar spread through the room, Ames reached into his pocket and produced the stock certificate. "I can deliver them now, Sir, and the dividends you can have soon."

Kelley, more concerned about his profits than his reputation, instructed Ames, "Hand them to the Chairman [Judge Luke Potter Poland] with the list of dividends, for my use."

Ames handed the list to the former Vermont jurist and then asked sarcastically, "If you say you don't own them, I don't see how you are entitled to the dividends."

Not to be deprived of what was his, Kelley publicly grasped the devil to his chest. "But you say I do own them, and I intend to make use of them."

Apparently "Pig Iron" knew his constituency; despite these revelations he was routinely renominated by the party and returned to Congress until his death in 1890.

Before the matter was finally powdered over on February 27, 1873, when Congress voted a censure motion only against Representatives Ames and Brooks, it had become apparent that a probable quorum of the House was supplementing its income with Crédit Mobilier dividends.

On February 25, Judge Poland delivered a two-hour explanation of why he was justified in not recommending action against additional congressmen. He admitted others had acted "with impropriety," but their acts, he claimed, were not of the kind specified in the narrow resolution Congress voted when setting up the committee.

This was the same lame duck Congress that during the next three weeks was engaged in what has come to be referred to as "The Salary Grab."[24] As the session was drawing to a close, a bill was pushed through that doubled the salary of the president, and gave representatives a 50 percent raise. Adding insult to injury, congressional increases were to be retroactive for the previous two years. Although the bill, as a result of this last provision, transparently violated the Constitution, Grant saw no difficulty in signing it. Only after cries of "steal" came from all sections of the country, did a chastened, if unrepentant, Congress reassemble to repeal the token of generosity it had bestowed on itself.

The impulse behind this congressional largess seemed to be a desire to have all, not simply the insiders, profit from power; Schuyler Colfax's perpetual smile had finally been explained. Surely there was enough merriment to go around for run-of-the-mill congressmen. After all, Representative James A. Garfield, soon to be president, had been a privileged Crédit Mobilier stockholder; even the Republican Speaker of the House, Maine's James G. Blaine, candidate for the presidential nomination at the next four conventions, was the recipient of railroad graft.

As the grease continued to be applied, Congress ladled out the national treasury with both hands: Jay Cooke's new Northern Pacific Railway was the beneficiary of even more munificent grants of public land. Cooke was able to gain approval for his land grab by means of lavish gifts of goods and money to such as Ohio's Governor Rutherford B. Hayes, another soon-to-be president, and a comprehensive list of politicians, including all already mentioned, plus newspaper reporters and editors throughout the country.

The *Times* financial reporter suggested, even while Oakes Ames was telling all about the Crédit Mobilier, that Jay Cooke's Northern Pacific 7.3 percent bonds were "a well secured and unusually profitable investment" for the average man. Cooke supported this estimate with the information that he had succeeded in selling the land given to him by Congress for $5.66 per acre, "which is at the rate of more than $100,000 per mile of road for the whole grant."[25]

Since it had cost Cooke less than $20,000 per mile to build the road, the *Times* recommendation seemed sound. But this good news for Grant's friend and entertainer[26] was not such good news for the despoiled taxpayer; without the bribery and excess profits, the rails could have been laid at a fraction of the final cost, the economy of the country would not have been disoriented, and thousands of people would not have been financially ruined.

What justice was there in allowing Jay Cooke to sell government land to homesteaders for $5.66 an acre when the government was willing to sell much the same acre, under the 1862 Homestead Act, for $1.25? In effect, Grant and his party cronies gave Cooke the money to build the railroad, and then guaranteed his profits; that was incredibly generous behavior for a second mortgagee.

Cooke was likewise generous to his powerful friend: Boxes of cigars, fast horses, rich food—even a fifty-thousand-dollar house in Philadelphia—were ordinary signs of his respect, and affection, for the president of the United States.

When the count was finally in, the government was revealed to have given 158,293,377 acres to the railroads,[27] not quite the size of Texas: state, county, and municipal partymen chipped in with extensive land grants, tax exemptions, outright donations of money, purchases of railroad stock, protection from competition, low-interest loans, and every sort of special privilege conceivable to a corporation lawyer's mind.

The record of criminal activity by Grant and his associates was far from complete by the time the 1872 election was held: The Whiskey Ring, the Treasury and War Department scandals were yet to come. Nevertheless, many of his former supporters, such as civil service reformer Carl Schurz, and Senators Lyman Trumbull and Charles Sumner, were completely alienated by what they already knew; they decided a second term for the decadent Grant could not be tolerated. Since the bosses of the Republican party did not share their view, nor their perception of right and wrong, the enlarging anti-Grant faction set about to create its own party; there was no way to challenge the iron grip that pro-Grant party professionals now had on the Republican nominating process.

In an attempt at descriptive accuracy, the disaffected named themselves the Liberal Republicans; which is not to say that, within their ranks, there was a complete absence of conservative opinion. Their platform called for a withdrawal of troops from the South without any further progress toward equality or protection for the freed slaves; its insistence on the resumption of specie payments, revealed the strength of Tory sentiment within the new party. Nevertheless, most liberal Republicans left Grant's shabby house to dwell in the new ark with Schurz and his brethren.

The original, somewhat idealistic party of Frémont, for free soil and free speech, was dead. What remained was a Republican party dedicated to the propositions that Jay Cooke knew the right way to do things, Jay Gould and his friends were fine fellows, and as long as that chummy Grant was in the White House, Chief Red Cloud and those Confederate felons would be the only occupants of federal prisons.

9

How Hacks
Produced Hacks

I don't care who does the electing as long as I do the nominating.

Boss Tweed[1]

In 1871 Thomas Nast, hot on the trail of Tammany Boss William Marcy Tweed, drew a cartoon of an obese clubhouse type with his thumb squeezing down on the skyline of New York; the caption challenged *Harper's Weekly* readers, "Well, what are you going to do about it?"[2]

The impotence of the average citizen was never more clearly demonstrated than it was during the following thirty years. The plunderers, the leaders upon whom no one could depend, were free to take over society, and they hastened to do so. In New York City alone, Tweed and his confederates stole perhaps as much as $200 million[3] (in today's dollars, undoubtedly in the billions) by means of padded bills, needless repairs, phoney payrolls, and whatever other forms of larceny were appropriate for the moment. Arrayed against him were a straggly group of civil service reformers, newspapermen, and maverick politicians—none of whom, at first, had the ability to more than delay the tide of public thievery.

Tweed's criminal success depended completely on his control of the New York Democratic party. For many citizens, it is disconcerting to entertain the thought that political parties may be the tools of criminals. Through a combination of self-serving advertising and the

117

willingness of most people to believe the best of public figures, leaders of political parties have often managed to clothe themselves in robes of civic purity. Tweed, however was too blunt and arrogant to trouble himself about appearances; and, as a result of his criminal flamboyance we are provided with a classic study of how parties actually function.

Tweed started out in precinct politics; originally a bookkeeper and saddler, he found the easiest path to success lay through the clubhouse door. He joined the volunteer fire department and parlayed his influence with this community organization into district status; his 7th Ward encompassed much of the Lower East Side of Manhattan.

When Tweed was elected alderman in 1851, his City Hall associates were already widely known as "The Forty Thieves." He by no means introduced corruption to a New York City that had known DeLancey, Burr, and Van Buren.

Although he served in Congress for one term, from 1853 to 1855, he was a man not enamored of the illusions of title and, instead, turned back to local politics, where the pickings appeared riper. By 1860 he was chairman of the county's Democratic central committee and was, thereafter, dictator of the municipal party. Elected to the New York Senate in 1867, he was, from that moment, leader of the state Democratic party, which he controlled from his hotel suite in Albany. It was there that Tweed and the members of his ring, the leaders of the Democratic party, decided that city contracts could be signed only if they had a 50 percent markup for them; within a short time the figure was raised to 85 percent.[4] Together with Jay Gould and James Fisk, he then began looting the Erie Railroad.

Tweed's hunger for graft was insatiable, and he had found the key to the mint. In a democratic society—regardless of the class or status into which one was born—it was possible for a determined crook to become a politician and be given control of the state's treasury, a bulging wallet to which he could otherwise not have access.

The genie in his Aladdin's lamp, that made this all possible, was his absolute control of the party. The cork bottling up the awesome power of the genie, and making it available only to him, was his control of the nomination process. If some gentleman wanted to be a judge, why, then pay Tweed's price. If a less ambitious striver wished to be an assemblyman, then never mind if he even knew where Albany was, as long as he knew who was the boss and how much the privilege would cost. The United States Senate nomination was auctioned off in the same manner. In fact, the Democratic nomination for any elective office in New York State, which was an absolute and rather exclusive requirement for a candidate's success, no longer had anything to do with the voters. In that all-important process, Boss Tweed cast the only ballot.

Tweed's raw tactics and the persistence of his media enemies led to his conviction November 5, 1872, on the eve of Grant's reelection. His abortive attempt to flee to Spain ended when he was wrapped in chains and returned to a New York jail, where he died miserably in 1878.

In one respect, Tweed was a somewhat unusual political boss; most are not interested in holding elected office. Their aim is fortune-building, and public ego-building can obstruct the achievement of that primary goal. There are thousands of such reticent politicos scattered around the country at any given time, and they are as little desirous of having their names and faces known as are any of the felons whose warrants decorate post office walls.

They are usually insignificant men who have failed at their first callings: lawyers waiting for clients who seldom materialize, journalists tired of the newspaper business, petty contractors dreaming of a municipal bonanza that will rescue them from bankruptcy—the disaffected and despoiled of every humble trade who see in the boss's den a haven in which plots for advancement are hatched and grubbers are turned into mayors, governors, and presidents.

Often young innocents are lured into these sanctums thinking they have entered some sacred democratic hall. Hoping for careers in government, they make their pilgrimage to the boss's inner temple, where his impact on them is devastating. If they are to remain, they must undergo severe character changes; their idealism is derided, or deviously exploited; they are forced to accept the values of the boss or leave politics.

The period of bondage experienced by the ordinary apprentice might last for years. During that time he must daily find new ways to humble himself. In short, he must, as quickly as possible, destroy his ability to function honestly. In the place of that desirable leadership quality he is habituated to accept the credo that the end, which increasingly becomes personal aggrandizement, always justifies the means.

The rich are the only major exceptions to this rule. Their money, should they deign to become directly involved in politics, purchases their independence although a surprising number slavishly conform to the leader's instructions.

At the 1972 Democratic National Convention in Maimi, Robert Wagner, former mayor of New York, confided that "rich men mostly want to rub shoulders with politicians. Give them the impression they are close to the action, invite them to a meal at Gracie Mansion, and their campaign contribution will be in the next mail."[5]

The more numerous Republican rich are usually involved in politics as merchants are involved in the marketplace: willing to pay a price for suitable merchandise. They are seldom a William Randolph Hearst, Averill Harriman, or Nelson Rockefeller in search of something missing from their ordinary dalliance with luxury. More often they are an Andrew Mellon, J. P. Morgan, or Jay Cooke; the head of some bank or oil company, determined to own a political party as one owns anything of worth.

The only other individuals who can function in politics without bending their knee to the boss are those who have achieved fame in some other field: athletes, movie stars, occasionally a literary figure. They frequently lend the glamour of their name to some candidate's campaign, much as they would endorse a commercial product. However, the same itch that makes them yearn for political notoriety often leads them to scratch to the boss's somewhat more muted command.

Women do not prosper in a field requiring so much calculated corruption. Some have suggested that the participation of women in party politics would raise its moral level. There is in this suggestion a lack of recognition about the debilitating effect of evil on innocence.

Women who enter politics must come to grips with the fact that the quality of the pros who make up the membership lists of the local parties can be matched in few places other than an encampment for Mafia soldiers. Thoughts of self-sacrifice are as rare in one place as in the other. Men who bind themselves in the service of a party boss seldom have aspirations more ennobling than to run some day for minor office or control their own clubhouse; the most successful of them are not as artless. The achievement of their goals is made easier by the careful choice of their companions; dishonesty does not flourish in the presence of sincerity; brutishness does not thrive in the presence of gentility. Women, in short, rarely find themselves welcomed in a clubhouse where the usual lack of surface cleanliness is merely a token.

Most men are equally repelled by the aroma of ordinary politics. It often takes a particularly calloused, amoral or simple son of Adam to find his home amongst such ethical squalor.

Some well-educated individuals, with the best of motives, do become involved in local politics: A civic issue attracts them—blocking an unwanted, politically inspired road through the most beautiful part of their region perhaps, or preventing the dumping of noxious materials. But whatever the source of their inspiration, it is usually based on a desire to "improve," to "clean up" politics. They recognize that the local politicians are often the main obstacle to this goal and, so, they become involved. The involvement, however, is rarely enduring. Their lives are shaped by the need to earn a living, or the demands of a healthy family life. They simply do not have the time, or the singleness of purpose, to overcome the predatory obsessiveness of the professional.

The largest number of partymen have about them a tragic aura; they are infrequently Richard Daleys with thousands of sycophants striving to please them: they are most often isolated Democrats in Midwestern conservative enclaves, or out-of-step Republicans in the solid South. Even in those areas where their party label matches the established faith, the pickings are so small that the most impressive rewards can be measured only in status symbols, such as who tells who to go out and get containers of coffee for the apathetic pros.

In short, party life, for many, is a form of diversion, which may not for much longer successfully compete with television. Unlike the night out with the boys at the bowling alley, however, it is an exercise, for most, tinged with covetousness and shaped by the basest motives. The major question that must sooner or later occur to members of society, who do not make a profit from this political racketeering, is: Why are such men allowed to choose the servants of the state?

That question first occurred with great force in America during the great surge of criminality surrounding Grant's administration. Yet time, indifference, and ignorance have thrown a protective mantle over Grant, and historians are prone to picture him as merely an unsuccessful president, which tends to mute the question; he was a man who accepted bribes; he did everything in the enormous range of his powers to obstruct justice when the destinies of his closest associates were involved; he lied with the frequency that a soldier curses, and saw nothing wrong with public officials growing rich from a broad spectrum of illicit activity.

Must we view him as a good man because he was our ruler? Must this criminal be clothed by our eyes in fictitious garments of virtue merely because those with felonious tendencies, who controlled the Republican party at that time, chose him as the successor of Lincoln?

The temptation to explain his failings as those of a simple, not a corrupt, man invites a repetition of the party irresponsibility which placed him at the head of the American government. Jailhouses in each of the fifty states are filled with simple men; these men are in jail not because they are simple, but because they are criminals. Grant's gullibility does not alter the fact that he was simultaneously a president and a criminal.

Despite this criminality the Republican party wanted to renominate him for a third time. But the greater crime was that the choice in this matter was now exclusively in the hands of just those men least able to exercise responsible judgment.

Was it reasonable to think they would never again choose a Grant?

10

An Opportunity to Inhibit Party Larceny

*From neither party, when in power, has the world any
benefit to expect in science, art or humanity, at all com-
mensurate with the resources of the nation.*

Ralph Waldo Emerson[1]

The most elementary fact of political life is that the average citizen
cannot possibly gain from the corrupt administration of government:
District leaders, clubhouse tenants, businessmen reaching for elusive
prosperity, lawyers in search of easy fees, gaggles of office holders,
even presidents can see an advantage in corruption; but for the taxpayer, the person concerned only with living a happy, productive life,
corruption is a drain worse than a spendthrift spouse or a weakness
for booze.

The waste is counted not only in money, but in objectives not
achieved, ponderous mistakes leading to wars and depressions, unsafe
cities, and the conviction that serenity can only be found on the other
side of the grave.

In the 1870s Grant's venal peccadillos convinced vast numbers of
Americans that some method must be found to limit the debilitating
impact of political parties on government. Their remedy was applied
half-heartedly, but was essentially correct. Led by Senators Carl
Schurz, Lyman Trumbull, and Charles Sumner, and reformers Whitelaw Reid and George William Curtis, they pressed for the creation of
a professional civil service system that would limit the ability of
spoilsmen to replace competent government employees with party
favorites.

123

The civil service movement was based on the concept of merit; it took its inspiration from the ancient Chinese, who subjected those who would serve the emperor to tests of competence. The leaders of the movement rejected Jackson's easy assurance that "qualified" government workers could be found behind any bush; they believed that greedy men would always reach for the control of riches available in government offices and were convinced that predacious drive was basically in conflict with efficient service.

If society was to function well, it was necessary to select men trained to understand that their interests lay in the direction of good performance. Sumner, Schurz, and Trumbull suggested that if party politics were banned from the bureaucratic process and men were forced to prove they were competent, government offices would be staffed with more capable personnel; no longer would the boss send someone to a supervisor in thrall to the party with instructions to place him on the public payroll regardless of his ability; no longer would such incumbents feel their first duty was to the clubhouse; no longer would public offices be emptied for weeks before election day as the troops deserted the national interest in order to serve the party.

As the 1872 election approached, Grant felt compelled to speak in favor of civil service reform; he was advised that there was a need to counteract the bad publicity arising from the scandalous behavior of his closest associates. Playing the game of politics in a traditional manner, he made gestures in the direction of good government; he appointed a Civil Service Commission in 1871, headed by George William Curtis, then editor of *Harper's Weekly*.

But as in the case of the tariff, which he lowered just before the election and promptly raised as soon as he was reelected, Grant's conversion to probity was merely a momentary lapse. With the election safely behind him, the Commission's recommendations were ignored and government jobs were filled on signal from the party.

In turn, party sachems, following a practice in effect since Jackson's time, levied assessments on those incompetents whom they were giving a ride on the public's back. The assessments were at a higher rate than those previously imposed, creating a greater thirst for boodle by those paying the tribute. In this manner, the Treasury was made a huge pork barrel for Republican organization men. Whitelaw Reid, who became editor of the *Tribune* upon Greeley's death (three weeks after Grant's victory over him), commented, "There is an utter surrender of the Civil Service to the coarsest use by the coarsest men."[2] The laxity of the times is indicated by the fact that the respected Reid barely edged out a job-hunting, disgraced Schuyler Colfax for the leadership of the most important paper in America.

Within a short while Curtis understood Grant had an active distaste for honesty, which made a mockery of his dreams of effective reform. He resigned as head of the Commission in 1875 when Congress failed to appropriate money for his work, and the country was surrendered to the spoilsmen.

Almost simultaneously, Michigan's Zachariah Chandler was appointed to Grant's cabinet, placing one of the country's leading political bosses in charge of civil service staffing—hardly a promising sign for those who wanted an elevation of the tone of government.

In this fashion the Grant administration went on its merry way.

Secretary of the Navy George Maxwell Robeson excelled in the selling of contracts to businessmen and finished his eight years of service to Grant several hundred thousand dollars richer than was legally possible.

Since much of the government's revenue depended on money realized from taxes on imports, the stewardship of the customshouses in New York and New Orleans were invaluable prizes for the party bosses who controlled them. They were, as a result, the worst sewers of corruption directly under Grant's supervision. When the larcenous activity of New York Port Collector Thomas Murphy was finally exposed, Grant's reaction was to accept his resignation "with regret."[3] A similar exposé of New Orleans Custom Collector Casey resulted in his reappointment. The country was being run as though it were a concession at a carnival. Sleazy people were in charge of seeing how quickly they could detach the multitude from their earnings.

With the collapse on September 17, 1873, of Jay Cooke and company, which owed much of its success to its party connections, the bubble burst; by 1876, the country's centennial year, the economy lay in ruins: there were over nine thousand business failures that year. James Russell Lowell, commissioned to write a poem celebrating the country's first hundred years, aimed his sarcastic comments at corrupt politicians:

> Show your State Legislatures, show your Rings;
> And challenge Europe to produce such things

As high officials sitting half in sight
To share the plunder and to fix things right;
If that don't fetch her, why you only need
To show your latest style in martyrs—Tweed:
She'll find it hard to hide her spiteful tears
At such advance in one poor hundred years![4]

The election of 1876 was to fix things right. The Republicans, realizing they had exhausted their credit with an impatient electorate, determined to nominate a mediocre, noncontroversial Civil War general, Ohio's governor, Rutherford Birchard Hayes. Hayes was a born compromiser, a quality highly praised by professional politicians, who place their faith in the principle that no one believes strongly enough in anything to be beyond the blandishments of a good offer. Prior to the war he was in favor of compromising with the South on slavery. Although sympathetic with the reformist aims of the Liberal Republicans in '72, he remained loyal to the tainted Grant and campaigned vigorously for the ticket.

The Democrats, short of generals at this point in history, turned to New York's governor, Samuel Jones Tilden. He had been much impressed with Van Buren during his sickly youth and had spent most of his delicate adult life as attorney for various railroads seeking to reorganize and refinance their watered ventures. His great service to the Republic came as Tweed's nemesis, and, as a result, during the years of the Grant administration, he developed a reputation as a reformer. While governor he exposed the operation of the "Canal Ring," a gang of politicians from both parties who were emulating Tweed's bill-rigging frauds, but this time in transactions arising from the repair of the state's canals.[5]

The Liberal Republicans, confronted with the fact that Hayes was generally considered honest, could find no reason to nominate their own candidate; which led Democrat Joseph Pulitzer to comment in the *New York World* about the only qualification of the next president, "Hayes has never stolen. Good God, has it come to this?"[6]

The Republican regulars fell in line. Even those soiled supporters of Blaine, who lost the nomination on the seventh ballot, as a direct result of his connection with a swindle involving the bonds of the

Little Rock and Fort Smith Railroad, had no excuse to object to a man of Hayes's demonstrated malleability.

The campaign was exceptionally bitter. The Republicans were not anxious to discuss the economic depression, which their ineptitude was intensifying, since the humane solutions for unemployment, mortgage defaulting, bankruptcy, evictions, and destitution involved probable financial losses for the wealthy backers of the party. Therefore, laissez-faire doctrinairism, already discredited in those early years of America's industrial revolution, was Hayes's only prescription for recovery. But he was realist enough to understand the unpalatability of such a nostrum. In a letter to Blaine, the leading quack in the party, he explained how his golden voice could be used to its best advantage in the campaign; in short, how he could best deceive the voters he had always specialized in deceiving:

"Our strong ground," the man who would be president said, "is the dread of a solid South and rebel rule. I hope you will make these topics prominent in your speeches. It leads people away from hard times, which is our deadliest foe."[7]

On November 7, after the ballots had been counted, it was obvious that guile had failed and Tilden had been elected; he had a popular majority of 250,000. The champagne corks were popped at Democratic headquarters.

The Democratic victory was obvious to everyone except Zachariah Chandler. He had noted a curious development: Although Tilden had, predictably, taken the Solid South and made significant inroads into the Republican North by garnering the votes of New York, New Jersey, Connecticut, and Indiana, there were still four states that had not filed definitive results. As matters stood Tilden had only 184 Electoral votes; he needed 185. If only these outstanding states—South Carolina, Florida, Louisiana, and Oregon—would end up in Hayes's column, he would win by one vote.

Although the celebrating Democrats could count as well as Chandler, the possibility that Tilden might not be the next president did not occur to them; he had substantial leads in Florida and Louisiana, and Oregon seemed likely to end up in his camp.

What they had not taken into account was the fact that Chandler, whose sticky hands had enriched him in a variety of ways, was not above stealing a national election. The morning after the balloting he sent the following telegram to his Republican counterparts in each of the four unrecorded states, "Can you hold your state?"[8]

Without any need for clarification, these men responded affirmatively. That afternoon, with the brevity of a ukase from the czar, Chandler issued a telegram declaring, "Hayes has 185 electoral votes and is elected."[9]

He had every reason to think his gambit would work: The South was still occupied by the Army, and each of the election boards in the three disputed Southern states were under Republican control. These boards found no difficulty in voiding enough Tilden votes to certify Hayes's victory. There was an ironic form of justice in this Republican practice, since Tilden's "victory" in several Southern states had depended upon the Ku Klux Klan's ability to terrorize blacks into staying away from the polls, where they would most certainly have cast their votes for Hayes.[10]

Since Oregon had probably been won by Hayes, no one's tender conscience was irritated when his Electors were sent to the national capitol.

In point of fact, on December 6, two sets of electoral returns were reported from each of the disputed states. Faced with this unprecedented occurrence, Congress determined, in the third week of January 1877, that an Electoral Commission would be created to arbitrate the claims of the contending blocs of Electors. It consisted of fifteen members, divided equally among the House, the Senate, and the Supreme Court; the fifth Supreme Court appointee was to be the commission's only independent; he was therefore expected from the beginning to be the only one of his peers who could be counted on to render an impartial judgment.

Unfortunately, Justice David Davis decided, instead, to accept appointment to the Senate by the Illinois state legislature, and the only other justice who could be found to fill that impartial spot was Joseph Bradley. Justice Bradley had entered politics as a Whig, in legal practice specializing in corporate law. He was conservative in all aspects of his public and private life.[11]

On the evening of February 8, 1877, Judge Bradley wrote a decision in the Florida dispute favoring Tilden. When the decision was read before the full commission the next day, the extended legal reasoning leading up to his conclusion was as it had been the night before, but his decision was in favor of Hayes.

A late-night visit from Grant's secretary of the Navy, Robeson, plus the pleadings of his wife, changed the direction of American history.[12] Those who think the individual insignificant, or women, before the Nineteenth Amendment was passed, politically impotent, should ponder Judge Bradley's conversion.

On the 16th, 23rd, and 28th of that month similar decisions were rendered in cases involving the other states. The only question that remained was, how could this first stolen presidential election be made acceptable to those whom it had victimized? The stability of the American system had been based on the universally accepted concept that once the majority spoke, everyone would support the successful candidate; but what was the defeated camp to do when it was in the majority?

Chandler's genius for intrigue was up to the challenge. His agents circulated among Southern congressmen, and other leaders of the Democratic Confederacy, offering a compromise. If they would accept Republican Hayes as the nineteenth president of the United States, he would end the Radical Reconstruction program: Federal troops would be withdrawn, a Southerner would be appointed to the Cabinet, and money would be appropriated for internal improvements below the Mason-Dixon line. It was an offer which could not be refused: If they deserted "Yankee" Tilden, their loss in the Civil War was to be wiped out. Nothing in the code of Southern chivalry seemed to stand in the way of such a profitable bargain.

Hayes was inaugurated on March 5, and the next day David McKendree Key, a former Confederate soldier, but then Democratic Senator from Tennessee, was appointed postmaster-general. Shortly thereafter, Sherman's rear guard was ordered to retreat.

Hayes, who was now popularly being referred to as "His Fraudulency,"[13] was never able to overcome the disreputable manner in which he had seized office. He compounded the error of his ways by rewarding every one of the members of the Louisiana election board that had certified his Electors. Similar gifts were given to others who had participated in the crime.

It was only natural that Hayes should attempt to redeem himself in the eyes of his countrymen. Unfortunately for the twenty-first president of the United States, Chester Alan Arthur, it was to be at his expense.

Arthur had been appointed collector of the Port of New York Custom House by Grant in 1871, as a gesture of appreciation for the extraordinarily obedient manner in which he had done everything the party had asked of him. His patron was New York's Republican boss Senator Roscoe Conkling. In his new position Arthur conceived of himself as Conkling's servant: consequently, the only way to be placed on the payroll of the Custom House was to come knocking at Arthur's door clutching a note from Conkling.

The matter of cheating his fellow citizens, which was involved in the employment of superfluous, unqualified personnel, never seems to have occurred to this future president. He simply added clerks, laborers, and supervisors to his staff as rapidly as Conkling could send them along. Soon the number of employees outpaced the vacant jobs—a minor problem for such an imaginative administrator.

Hayes thought this type of corruption unforgivable; he ordered Arthur to trim the fat. Since this was equivalent to a blow against the party, Arthur refused. In turn he was ousted; thus did a future president place his party in obligation to him.

Arthur was considered a hero by Republican regulars; he had been a victim of an ingrate. As the June 2, 1880, Chicago convention approached, Conkling was determined that a man of such sterling loyalty must be rewarded. He would have preferred that the party nominate him, or, if blind to his qualities, turn to men of equal virtue, James G. Blaine or Ulysses Grant. Grant was proving himself as inept a private citizen as he had been a president. He had mismanaged his affairs to the point where he was near bankruptcy and would shortly be a candidate for charity. Sooner than have that happen, Conkling, Cameron, Chandler, and Boutwell, the moral leaders of Republicanism, decided to place Grant back in the White House.

Washington's hand reached out from the grave to hold him back. Grant's opponents argued that if the father of his country, a man of indisputable ability, would not allow himself to be nominated for a third term, how could that honor be given to a man such as Grant?

When all the compromises were effected, after thirty-six ballots, the ticket consisted of Civil War General James Abram Garfield and New York's own Chester Alan Arthur. Hayes had committed himself at the time of his nomination to serve only one term, and although he might very well have changed his mind, neither Conkling, Cameron, Chandler or Boutwell thought it necessary to inquire.

Garfield's sordid career was typical of the presidents who came to power post-1840. He had a bland, broad face framed by a neatly trimmed beard and mustache; the effect was visually heroic and reinforced the frequent references, in his campaign material, to his wartime service. In all matters of mind and heart, however, he was extraordinarily ordinary.

Soon after he entered Congress, in 1869, as representative from Ohio, Garfield was placed on the Appropriations Committee. From this fulcrum of power he managed to implicate himself in enough transgressions to send a platoon of his Civil War draftees to the stockade.

The *New York Sun* was first to point out the deficiencies in Garfield's character. At the height of the 1872 campaign the *Sun* accused him of having accepted a bribe from Oakes Ames in the form of shares in the Crédit Mobilier. Ames was in the process of being exposed, and chose in the early stages of the investigation to conceal as much as possible, apparently in the hope of gaining the covert support of his numerous congressional accomplices.

On December 17, 1872, he began speaking of Garfield to Judge Poland's committee. "I agreed to get ten shares of stock for him and hold it until he could pay for it. He never did pay for it or receive it."[14]

This was hardly a forthright defense of the Ohio congressman. None of the lawmakers Ames bribed ever paid for their share of the swindle, and most of them conspired to have Ames hold their anonymous certificates since they believed him reliable enough to deliver their *dividends* in the correct amount at the appointed hour.

Ames, determined to avoid the penalty of perjury, answered questions gingerly.

Q. He received no dividends?
A. No sir; I think not. He says he did not. My own recollection is not very clear. . . . He had some money from me once. Some three or four hundred dollars, and called it a loan. He says that is all he ever received from me and that he considered it a loan.

Garfield professed outrage and demanded the right to rebut his accuser. He was given that opportunity January 14, 1873. He admitted

Ames had offered him stock in 1868 and described the terms. He could pay $1,000 plus interest on delivery, *or* he could simply wait until dividends had accrued to the face value of the stock and then wipe out his indebtedness. How many pressed speculators have fruitlessly dreamt of similar generosity by their brokers?

Then in a burst of seeming candor that was finally punctuated by obscurity, he confessed. "I probably should have taken the stock if I had been satisfied in regard to the extent of pecuniary liability."

Some laggard on the committee, apparently confused by the meaning concealed in his last two words, inquired whether he had suspicions about the origins of the Crédit Mobilier's profits. Garfield evaded answering and his colleagues were too polite to press him.

He did describe the terms of the *loan* to which Ames had referred. "Mr. Ames stated to me that if I concluded to subscribe for the Crédit Mobilier stock I could allow the loan to remain until the payment on that was adjusted." In short, Ames was to give him money, and he was not to repay it. Some might call this a loan, to others it appeared little more than a traditional bribe.

This gentle game of public deception went on until January 22, when the panicked members of the Crédit Mobilier's board of directors righteously announced they were going to demand an accounting of all the stock Ames claimed to have given to congressmen. This was the equivalent of having the head of a numbers mob call in Price Waterhouse to check on the dependability of his collectors.

It had the effect, however, of compelling a greater amount of concreteness from Ames, who was now intent on clearing himself before those whose opinion he most valued: his Crédit Mobilier paymasters. Records, checks, memorandums, thought by those congressmen involved to have been so far down the biodegradeable line that their safety was guaranteed, suddenly appeared on the committee table in front of a perspiring Ames.

When questioned again about Garfield, his tone had become firmer and his memory clearer. Garfield, he swore, had taken the ten shares of stock and, as in the case of other congressmen, he had "carried it for him." There had quickly been a $600 cash dividend, which combined with $776 due the incognito Garfield as a bond "bonus" for his *purchase* of the original shares, placed the fortunate congressman in the position of receiving a balance of $329 in cash, plus the clear ownership of ten shares of the glamour stock of his day—all of this without his having risked a single cent.

Ames remarked ironically, "He calls this a loan."

In the face of these much more specific accusations, Garfield chose not to risk a second appearance before Judge Poland's easily satisfied jury. This unwillingness to defend his honor under oath was generally taken as a confession of his guilt. The *Times* editorialized on February 19, 1873, "Of the members referred to, Messrs. Kelley and Garfield present the most distressing figures."[15]

For these felons there was in the Crédit Mobilier affair at least the comfort of company: however, in the winter and spring of 1874 the soon-to-be-president revealed his willingness to go it alone when there was a profit to be made.

The matter came to light when a joint congressional committee was looking into allegations of extravagance and laxity in the letting of District of Columbia paving contracts. In its capacity as overseer for the district, the committee was particularly concerned about a recent contract given to a G. R. Chittenden. He had convinced local politicos of the superiority of a new process, called "DeGolyer pavement," wherein wooden blocks were laid down to form (he claimed) a more durable and smoother roadway.

In order to obtain the contract, Chittenden had hired Congressman Richard C. Parsons of Cleveland to act as his agent. From the spring of 1872 on, Parsons exerted himself to win the $700,000 prize for his employer, when at the same time he was supposedly exerting himself on behalf of the citizens of Cleveland. It was an age of great confusion for many politicians on, what was for them, the much too subtle issues surrounding the question of conflict of interests.

The main reason for hiring Parsons seemed to have been to gain access to his Ohio colleague, the pivotal head of the Appropriations Committee, James Garfield. Without his endorsement it was extremely unlikely government money would ever make its way into Chittenden's pockets.

At the conclusion of his successful lobbying efforts, Congressman Parsons received $16,000. Without a moment's hesitation he deposited $5,000 of it into Garfield's bank account. The committee investigating the matter determined that in excess of $72,000, or approximately 1/7th of the total value of the contract, was paid out to citizens with no other roadbuilding talents than their influence.

The *New York Independent,* July 30, 1880, took the occasion of Garfield's bid for the Republican presidential nomination to look back six years and evaluate his qualifications for a deluxe accommodation in the federal penitentiary: "Of course Mr. Garfield's argument was successful. How could it be otherwise? He was chairman of the Committee on Appropriations. Every cent of money voted to the district had to come through him. They could not afford to refuse him anything that he asked, and Mr. Garfield knew it when he asked and received for his services a fee which would have been grossly extravagant but for his official position as guardian of the Treasury of the Nation. . . ."

Garfield's defense was stated in a letter to the *Chicago Tribune:* "The fact of my being a member of Congress does not disable me from the legitimate practice of law and this was as legitimate as any other practice."[16]

There were some lawyers who took offense at this explanation. Most of those few, however, were in no position to affect Garfield's destiny. His career had been besmirched just enough by the Crédit Mobilier and DeGolyer paving contract scandals to make him a potential candidate for the handful of men who now chose the president.

The party's debt to him had been incurred on an almost daily basis, so regular and dependable were his partisan instincts. When Rutherford B. Hayes's Electoral votes were being challenged in November 1876 by those petulant Tilden guerrillas, the Republicans selected General Garfield as their representative in Louisiana to make sure that the count came out right.

Despite those eminent qualifications it took Grant's phalanx until September 1880, more than three months after the Chicago convention had officially chosen Garfield, to accept his nomination over Grant and recognize him as the party's candidate. It is clear that without the inclusion on the ticket of Conkling's protégé, Chester Arthur, a substantial pro-Grant segment of the party would have sat out the election.

His 214-to-155 Electoral victory over three opponents was not as one-sided as those figures would indicate. His chief adversary was General Winfield Scott Hancock, a genuine Gettysburg hero. The Democrats had somehow managed to persuade him to let them use his prestige to convince the Northern multitude they were not lepers. Running on a platform almost indistinguishable from Garfield's, he collected 4,442,035 votes, a mere 7,018 less than the successful candidate. When the total of two new minority parties was added to the equation—308,578 for James B. Weaver and the Greenback party, and 10,305 for Neal Dow of the Prohibitionists—[17], it was incontestable that a substantial majority of his countrymen did not want Garfield to be president.

No sooner was Garfield sworn in than it became apparent he intended to conduct himself in a manner which would make the Grant administration seem honorable. On March 5, as almost his first act in office, he appointed James G. Blaine secretary of State. This was considered a slap in the face of Conkling and his friends, but in reality it was a body blow to the good government forces.

Blaine was a fixture in the Republican party for over thirty years: during all that time he dominated committees, selected candidates for high office, shaped issues and acted as a spokesman for the party. Yet it would take superhuman effort to discover a single occasion on which he acted selflessly for the benefit of the nation. He was the epitome of the mindless, unethical, scheming politician, quick to use his superb oratorical talents to extol the virtues of party loyalty, while equally adept at whipping his audiences into a vendetta over issues such as the British and Jefferson Davis.

Despite his years in Congress, there is no legislation of consequence which bears his name. He was a selfish man who could not see beyond his own needs and could act only when his interests were involved. Using hatred as his chief vote-getting contrivance, and spoils as the energy source for his political machine, he was perhaps the most successful politician of his era, and certainly one of the most dissolute.

Garfield's choice of him to occupy the senior-most position in the cabinet was a blow to the reform movement; it was also a signal that Conkling's wing of the party was to be deprived of patronage. The pot came to a boil within a month when Garfield appointed Conkling's enemy, William Robertson, as collector for the New York customshouse. Conkling was in a rage and, from March 23 to the middle of

May, he fought the appointment in Congress. When Garfield finally prevailed, Conkling resigned from the Senate in a peevish attempt to demonstrate his outrage.

The situation was chaotic. In effect Conkling had retired from politics on the issue of customshouse spoils, while his puppet, and former customshouse bagman, Chester A. Arthur, was vice-president of the United States—but not for long.

On July 2, 1881, scarcely four months after he had taken office, Garfield was shot. Charles J. Guiteau, a somewhat insane supporter of Conkling, who described himself as "a lawyer, a theologian, and a politician," had walked up to Garfield in the Washington railroad station and shot him, declaring, "I am a Stalwart (Conklingite), and Arthur will be President."[18]

Guiteau had his way; Garfield died slowly and agonizingly on September 19. Guiteau was convicted after a sensational trial that gave full satisfaction to his thirst for publicity. While waiting in jail to be executed, he wrote a short book entitled *The Truth and the Removal*, in which he gave additional reasons for killing Garfield. "I say the Deity inspired the act and forced me to do it. . . . I say Garfield deserved to be shot, and I was God's man to do it."[19]

He demonstrated his insanity anew by publishing his literary Rorschach at his own expense and selling it only from his jail cell. The price of the book was two dollars, and he offered the 1,000 subscribers, practically from the gallows, the opportunity to purchase "photographs with autographs $9 per dozen or $1 each."

His execution on June 30, 1882, accomplished something his diseased brain never imagined. Garfield's assassination dramatized the foolishness, if not the sheer lunacy, of staffing the American government periodically with large numbers of incompetents—some marginal few of whom, like Guiteau, were potential assassins—whose only qualification was that they supported the winning side.

The spoils system had been under systematic attack for at least two decades. Lincoln had warned it was "going to ruin republican government,"[20] and Charles Sumner had introduced a civil service reform act into the Senate as early as 1864. It was spoils-seeking Guiteau, however, who jolted Congress into action; and on January 16, 1883, "Gentleman" George Pendleton's reform finally became law.

A three-man Civil Service Commission was created to administer a series of competitive examinations for approximately 12 percent of the federal bureaucracy. Future presidents were given the power to place additional jobs under the protection of the act: Cleveland, Wilson, and the two Roosevelts were responsible for raising the number of eligible civil servants from the original 14,000 to approximately 2,600,000 by 1974. A key provision of the bill outlawed the levying of political kickbacks, an activity in which the now President Arthur specialized.[21]

The theory of the Pendleton Act was beyond reproach. Morale in the civil service rose sharply as depoliticized workers realized they could not be fired merely because they had bet on the wrong horse. At the same time the efficiency of government workers improved; a person who acquired his or her job after studying for a difficult test was far more likely to be capable of meeting the demands of that position. If promotion within an agency was based on knowledge and demonstrated ability, then a cadre of responsible government workers could quickly replace the patronage leeches.

The major defect of the reformed civil service system was its inability to eliminate political influence, especially at the summit of the structure. No matter how thoroughly the concept of merit was accepted for the mass of jobs within any particular agency, those men in control of policy were always appointees of the chief representative of the party system: the president, the governor, or the mayor. The theory persisted that those top-level administrative jobs should be responsive to the shift of political opinion as reflected in the latest elections.

The fact was that democratic theory had nothing to do with the function of most government employees. Whether a man was a Democrat or a Republican, whether he was "rotated" according to the results of an election which was won, perhaps, on nothing more substantial than a candidate's personality, did not affect his ability to devise a postal system that would operate more efficiently. An independent, who had spent his life dealing with ordnance, was better qualified to make final decisions on new weapons than some representative of a victorious party, whose reward for faithful service was the office of secretary of the Army.

Overlooked in the criticism of the spoils system, before 1883, was the fact that a large number of government employees retained their jobs despite the shift of power from one party to another. It was simply impractical to fire everyone; nor was it necessary. There were enough jobs to satisfy the clubhouse gang and retain a somewhat basic staff to give continuity to government service. Although the parties were denied complete control of all jobs down to floorsweeper, which they had previous to the Pendleton Act, their control was to remain almost as decisive as it had ever been, since the key jobs—the most profitable and pivotal ones—were still at their disposal.

Despite the spread, after 1883, of the civil service competitive examination concept to state and local government, party influence was strong enough to restrain the reformers from instituting a top-to-bottom merit system; for example, the hiring of provisional appointees, who were not obligated to take any exam, but received comparable pay, became a common abuse.

In many respects halfhearted civil service reform provided partymen with an aura of respectability that concealed a patronage system operating on much the same principles, and with much the same opportunities for plunder, as had existed in those halcyon days when Roscoe Conkling routinely sent word to his candidate for president to make room for another feeder at the public trough.

11

Emergence of the One-Party System

Were parties here divided merely by a greediness for office, as in England, to take part with either would be unworthy of a reasonable or moral man. . . .

Thomas Jefferson[1]

Once in control of the nominating process, the party leaders wielded their power as might have been predicted. Following Van Buren in 1838 were a group of nonentities, whose best description is a mere listing of their names: William Henry Harrison, John Tyler, Zachary Taylor, Millard Fillmore, Franklin Pierce, and James Buchanan.

The only president of that pre-Civil War era who raises his head above that limp collection of handpicked hacks is Polk, likewise a handpicked hack, distinctly second-rate, but whose aggressive willingness to push Mexico around in 1845 resulted in the expansion of the national boundaries. That interim was a long time for a growing nation to be deprived of substantial leadership, and may well be one of the reasons why slavery, which was ended in the British Empire by act of Parliament, could be ended in America only with the shedding of blood.

Lincoln temporarily interrupted this succession of convention-chosen inadequates; however, before he could be elected, it was necessary to create a new party. In its fledgling state the inexperienced Republican organization, acting under the inspiration of an extraordinary issue, selected an outstanding leader.

Grant's administration—chosen when the new party was little more than a decade old—represented a return to form. The selection of the president was once again in the hands of clubhouse loiterers, who every four years rubber-stamped the choice of the handful of men to whom they owed the most.

Their preference for Hayes, Garfield, and Arthur confirms their taste for the obedient and the opportunistic. With the selection of Hayes, and Arthur's accession to office, after Garfield's brief tenancy, the party leaders were confronted with a new problem. Although Hayes and Arthur were both men of blemished background, they made some effort, once in the White House, to behave as honestly as men beholden to political parties could—too honestly to permit the men who controlled the nominating process to allow either of them to run for reelection.

Instead, in 1880 the Republican kingmakers picked the more dependably corrupt Garfield to succeed Hayes, and in 1884 they settled for James Gillespie Blaine to take apostate Arthur's place at the head of the Republican ticket. Blaine was entirely unacceptable to the independents, who had demonstrated their tenderness on the honesty issue by previously creating the anti-Grant Liberal Republican party.

When the Democrats, desperate to break the drought that had lasted since they had placed Buchanan in the White House, nominated New York's governor, Grover Cleveland, the independent Republicans fell in behind him. Labelled "Mugwumps" because, according to one wit, they had their mugs in one party and their wumps in another, they cried that civil service reform was more important than party loyalty. Led by Carl Schurz, Charles Francis Adams (the latest blossom on the Adams tree), and George William Curtis, they spoke tirelessly against Blaine, maintaining he symbolized all that was evil in government.

Within a short time publication of the notorious "Mulligan letter," incriminating him in a railroad swindle while he was Speaker of the House, confirmed the Mugwumps in their indignation. One of these messages from Blaine had instructed the recipient, in a cautious postscript: "Burn this letter."

Once again Blaine's honor was brought into question; and once again this man, who would be president, was unable to clear himself. It was a situation in which a thief, who happened to be a politician, was running for the presidency. In this endeavor he had the enthusiastic support of most leading Republican politicians, who apparently saw nothing but advantages to having a man of his propensities at the head of the government.

Democratic rallies and parades were stirred with chants underscoring Blaine's character deficiencies.

> Blaine, Blaine, James G. Blaine
> The continental liar from the State of Maine
> *Burn this letter!*[2]

Now barrister Conkling, seldom known to make this distinction before, when asked to campaign for Blaine, responded, "I don't engage in a criminal practice."[3]

The Republicans, perhaps attempting to prove Democrats could also violate accepted codes of conduct, publicized the fact that Cleveland had fathered a child by a woman not his wife. This had apparently occurred while he was a young bachelor in Buffalo, a city where he developed a reputation as a straitlaced, exceedingly upright sheriff and mayor. Cleveland promptly admitted the truth of the accusation and was shortly elected president; the fact that women did not vote might have been an influential factor in Cleveland's success. Perhaps even more important was the quality of the candidate opposing him.

Blaine, a man incapable of accepting responsibility for his failures, persisted in thinking the reason for his defeat was a visit by the Reverend Samuel D. Burchard to his Fifth Avenue Hotel room on October 29, 1884. After a short sojourn with a smiling Blaine, Reverend Burchard had emerged to tell the press that, in his estimate, the Democrats represented the party of "Rum, Romanism, and Rebellion."

Offered the Hobson's choice of repudiating the parson and offending the Protestant communion, or endorsing his view and outraging Irish Catholic electors, who might rouse themselves to desert their "rum" long enough to vote against him, Blaine chose to remain silent. This proved to be too neutral a position for many New Yorkers of the Roman persuasion, and they demonstrated their rebellious nature by trooping to the polls. Blaine lost New York by 1,149 votes out of a 1,125,000 total, which was enough to tip the Electoral College balance in Cleveland's favor, 219-182.

The popular vote was extremely close: Cleveland had 4,911,017;

however, when Blaine's 4,848,334 was combined with the 325,739 total of the Prohibition and Greenback party candidates, it becomes clear that once again, as in most of the elections which took place in those middle years of the Republic, the winning candidate did not have a majority.

The closeness of these tallies denoted, as much as anything, the inability of the American voter to detect substantial differences in party positions. To the mass of farmers and urban workers, who comprised most of the adult population, neither party was a reliable advocate of their interests. No longer excluded from the electoral process by property qualifications, the working man was closed out of political decisions just as completely by his inability to influence party judgments. Neither of the major parties made more than a pretense at representing him.

In fact, both parties straddled most issues. The Democrats championed lower tariffs until Cleveland took over and then did nothing to lower them. Both parties publicly claimed to be in favor of civil service reform, but neither allowed this to stand in the way of patronage requirements. Cleveland spoke bravely of expanding the number of federal employees to be covered by the merit system, but managed to fire 15,000 Republican postmasters to make room for needy Democrats. His successor, Benjamin Harrison, grandson of William Henry Harrison (and therefore automatically presidential timber), did a more thorough job and, within a year, had dismissed 30,000 postmasters who did not meet the standards set by party leaders.

The real rulers of America were its businessmen, and although they had a preference for the Republicans, they did not allow that label to influence them against a potentially cooperative winner merely because he was a Democrat; contributions from the largest corporations flowed into the campaign treasuries of both parties.

Once in power, the contributor could depend on a Republican Hayes to break "The Great Strike" of 1877 or a Democratic Cleveland to break the Pullman strike of 1894. Republicans or Democrats from Grant through William McKinley were equally unsympathetic to the plight of men not of their circle. Both parties viewed workingmen as potential enemies of the state who, out of malice, or without understanding what they were doing, might bring the country's commerce to a halt. The viewpoint of the stock market manipulator had largely become the viewpoint of the politician.

The Republican presidents of this era were, without exception, in the service of the robber barons then pillaging America. Congressman William McKinley, chairman of the Ways and Means Committee, saw nothing unethical in catering to the wishes of his Cleveland industrialist friend, Mark Hanna. Since Hanna wanted a high tariff, and had the money to purchase it, McKinley, in 1890, pushed the tariff bill, which bore his name, through Congress.

Hanna, never one to ignore the opportunity to express his gratitude, eagerly raised money in 1893 to redeem defaulted notes McKinley had endorsed for a friend.[4] His willingness to accept money from a man whose fortune had been enlarged by his congressional efforts endeared McKinley to those charged with finding an acceptable Republican candidate after the death of the party favorite, Blaine. McKinley soon showed the disadvantage of coming up through the party organization; he led America into a war that he personally opposed, because the jingoists in his party insisted, and was, to the day of his death, an undistinguished partyman of dubious ethical standards.

It is the act that is important, not the stated intention; and most of the important acts of those chief magistrates added to the wealth of their business sponsors, while they simultaneously impoverished the Midwestern farmer and the city workers: Trusts grew, violent elimination of competition went unchecked, the power of government was used to destroy unions and prevent the introduction of safety devices in factories and mines, interest rates rose until the worker's income was dissipated while fiscal frauds and tax manipulations were developed and elaborated.

Exceptional men were rarely able to get by the screening process of the national convention. Teddy Roosevelt, despite the strenuous efforts of party leaders, was the first of these; his exploits as a "Rough Rider" in the Spanish-American War had made him so popular that Hanna's opposition was not sufficient to deny him the 1900 vice-presidential nomination. However, it was the assassination of McKinley in 1901 that gave Roosevelt the presidency the party leaders would otherwise have denied him. During the time between the Grant administration and the turn of the century, each president, carefully chosen for office by the political leaders of the Democratic and Republican parties, was an unrelievedly dreary mannikin, without the brains or energy to intelligently direct the awakening industrial giant.

Even more discouraging was the quality of the men selected by these bosses to run the political establishment. The underpinnings of the American government—city councils, state legislatures, and Congress itself—were mired in corruption that was encouraged, in fact required, by party leaders. The men provided by party machines to service the American people were most often incapable of distinguishing between right or wrong; some, who could make that distinction, preferred not to.

Henry Adams wrote in his novel, *Democracy,* of those political types he knew so well. His heroine, Madeleine Lee, was proposed to by Senator Silas P. Ratcliffe, a facsimile of Grant's secretary of the Treasury, George Boutwell. In order to win her, he confessed securing reelection to the Senate by dishonest means, and, to further prove his candor with her, told of voting a steamship subsidy to gain a large donation to the party. Adams described Miss Lee's reaction: ". . . the more she saw of him, the surer she was . . . that he talked about virtue and vice as a man who is colorblind talks about red and green."

With a burst of Victorian righteousness, she rejected the Senator's proposal. But Ratcliffe, driven by his passion for the beautiful Madeleine, pressed his suit, finally to be repulsed in a manner that pleased readers throughout the world.

"Mr. Ratcliff! For one long hour I have degraded myself by discussing with you the question whether I should marry a man who by his own confession has betrayed the highest trusts that could be placed in him, who has taken money for his votes as a Senator, and who is now in public office by means of a successful fraud of his own, when in justice he should be in a State's prison. I do not doubt that you will make yourself President, but whatever or wherever you are, never speak to me or recognize me again!"[5]

That the Ratcliffes, after the Civil War, were making themselves president with increasing frequency finally depended on one factor: their selection was in the hands of a group of men anxious only to find a candidate who, in return for their favor, would pour money into their pockets.

The Congress, mostly under control of state and large-city machines, consistently positioned itself to more accurately reflect this mercenary viewpoint. Each party had its cadre of special-interest representatives sitting in the Senate. This was not too difficult to arrange, since senators were still chosen by majority vote in the state legislatures, and even the minor restraint of going to the people on election day did not exist; Senate seats were regularly bought from party leaders by those most able to pay the price.

That there were men of integrity in the Senate is attested to by the presence of Carl Schurz and Lyman Trumbull, two of the most virtuous spirits in American history. Both of them, however, were out of the Senate by 1875; thereafter, the tenants of that temple were a singularly shady group. For the last thirty years of the nineteenth century and the first decade of the twentieth, before the Constitution was amended to allow for the popular election of senators, mostly lobbyists and political bosses occupied that chamber, making of it a commercial exchange where votes were brought and sold.

In this grubby atmosphere, parties were largely indistinguishable; differences over issues had all but disappeared. In its place was a consensus that the words *money* and *success* were synonyms. Lawmakers extended their hands not as a sign of openness, but as an indication they were ready to receive tribute. It would have been difficult to find another group of that size anywhere in the country, including inmates of county jails, who had been so deeply involved in such a multitude of substantial crimes: conspiracy, bribery, obstruction of justice, and perjury were only some of the more frequent felonies practiced by these master politicians.

Each of them wore a party label prominently, but it no longer had great meaning; there had been a merger of the two-party system: there were sugar, lumber, railroad, mining, banking, and oil senators, not Republican or Democratic senators. Congressmen with ambition courted the most powerful special interest representative in their district, and swore their allegiance.

In the South, after the mid-1870s, there was, without any pretense, a one-party system. The Democrats, with the help of nightriders of the KKK, effectively outlawed the Republicans. Using "white supremacy" even more effectively than the Republicans used "the bloody shirt" in the North, there was so little challenge to the Democratic candidates that the November elections were meaningless; the issue of who would be elected was decided in springtime Democratic primaries, where Republican voters were completely disenfranchised. The mass of Southern whites were as victimized by this one-party arrangement as were the blacks; for many of them were blocked from voting by poll tax levies, which required them to pay for the privilege of voting for some Democrat who was, in reality, designated for nomination by the local landowners, bankers, and assorted men of wealth.

John Sherman, unlike his brother General William Tecumseh Sherman, sought the Republican nomination in 1880, 1884, and 1888. He was, nevertheless, appalled at the influence of money in the selection of office holders. A man of abiding conservative instincts, he served in the Senate with distinction for all but four years between 1861 and 1897. After Harrison's election in 1888, he commented grimly that the country had "reached the last stages in the history of the Roman Empire when offices were sold at public auction to the highest bidder."[6]

Of no concern to the bidder was the party designation of the chattel on the auction block; in the South he was buying Democrats, in the North, Republicans. It was still possible to be a voter and believe there was something special about the party of Lincoln, or the party of Jefferson and Jackson, but the men who controlled the access to office did not burden themselves with such fantasies. For them party politics had become a business; and like most of the largest businesses of the day, it had become a monopoly, disguised as much as it could be to confuse casual observers, but essentially a system closed to outsiders.

12

The Myth of the
Imperial Presidency

A politician in this country must be the man of a party. I would fain be the man of my whole country.

John Quincy Adams[1]

Those who concentrate their attention on the glitter and noise emerging from the White House and on the secretive duplicity of the Nixon administration profess to see the growth of an imperial presidency. Jimmy Carter, in an attempt to dispel this regal image, took to carrying his own suit bags on Airforce I trips and playing in softball games with his brother Billy. Underlying this perception is the belief that our chief magistrates have increasingly, since Lincoln's time, accumulated powers, at the expense of Congress and the people, to a degree that might eventually threaten the democratic nature of the Republic.

Most pessimists among those theorists insist that irresistible power is flowing into the hands of this imperial potentate who now sits in Lincoln's chair. They claim that the mass of citizens are defenseless in the face of his enormous might and that democracy which had seemed so promising, two hundred years ago, is about to dead-end at a cliff overhanging a dark totalitarian sea. Their conclusion is that a demi-emperor reigns where once a citizen-president governed.

Since so much of the real power in American society is demonstrably concentrated in the hands of its mostly anonymous bankers, industrialists, and labor leaders exercising their power through party bosses, the attempt to conjure up the vision of Jimmy Carter as an

147

all-powerful ruler concerned with sending his opponents to the dungeon invites laughter.

There are misconceptions about the presidency that generate this fear: The first, perhaps, is that people want weak leadership. It is based on the idea that the president is an enemy of the people who must be thought of as a potential tyrant, and that, given the opportunity to seize power, he will; therefore, wise citizens desire a weak leader, who does not have the energy to think in such grand and oppressive terms. It is a variation of the fear expressed by some members of the Constitutional Convention when they contemplated the possibility that they were creating an "elected king."

The second misconception is that if the president is not strong and decisive, the people and their legislative representatives in Congress will be: This is a seesaw theory of politics. The theory seems to gain some force from Rousseau's belief that the people are innately good and knowing, and anyone who acts as their ruler has put them in chains. It also attributes to legislative bodies a wisdom and cohesiveness the lack of which, paradoxically, is frequently their most glaring shortcomings. Overlooked by that theory is the fact that people accept government, they obey rulers, precisely because as an unorganized mass they easily fall victim to the predators living within their midst.

Even as supposed head of his party, which may have majorities in both Houses of Congress, the president is not all-powerful. No matter how important he feels a legislative decision is, he is not able to call on party discipline, such as English party leaders have at their command, to exact obedience to his wishes. Each member of Congress, when confronted with a demand for support by his president, even if the president is of his party, first thinks of what reaction his vote will cause among the important people of his home district; and those important people are seldom the mass of voters. Before the president can list a congressman on his side of the tally sheet, he knows that congressman will have consulted with the party boss to whom he is most in debt, whose response will pivot on the thought: Will it offend or delight the people from whom I expect the donations that will finance the next campaign?

Even the most charismatic president must face the truth that his party is seldom of aid to him in organizing constructive political activity; it is more often a force to be overcome. Where the British prime minister can rely on his party to produce a majority vote for every part of his program from the day he assumes office until the day he relinquishes it, the president can only hope for a prolonged "honeymoon" at the beginning of his administration, during which exuberance and gratitude may win him the support of a temporarily benign Congress. Such power does not a Caesar make.

The writers of the Constitution had experienced enough drift and dizziness from the leaderless Confederation to know that vigorous executive leadership was necessary if the country was to survive. If it was true in those relatively uncomplicated days, how much truer is it now when indecisiveness can quickly lead to runaway inflation, to fuel shortages that bring the economy of the country to a halt, or to the threat of atomic annihilation. Some of our early presidents were extremely decisive, and stretched powers not so clearly granted to them, when they were confronted by special situations. Jefferson's decision to double the size of the country with the purchase of Louisiana is an oft-cited example of such an act.

Jackson was as decisive as his times would allow; it is doubtful a president has ever been so strong-minded and sure of his direction. Polk was grim in his determination to accomplish the task he had set for himself: Congressional sensibilities were shoved aside, diplomatic authority stretched beyond the breaking point, and executive powers tested to limits never before explored.

In short, even before Lincoln's terrible trial there were occupants of the White House who displayed what some critics of modern presidents must concede were imperial tendencies. Yet we think of these men as the most impressive to have occupied that office.

After Lincoln there was a stretch of thirty years during which men of minor substance posed as presidents; it was precisely at that point in our history that Congress dominated the scene. The result was a horror of inefficiency, selfish individualism, and monumental corruption. For although Congress was dominant, individual congressmen were under the domination of local party leaders. This bondage to the clubhouse resulted in congressional irresponsibility. Combined with an abdication of leadership by a series of party-chosen White House mediocrities, this produced an era of industrial injustice and economic depression: Farmers were bled, workers were brutalized, all under the lackluster hesitations of some exceedingly unimperial presidents.

On the other hand, presidents normally thought of as enlarging the powers of that office were seldom awesome or threatening, and were always least responsive to party orders. Theodore Roosevelt, the first of these modern "strongmen," was an inspirational figure: He was vital, courageous, sophisticated, and essentially honest. Yet, at the same time, he was a master of self-advertisement, certainly not a modest man, who made a point of never living up to his professed belief that if you "speak softly and carry a big stick, you will go far."[2]

Carrying a big stick, he, nevertheless, spoke in an exceedingly loud voice about anything involving his strong convictions: He insisted on conservation of natural resources when most Americans thought our resources were inexhaustible; he wanted a canal built through the diseased and desolate wastes of Panama, and would not restrain himself from accomplishing this epic service for mankind; he was the first president to attack the rapacious activities of socially irresponsible business combinations, a stand not popular with the leaders of the Republican party. Yet he did not consider himself some sort of secular deity, and his determination to act on his convictions did not convince him the convictions of others were valueless. He was pragmatic, inquisitive, and zestful: a joyous man, an exceptional leader.

When he turned his office over to William Howard Taft in 1909, and went on a hunting trip to Africa, thoughts of returning to the political wars were far from his mind. His former secretary of war and personal friend, the rotund, benign Taft, would do the job, so he thought. Taft, however, was the antithesis of the vigorous leader; during his four years in office he served as a cautious administrator rather than the leader of his country. In most matters, he was a good-natured procrastinator of conservative instincts, whose anti-labor attitudes were a measure of the distance between him and most voters.

The "imperial" Roosevelt came charging back to stage center in 1912. Convinced Taft had betrayed his trust, he offered himself as an alternative at the Chicago Republican convention. There is little doubt he was the most popular Republican in the country, and if nominated, would most likely have easily won; however, the party leaders, intent on proving they were the only ones who mattered, wanted the more pliant Taft, and so, they turned from the natural, most competent leader.

Despite Roosevelt's heroics, the bosses were able to control the convention; their most important allies were found in the feeble "rotten borough" Southern delegations, which seldom produced an electoral vote for the party on election day, but which had equal voice at the convention with more effective Republican vote-producing delegations from the North and West. By means of bribery, the exchange of votes for job pledges, and an assortment of other devices skillfully used by his political opponents, Roosevelt was deprived of the nomination.

In a fury, shouting "thievery," he bolted the convention and resigned from the party. Within six weeks he was back in Chicago standing before the convention of the new "Bull Moose" Progressive party, dedicated, he thundered, to "social and industrial justice."[3] On August 5, 1912, he was nominated and proceeded to conduct an issue-oriented campaign, which was marred, on October 14, by an attempted assassination in Milwaukee.

The assassin, upset because Roosevelt was seeking a third term, and, because, in a dream, McKinley had told him that he had actually been killed by Roosevelt, walked up to the smiling candidate, as he was about to enter his car, and shot him in the right breast. After calming the crowd, which wanted to lynch his assailant, Roosevelt made his way to the auditorium where thousands awaited him. Dripping blood from the wound—the bullet was still lodged in his muscle tissue—Roosevelt disdained his doctor's instruction that he must immediately be rushed to a hospital, declaring, "I will deliver this speech or die, one or the other."[4] He survived, as did the vanity that allowed him to make that statement. Given the opportunity to have his heroics worshipped by thousands in whom he had produced a passion, he could not resist.

The results of that campaign showed nothing more clearly than the power of the men who dominated the major parties and the effectiveness of the machinery they had developed to stifle opposition. In losing, the imperial-like Roosevelt received more votes than Taft: His electoral total was 88, compared to Taft's 8. But Roosevelt's effort had only made possible the election of Woodrow Wilson, a minority president in terms of popular vote, who, nevertheless, had the largest electoral majority, with 435 votes, to that point in American history.

Wilson was an extraordinary man. While governor of New Jersey, he boldly challenged the cozy arrangement between business and party politics. On August 29, 1912, he voiced his doubts about parties in a speech at Williams Grove, Pennsylvania. "I thank God that we have lived to see a time when men are beginning to reason upon facts and not upon party tradition."[5]

Only desperation had driven Democratic party bosses to nominate him for the presidency. It took 46 ballots to drag from them their reluctant consent; the party system produced a Wilson in spite of itself. Since Buchanan's administration, only Cleveland had temporarily given Democratic leaders the opportunity to dip their hands in the federal patronage pot. They reasoned that honest men, who had spoken of reform before elections, had most often yielded to expediency after assuming office, and gambled that Wilson would prove as tractable.

He must have worried them in his inaugural address on March 4, 1913, when he said, "The success of a party means little except when the nation is using that party for a large and definite purpose."[6]

Those supporting the theory of the imperial presidency profess to see in Wilson one of the chief examples of such a power-hungry leader. Sigmund Freud and William C. Bullitt wrote a study of Wilson's character that lent support to the vision of him as a puritanical, grim, righteous person intent on superimposing his Calvinist values on the world.

A president with such a character, in office during the worst war in history, could have easily exceeded Lincoln's wartime acquisitions of power. Wilson's detractors, those who see in this brilliant idealist an admirer of elected monarchy, should be able to support their claim by citing a series of dictatorial acts, or at least acts that suggest authoritarian tendencies. Instead, we see in Wilson the prototype of a confident, informed, self-assured leader, who although firm in his conduct of the war made the brutish exercise something like a democratic catharsis.

Even in this area, so foreign to his training and disposition, Wilson proved the ideal leader; he mobilized the nation in months and made a major contribution to the Allies' success. This was done with a minimum display of imperial truculence; in fact, each decisive move was explained in the most sincere and inspired democratic terms.

Even his innovative plans for peace, supported with all his strength, were pursued in a democratic manner. With the exception of Lincoln and Roosevelt, it seems doubtful that any White House resident selected by political bosses over the previous seventy-five years, would have been able to display a generosity of nature and breadth of vision expressed in his Fourteen Points. The League of Nations, despite its failure, was a quantum leap in international relations.

Those who inveigh against the imperial president must consider the events of the next year and a half when Congress, and its party masters, were free to conduct the affairs of the nation without any interference from a bed-ridden Wilson. As he lay incapacitated, scarcely able to speak, seen for weeks on end only by his doctors and newly wedded second wife, Congress did everything it could to avoid stepping into the breach.

The truth is that strong, wise executive leadership—profitable to the people of any country—is particularly important in a modern industrial nation, and the restraining influence of Congress works best in such a situation. Being called on, however, to be decisive and quick, when it is by nature contemplative, prone to compromise, susceptible to party pressure, and slow, makes unreasonable demands on this group of elected lobbyists. The failure of Congress during the period of Wilson's incapacity strongly suggests that Madison and his confederates had correctly chosen to provide the new government with an executive capable of acting decisively.

At the same time Congress provides the American people with a champion, albeit a much battered one, against usurpation of power by an out-of-control chief magistrate: His vetoes can be overridden; money for his projects can be withheld; confirmation of his nominees can be denied; opposition to his proposals can be loudly voiced in a protected assembly; his mandate to rule lasts only four years, and, finally, he can be removed from office.

The men who wrote the Constitution were far from certain they had fashioned the best possible institutions for every conceivable situation. In terms of the presidency, they recognized the limitations of legal restrictions written by a group of men who had passed from the scene. They depended even more on the democratic training each occupant of the White House would have before aspiring to that office. Such a commitment to democracy would be the strongest protection against any movement to convert a president into an emperor.

In effect, they had created an elected monarch, who was capable, under the powers they had given him, of all the excesses committed by the tyrants of their day: He could declare war, although prohibited to do so; ignore Congress, although ostensibly only its coequal; shape the direction of the economy and destiny of individuals at his whim, although theoretically the servant of all. During his term in office he was virtually invulnerable to criticism, although personal traits might make him willing to yield to it. With the abortive impeachment of Andrew Johnson, it had become clear that presidents were even less likely to be dismissed from office before their term expired, than a monarch would be expelled by revolution before death terminated his reign.

The potential for imperial expropriation lies in any executive position. Men who serve in such a capacity may yield to that temptation. But the real threat to a healthy democratic nation probably lies in the other direction. Who is more frightening—the president who acts resolutely at the proper time or the one who does not act when he should? The thing to fear is that craven, enfeebled, and corrupt men will occupy that office. That is a real menace—not a theory, not a phantasmagoric imperial vision, but democratic reality; for political parties produce such men, and the label "President" should not be allowed to disguise their fundamentally imperfect credentials.

The theorists of the "imperial presidency" ignore the fact that most of our presidents have been figureheads, titular leaders responding to the directions of party leaders. Those party leaders have most often chosen men who mirror their partiality for booty, dissolute decisions and easily abandoned convictions.

It is presidents produced by this debased party structure who have recently, and increasingly, projected this surface image of imperial splendor. More important has been the inner venality of these men; that is the quality sought by party leaders.

As long as tainted professional politicians maintain a stranglehold on the selection process, American presidents will tend to be facsimiles of the worst in our society, packaged gaudily, with mellifluous voices and handsome faces, but essentially compromised counterfeits of the models we would all want as our national leaders.

13

A Fool as President

I believe in political parties. They were the essential agencies of the popular government which made us what we are.

Warren Gamaliel Harding[1]

Warren Harding was the ideal candidate for party leaders, the man they would choose to be president every time, if only providence would produce such perfection, and the public would allow itself to be saddled with its consequences.

Born in 1865, he grew up poor in rural Ohio. At graduation from tiny Iberia College, his education had prepared him primarily for unemployment. He began to hang around the town's printing shop where, by dint of sweeping floors and practicing the other skills of a printer's devil, he learned the trade. He bought the ailing *Marion Weekly Star* in 1884, while still under twenty, and by this stroke found his salvation. He was not as lucky in his choice of a bride.

Florence Kling De Wolfe, daughter of the town's capitalist, had made an unfortunate first marriage to the town's drunk, as a consequence of a dalliance which brought into play a shotgun and resulted in a six-month pregnancy. Florence, a plain, ungainly, sharp-tongued grimling, shook free of her shiftless husband after four years of inattentitiveness.

Harding, although her social inferior and five years her junior, captured her heart soon after he purchased the *Star*. From that moment on, she was in hot pursuit. He, in turn, neither fled nor pursued. He was content to frequent houses along the railroad tracks where professional services were available, or visit girls in nearby towns who were attracted by his virile good looks, already accented by a streak of white hair starting at the center of his forehead.

He finally married her in 1891, and spent the rest of his life being guarded and tormented by her, although he never made any pretense of changing his bachelor taste for varied sexual liaisons.

He quickly began calling her "Duchess," rarely as a sign of affection. Driven by her ambition, and the beneficiary of a boom in Marion's population and wealth, he converted the *Star* into a daily and soon found himself prosperous and of some note in his small pond.

Politics entered his life as a diversion. He made his first mark when he successfully ran for the state senate in 1898, while his Buckeye neighbor, McKinley, was sitting in the White House publicly acknowledging his debt to Mark Hanna and the Ohio machine.

At that time, the legislature of almost any state was a poor place in which to mold the morality and social habits of a future president. The Ohio legislature had a particularly boss-ridden, repellent atmosphere; Columbus was, more than anything, a clearinghouse for businessmen in need of governmental favors. Six-foot, robust Harding found this atmosphere entirely to his liking.

The crucial event in Harding's life occurred one week before the 1899 election when chance brought him and Harry Micajah Daugherty together in the hamlet of Richwood, a few miles from Marion. They were there to attend a rally in the local opera house.

Daugherty was a well-known figure in Ohio politics; he had been chairman of the Republican state committee and selected by Hanna to deliver the nominating speech when McKinley had run for governor six years earlier. A lawyer by profession, he was on the payroll of the largest corporations doing business in Ohio: among others, American Tobacco, Armour, American Gas and Electric, and the telephone company.[2] His three years in the state legislature had familiarized him with the wheels within wheels that made the machinery of that politically sophisticated state move; corporations in trouble in Ohio beat a path to his law office.

In his alternately frank and disingenuous reminiscence about

Harding, *The Inside Story of the Harding Tragedy,* he wrote of his professional life. "I was offered positions on the bench by two Presidents and refused them, having grown to love the battles on the floor of a convention. I became a political leader instead of an office-holder—from choice. . . . I frankly confess to a leadership in the so-called 'Ohio Gang' for about forty years."[3]

He came upon Harding, he related, in the cluttered backyard of the Globe Hotel, where they had both spent the night waiting for the rally. Daugherty was there seeking water from the hotel's pump, since luxuries such as indoor plumbing had not yet been installed in Richwood's only elegant public house.

He found Harding polishing his shoes. He was warmly greeted and offered a chew from Harding's tobacco plug.

Stocky, square-headed Daugherty looked at the stranger through one brown and one blue eye, his aggressive chin thrust out, his small mouth turned down perpetually as a sign of unrelenting doubt; and Daugherty recalls that as Harding's graceful figure disappeared from view he remarked to himself, "What a great-looking President he'd make!"

Daugherty's reputation for moral ambiguity was already well established. However, this helped him within the party, where any other kind of reputation would have aroused suspicion. One of the members of the legislature who had served with him labelled him "paymaster for the boys."[4] Columnist Mark Sullivan, who knew Daugherty well, described his *modus operandi:* "He almost never appeared himself in court nor before a legislative committee or public utility commission; but always he knew who could make the appearance with the best advantage; always he knew what wire to pull; always he kept a web of wires running from his office out to all sorts of men who occupied places of leverage; always he knew how to get results."[5]

He quickly decided the result he wanted most was to advance Warren Harding's political fortunes. The future twenty-ninth president of the United States had found his kingmaker.

Daugherty's first coup for his friend was to win him the nomination as lieutenant-governor. Harding entered that office in 1903 and served for one term. Although he wooed the party bosses ardently, under his mentor's alert guidance, he was not offered another opportunity for office until 1910, when he ran unsuccessfully for the governorship.

His party loyalty, his physical attractiveness, and his ability to make melodious speeches filled with empty phrases offensive to no one won him election to the U.S. Senate in 1914.

How he loved that cozy spot! Lazy by nature, the Senate suited his disposition; seldom on the floor, he spent his time with cronies playing cards, drinking with modest intensity, and dallying with the two loves of his life, neither one of which was his wife.

Carrie Phillips was a statuesque beauty married to the owner of the most successful dry goods store in Marion. Harding and her trusting husband, Jim, were close friends. His friendship with Carrie was closer; between 1905 and 1920 they were lovers.[6] The relationship was tempestuous. This affair was explored in some detail by Francis Russell, although its full flavor is missing from Russell's biography because of his inability to quote from Harding's boudoir letters to Carrie. A nephew of Harding's had gone into court to protect from exposure the "naive . . . eroticism"[7] of his long-dead uncle.

Harding's second major tryst was with Nan Britton, a miss from Marion, thirty-one years his junior. Nan had been infatuated with the town's most prominent citizen from the outset of her puberty. In her somewhat remarkable memoir of their escapades, Ms. Britton spoke of those first moments in 1910. "Certain people . . . could tell you of the spectacle I made of myself those months, and indeed in years that followed, for I talked about [Warren] incessantly; no, I did not talk, I *raved*. I was fourteen years old, or going on fourteen. . . . But I remember well when Mrs. Sinclair telephoned my mother, and with friendly solicitude advised her to curb my girlish enthusiasm, or at least try to quiet me vocally, for my own sake!"[8]

With Carrie off in Germany, Harding's libidinous attention became riveted on the blooming Nan. The loss of her husband, and the responsibility of raising four children, had made Nan's mother grateful for Harding's apparently altruistic concern about her youngest. By the time Nan was sixteen, Warren was sending her surreptitious letters, and by 1916 he took the twenty-year-old Nan as his mistress.

The year 1919 was an eventful one for Harding. On January 6, Teddy Roosevelt, once again in the leadership of a reunited Republi-

can party, and the obvious candidate for the 1920 nomination, suffered a heart attack and died. Harding attended the Oyster Bay funeral
as a representative of Congress. The same day he received a note from
Daugherty, who seemed far from despondent. "I have some ideas
about this thing now which I will talk over with you."[9]

There was no obvious candidate to replace the dynamic Roosevelt.
Leonard Wood, his friend and companion in the Spanish-American
War, strutting about in uniform, his riding crop thrust under his arm,
looked like the man to beat. He had a reputation for efficiency and
unbending rectitude that made him completely unacceptable to the
party bosses; his sponsorship by the Ivory Soap millionaire, William
Proctor,[10] nevertheless, made him a formidable adversary.

Hiram Johnson, California progressive, was extremely popular,
but not with the party leaders. His independence, epitomized by his
split from the party in 1912 to follow Roosevelt into exile, had
permanently alienated the regulars.

Frank O. Lowden, governor of Illinois, was the third major candidate. He had an outstanding record as a reformer and a reputation for
probity. Moreover, he suffered from much the same liability as the
other two, a reputation for independence that made him equally
unacceptable to the men who were going to make the final choice.

Harding's Texas friend, Frank Scobey, wrote to the bewildered
Harding soon after Roosevelt's interment, "It looks to me like if you
want to be President now, here is your opportunity. Ohio is a pivotal
state and they know that you can carry it. If you are going to be a
candidate you ought to start soon."[11]

But Ohio's favorite son was not sure he wanted to be anything more
than a senator. "I must assert the conviction," he wrote to a friend,
"that I do not possess the elements of leadership. . . . I think I owe it to
the Party to say these things, because I know better than some who
over-estimate both my ability and availability."[12]

A week later he wrote, "I have such a sure understanding of my own
inefficiency that I should really be ashamed to presume myself fitted
to reach out for a place of such responsibility."[13]

Senatorial life was pleasant. Ms. Britton quotes his response to her
remark that some day he would be president, "Say, you darling, I've
got the best job in the United States right now!"[14]

He had status without responsibility; whatever he might not do, one or another of his ninety-five colleagues might. Washington was such an enchanting playground for a small-town boy and Nan was present to distract and delight him. His reward, in this all too eventful year, was an announcement from Nan that they were going to have a baby.

"We went over to the Senate office in the evening," she reminisced. "We stayed quite a while there that evening, longer, he said, than was wise for us to do, because the rules governing guests in the Senate offices were rather strict. It was here, we both decided afterwards, that our baby girl was conceived."[15]

Money to keep Nan going during her pregnancy was in somewhat short supply. In mid-1919 Harding was writing to Scobey that he would like to take a "flyer" in some Texas oil gambit, because "I need somehow to make some easy money."[16] Was there ever a more appealing plea made to an operator in search of a politician around whose neck to put his leash?

Many Americans were suffering from a similar money problem. After every war the exploiters move in—Continental currency speculators after the Revolution, land and bank speculators after 1815 and 1848, every kind of speculator after the Civil War—but the end of the First World War saw the rampaging spirit operating at its optimum. There was an immediate inflation, as too much money sought out too few goods. This was followed by harsh private bank credit controls, which resulted in a disastrous deflation. Overly inventoried domestic markets with few customers, a decline in exports as European farmers and manufacturers got back into peacetime production, and high unemployment rounded out the dismal economic picture. The times called for an inspirational president; Republican leaders did not choose to hear that call.

The party's most important boss was Senator Boies Penrose. In many respects Penrose, the heir to the corrupt Pennsylvania machine of Simon Cameron and Matthew Quay, was the epitome, if not the consummate caricature, of the venal politician. Born to a rich and prestigious Philadelphia family, Penrose was showered with the advantages normally associated with such luck. Unfortunately, he had the fullest measure of the deficiencies occasionally visited on the offspring of inherited wealth.

Penrose acquired an indifferent education at Harvard; after fitfully preparing himself for the law, he allowed his preferences to lead him into gutter politics. He was elected to the state legislature at age twenty-four and quickly became its boss. The Carnegie and Rockefeller interests funneled their bribes to legislators through him. Penrose was a most unabashed degenerate, practicing his whims on the scene during the thirty years he controlled Republican politics. A regular client at Harrisburg and Philadelphia brothels, he advertised his presence by handing out autographed pictures of himself with permission to prominently display them.[17]

It was difficult to judge which he enjoyed more, politics or eating. He gorged himself at each sitting, and believed that an appetizing meal consisted of seven pounds of steak, made digestible by the consumption of a quart of bourbon.

During the years he sat in the Senate with Harding, he tipped the scale at 350 pounds. A specially constructed sofa was placed at the rear of the chamber for his personal use where deals that would determine the country's future were arranged.

In August 1919, he summoned Harding to his bachelor apartment in Washington's Wardman Park Hotel. They sat in the stifling heat, their shirts wet with perspiration, men of remarkably similar tastes in women and whiskey.

"Warren, how would you like to be President?" Penrose asked.[18]

In that sentence was summed up the true power structure of American politics. For there is every reason to believe that Boies Penrose had the capacity to fulfill Warren Harding's desire.

The fifty-eight-year-old, six-foot four-inch Penrose sat there listening to Harding explain he had no money for such a grand enterprise. Besides, he would be more than happy to merely win reelection and return to his sinecure under the Capitol dome. Penrose brushed aside his hesitations. He would supply the money. "I'll look after that."[19]

Well on his decline to a premature grave, Penrose eyed his would-be president and told him why he liked him and how the deed would be accomplished. "You will make the McKinley type of candidate. You look the part. You can make a front-porch campaign like McKinley's and we'll do the rest."[20]

On October 22, Nan gave birth to their child, Elizabeth. She was now in Chicago, safely out of sight, if not mind.

In the meanwhile, Daugherty had gone to the Duchess, knowing that "If she backed our candidate he would make the fight." But

Daugherty knew she would be reluctant to give up the ease of "being a Senator's wife."[21]

"She looked at me steadily for a moment," he wrote. " 'You are going to ask Warren to run for the Presidency—' " " 'The people of Ohio will demand it—' I broke in. 'You're the people of Ohio now. The others will call for him if you say so.' "[22]

Daugherty could only listen and agree; he knew that men such as himself would pick the next president. In a revealing moment he described the presidential-selection process as it had evolved since Washington's time.

"We live in a hard-boiled age. No man in this country is ever called to the Presidency by the clamor of millions. No man is so great in our democratic society that his name excites the masses.

"All Presidents are made by organization. Our system of Party Government makes this inevitable . . . a political leader sees in his favorite statesman a presidential possibility, grooms him quietly for the office, and springs him on the party at the right moment.

"The idea that Presidents are made by a spontaneous outburst of public opinion is no longer believed except by a few amateur political writers."[23]

In November, after the adjournment of Congress, Daugherty called Harding to his Columbus home. He summoned up his most persuasive manner to convince him he should start acting like a candidate; but the senator still held back. He said he was not fit for the job, a comment he made frequently, despite the fact none of his friends seemed to notice.

Daugherty wrote of the six-hour conference in his memoirs. At first Harding asked, "What would you do in my place?" When that question got the only kind of answer Ohio's political boss was willing to give, Harding pressed his indecisiveness further, and elicited an exceptionally frank response.

" 'Come down to brass tacks,' Harding ordered. 'Am I a big enough man for the race?'

" 'Don't make me laugh! The day of the giants in the Presidential Chair is passed. Our so-called Great Presidents were all made by the conditions of war under which they administered the office. Greatness in the Presidential Chair is largely an illusion of the people.' "[24]

On December 16, Harding announced he was a candidate, simply, he averred, to fulfill his obligation to the Republican leaders of Ohio, who so desperately wanted him to take on that role.

Daugherty began touring the country in search of second-place votes, for it was obvious few thought of Harding as their first choice. He wrote of his strategy, after officially being appointed Harding's campaign manager. "Harding did not know much about what I was doing; I never bothered him, just went ahead, and when I learned what the situation was I told him about it. . . . The real work was done months before the convention when the pins were set up all over the country for second, third, and fourth choices for Harding among the delegates and influential men of the various communities. . . . The simplicity of his campaign was so pronounced that nobody knew about it until we began to collect the second-, third-, and fourth-choice votes when we got the convention tied up."[25]

The swaggering Daugherty was even more forthright when he told two reporters of another pivotal event toward which he was working in his campaign to nominate Harding. In his Waldorf-Astoria room, he spoke of what was to be the culmination of his months of effort:

"I don't expect Senator Harding to be nominated on the first, second, or third ballot, but I think about eleven minutes after two o'clock on Friday morning (the fifth day) of the convention, when fifteen or twenty men, bleary eyed and perspiring profusely from the heat, are sitting around a table some of them will say: 'Who will we nominate?'

"At that decisive time the friends of Senator Harding can suggest him and can afford to abide by the result. I don't know but what I might suggest him myself."[26]

This was the perfect description of the smoke-filled room, related by a man who had been in many of them. Although Harding hastened to categorize the published version as being based on misquotations, Daugherty's scenario for the final nominating council of the party was prophetic.

By the time the so-called Dark Convention convened in Chicago on Tuesday, June 8, 1920, Penrose's health had deteriorated to the point where he was close to death. Nevertheless, he maintained contact, from his Philadelphia bedroom, with the leaders of his delegation, and as the bargaining grew more intense his health showed signs of improvement.

The delegate count was to Daugherty's liking: out of a total of 984, a majority, 508, were uncommitted; Wood had been able to round up only 125 votes, a bad showing for the front-runner; Johnson had 112 and Lowden 72; Harding was the leading dark horse with 39 votes (mostly from Ohio),[27] which he had managed to win from Wood by barely 15,000 votes, out of a primary total in excess of 250,000.

Chauncey Depew, age eighty-six, but still missing the point as badly as he did when Commodore Vanderbilt was calling the shots on his Senate votes, pontificated to the press on the meaning of the delegate count. "You wanted an unbossed convention. Now you have it, what are you going to do with it?"[28]

This was the perfect convention from the viewpoint of party bosses; no independent primary candidate had been able to sweep into an unbeatable lead on a burst of popular enthusiasm, which is the occasional undoing of the most carefully hatched backroom schemes. Instead the bosses were free to block Wood, Johnson, and Lowden, either of whom would have been a president possessing numerous desirable qualities. In the place of these upright men, Penrose and his handful of peers were fingering the muck at the bottom of the barrel to see what limp object they might find to place in the White House.

As the bosses continued to haggle over the presidency, Wood's managers were quoted as saying that the price of a delegate was $5,000.[29]

William Allen White, a journalist temporarily posing as a delegate, opined that, in his experience, never had a convention been "so completely dominated by sinister predatory, economic forces."[30] He also described meeting an inebriated Harding in a hotel elevator, bewhiskered, his eyes bloodshot, looking "like the wreck of the Hesperus."[31]

The results of the first ballot lifted Daugherty's spirits: Wood 287½, Lowden 211½, Johnson 133½, Harding 65½, Sproul 83½, Coolidge 31, LaFollette 24, Hoover 5½, and another hundred votes scattered among five additional candidates. The Daugherty prediction of a deadlocked convention seemed near realization.

After the fourth ballot, Wood and Lowden were listlessly floating near their eventual crest, 314½ for the stiff-backed general, 289 for the aspiring governor. Daugherty was insisting to every delegate in sight that Warren Harding was the only man who could end the torments they were going through. In the broiling Chicago inferno, Daugherty's solution took on a growing appeal.

The kingmakers of the Dark Convention met at 8 P.M., Friday, June 11, in Suite 404 on the thirteenth floor of the Victorian Blackstone hotel. The rooms were paid for by Colonel George Harvey, an editor bankrolled by J. P. Morgan, the same man who promoted Wilson as governor of New Jersey, but who now regretted his error. A group of senators, led by the convention's chairman, Henry Cabot Lodge, dominated the discussions which rambled on until 2 A.M. Saturday. Dozens of men wandered in and out of the smoke-filled room; though Prohibition was in effect, empty whiskey bottles quickly cluttered the floor.

Daugherty insisted that Harding was the ideal man to break the deadlock since he could be trusted to go along. Connecticut's Senator Frank Brandegee, tired, and beyond the point of discrimination, explained why he would finally support Harding. "There ain't any first raters this year. This ain't 1880 or any 1904 . . . we got a lot of second-raters and Warren Harding is the best of the second-raters."[32]

At 1 A.M., less than ten fatigued men, most of them inebriated, struggled to their feet to record their carelessly exercised judgment that Harding should be the next president. That vote was more significant than any to be taken later in the day at convention hall, and infinitely more important than any aggregate of citizen's votes cast at the polls months later.

For all significant purposes, when the inveterate schemer George Harvey summoned Harding to Room 404 at 2 A.M., eleven minutes short of the time predicted by Daugherty, and, in a half-drunken state, in the privacy of his bedroom, informed him of his probable nomination the next day, the mantle of power was being placed on Harding's moist brow.

Harvey's friends, however, had been hearing rumors and wanted reassurance. "Before acting finally, we think," the Wall Street errand boy said slowly, "you should tell us, on your conscience and before God, whether there is anything that might be brought up against you that would embarrass the party. . . ."[33]

Having made it a matter of conscience, Harding was forced to ask for time to consider his answer. Left alone in the bedroom, it took him ten minutes to consider the catalogue of his sins before he could open the door and provide Harvey with the necessary reassurance.

Euphoric and guided by Daugherty's clubhouse wisdom, Harding descended several floors to Johnson's suite; reconciliation was his aim. A flushed and angered Johnson told his financial backer, Albert Lasker, what had transpired.

> ". . . I can't conceive of his being President of the United States. He's done nothing to deserve it. He tells me they have just agreed upstairs to make him President, and *he* came down here to ask *me*, wouldn't I run as vice-president. Of course I indignantly refused."[34]

Faced with a fait accompli, Johnson was incredulous. Progressives such as Johnson had spent their lives smashing at the bosses who had produced those deficient, often disreputable presidents of the post-Civil War era. They had elected Teddy Roosevelt and Woodrow Wilson; they had formed their own party, invented new political devices, and fought to insure an improved level of decency in political life; yet here, after a mere twenty years of improved government ethics and operation, the country was about to be turned over to "the Ohio gang."

Penrose hesitated. He had been mortally ill all Friday, but reached out to maintain his grip on events which were soon to pass him by. At 10 P.M. he placed a call to Wood's headquarters. The general refused to take the phone, but authorized his secretary, John Himrod, to speak for him. "You may say to General Wood," Penrose said, long past the point where he could be offended by such a snub, "if he were nominated tomorrow would he give us three Cabinet members?"[35]

Himrod relayed the message, and waited with hand over the mouthpiece. General E. F. Glenn, who stood at Wood's side, and understood the desperateness of the convention floor fight, said, "Now, General, one word will make you President of the United States!"[36]

How men became president was, at this moment, even clear to an army general. Wood, nevertheless, uncompromisingly called out to

Himrod, "Tell Senator Penrose that I have made no promises, and am making none."[37]

Penrose, expecting shortly to face his Maker, had made a gesture toward responsible behavior. How much more could be expected of him? He expressed his sorrow that a deal could not be arranged, but assured Himrod that if Wood was not the Republican to give him his three cabinet seats, he would find one who would.

Hours later, wheeler-dealer Harvey went down to the dining room to have breakfast with TR's daughter, the leader of Washington society, Alice Roosevelt Longworth. She listened to his description of the negotiations which had gone on in the smoke-filled room, and the bosses' decision finally to work for Harding's nomination.

"I sputtered," she wrote years later, "and asked why, if 'they' were strong enough to put Harding over, would they not have selected some 'dark horse' such as Knox who would seem to have higher qualifications for the Presidency. The reply to that amounted to saying that Harding could be counted on to 'go along.' In other words, he could be controlled."[38]

Her outrage did not keep her from including him on her invitation list in the years to come. When she finally wrote of him in her 1933 memoir, *Crowded Hours*, she concluded bluntly, "He was just a slob."[39]

The word spread quickly that Princess Alice's slob was to be the nominee; Daughterty made sure each delegate understood the bosses' preference. During the afternoon he visited at the Pennsylvania delegation's headquarters and was put on Penrose's private line. The ailing chief read a Harding endorsement he was about to release. Daugherty urged him to withhold it until after the deciding ballot so that the afternoon papers would not seize on this as proof Harding was being chosen in a sinister fashion.

As the tenth ballot got under way, the tide turned toward the Ohio senator; that tide, however, was still not irresistible. The delegates were tired and wanted to go home, but the crusher was needed. Boss Penrose provided it. At 6:15, as the clerk asked how Pennsylvania voted, Penrose's surrogate answered, "Pennsylvania casts 61 votes for Warren G. Harding," and the matter was settled.

Back at the LaSalle, where he was now staying in a larger suite engaged by Daugherty, Harding greeted well-wishers, the Duchess at his side. Speaking of what had transpired in terms most natural to him, he said, "We drew to a pair of deuces and filled."[40]

His major concern was not about campaign strategy—that could be left to Daugherty—but Nan. He went off to see her, making elaborate arrangements to throw a horde of reporters off his scent. They made love in Nan's apartment and he warned her she might find herself being "shadowed"[41] by the desperate agents of that other party. He told her to go to a secluded hotel in the Adirondacks and rest for at least eight weeks until the roses came back to her cheeks.

The campaign strategy was simple; Harding returned to Marion and spent the weeks before Election Day sitting on his front porch, greeting callers, and saying as little as possible most agreeably.

The Democrats had nominated Ohio's Governor James M. Cox in San Francisco, June 28, after forty-four excruciating ballots. He was, perhaps, more conservative than Harding. Since the Republicans had chosen as their vice-presidential nominee Massachusetts Governor Calvin Coolidge, noted only for his breaking of the 1919 Boston police strike, the Democrats filled that spot with Franklin Delano Roosevelt, the assistant secretary of the Navy, noted mainly for having the same last name as the century's most popular figure.

The election results justified the cynicism of the party leaders: Harding received 16,152,200 votes; Cox, who was never in the contest, received 9,147,353.[42] Eugene Debs, running once again as the Socialist candidate, but this time from behind the bars of the Atlanta federal prison, where he was serving a ten-year term for engaging in "seditious" activity during the war, collected 919,799 ballots.

More significant, over 50 percent of those eligible to vote did not bother. Republican leaders had come to rely on the fact that vast numbers of voters saw little reason to make the effort necessary to record themselves for any candidate. Those who stayed home, for the most part the ill-informed, the discouraged poor, the distracted and overworked lower middle class, would most likely vote Democrat if they summoned up the interest and energy to register their dissatisfaction. How delightful for Harding that they wouldn't, and how profitable for Harding's friends that they didn't.

The choice of who was to sit in the Cabinet and head the most important agencies was critical; without a leader of substance in the White House, the chiefs of these departments were bound to have more responsibility and greater latitude in arriving at decisions. It was, however, beyond Harding's ability to discriminate between the real and the dross.

He was determined to have Harry Daugherty as attorney general. This was a choice that outraged reasonable men; Daugherty's reputation for easy morality was well-known. It was one thing to have him as campaign manager, another to place law enforcement in his lawless hands.

Senator Harry New of Indiana and New York's Senator James Wadsworth counselled with the president-elect in Marion at Christmastime. During a night walk along the silent streets of the town, they spoke of their objections to appointing Daugherty to such a sensitive position, warning that the bar association was bound to express strong disapproval.

Harding responded angrily, "Harry Daugherty has been my best friend from the beginning of this whole thing. I have told him that he can have any place in my Cabinet he wants, outside of Secretary of State. He tells me that he wants to be Attorney General and *by God he will be Attorney General!*"[43]

Daugherty was too valuable to be discarded, no matter how fiercely the bells rang in the night. His services went far beyond politics. As he awaited inauguration, Daugherty was sent on a personal mission, which illustrated his real place in Harding's life. Francis Russell described the matter: "Several sportive letters that he had written as a senator to a Washington woman of clouded reputation were now being offered for private sale in New York at an asking price of $1,000. Daugherty's . . . mission was to undertake to get back the letters. Eventually they were recovered and destroyed, but Harding could not conceal his uneasiness during the negotiations."[44]

Here was a president-elect, long an associate of shady individuals, held in low regard by his colleagues in Congress, chosen for his high office by the worst elements in his party after a series of backroom deals which might have made Tweed blush, who was, in addition, the target of ordinary blackmailers.

Nevertheless, with all his doubts temporarily submerged in a chorus of party assurances that he was the man of the hour, he was about to assume the powers of that office. The twin summits of party supremacy and party irresponsibility had been reached at the same time.

14

The Criminal
Administration

*When I was a boy I was told that anybody could become
President; I'm beginning to believe.*

Clarence Darrow[1]

Nowhere is the shibboleth that high office raises weak men to the
needs of the moment more thoroughly disproved than in the case of
Warren Harding. In office he surrounded himself with the same gang
to which he had grown accustomed. They had nominated him and
been in the game with him from the beginning; therefore, according
to the rules by which he played, they deserved a share of the pot.

Daugherty suggested the nature of the disaster when he soberly
remarked, "If the political strategists of Ohio who led in nominating
Harding for the Presidency are criminals, our system of government is
a crime."[2]

Charlie Forbes, Army deserter, charmer, and confidence man, was
one of the men on whom Harding came to depend. He had met Forbes
in 1915 in Hawaii where he and the Duchess had gone on a senatorial
junket. Having somehow buried his past, Forbes was in charge of
construction at Pearl Harbor. He ingratiated himself with the non-
discriminating senatorial couple by smiling constantly, and escorting
them on a nonstop tour of the islands.

During the 1920 campaign, the peripatetic Forbes had been Harding's campaign manager in the Northwest. As his reward, the president offered him the governorship of the Alaska territory. This frigid

environment did not appeal to Forbe's passionate temperament, and his poker partner agreed instead to appoint him chief of the Bureau of War Risk Insurance based in Washington, D.C. Within a short time Forbes had convinced his friend that all veterans' services should be consolidated under one agency, the Veterans' Bureau, with him at its head.

The conniving Forbes immediately placed veterans' legal matters in the hands of Charles Cramer, who with his first act on arriving in Washington insured his welcome; he paid $60,000 for Harding's old Wyoming Avenue house—a bargain in later days, but not at that time.

Although the quartermaster general had been in charge of the purchase of Army supplies, and the disposal of surplus materials, Forbes persuaded Harding to burden him with that onerous duty. He immediately became the custodian of more than fifty huge warehouses at Perryville, Maryland.

Forbes decreed that most of the surplus was useless and must be disposed of quickly. Once having set this as a patriotic objective, he contracted with Thompson & Kelley, of Boston, to bring in their freight cars and rapidly empty the facilities. One witness later told of seeing so-called surplus bed sheets being loaded on boxcars at one end of a Perryville warehouse, while new sheets were being unloaded at the other end of the same building.

Thompson & Kelley eventually paid the government $600,000 for goods worth approximately $7,000,000.[3] For each dollar of profit they made, Harding's high-living friend received his rake-off. He was the entrepreneur par excellence, running the government business as incompetents and crooks have always run it, with no thought of balancing the public ledger but every intention of showing a private profit.

A disgruntled member of the Ohio gang first whispered the news of Forbes' activity into Harding's ear, since he presumed the Perryville improprieties were unknown to the president. Harding's reaction was to brush aside the charges. He assigned two Army officers, selected by Forbes, to conduct an "investigation." Their report could have been written in Forbes' office; then Harding proclaimed the charges against his friend, which were beginning to appear in the papers, an "abominable libel."[4]

His attention was distracted by Nan. Her visits to the White House, according to her, were made with greater frequency than those of the secretary of state. She commented upon the arrangements made by the president to receive her and his fear that his behavior might disappoint the party:

"Mr. Harding said to me that people seemed to have eyes in the sides of their heads down there and so we must be very circumspect. Whereupon he introduced me to the one place where, he said, he thought we *might* share kisses in safety. This was a small closet in the anteroom, evidently a place for hats and coats, but entirely empty most of the times we used it, for we repaired there many times in the course of my visits to the White House, and in the darkness of a space of not more than five feet square the President of the United States and his adoring sweet-heart made love."[5]

At the same time her constant request that he acknowledge their daughter, Elizabeth, and make an arrangement for a more public role for herself left him with a variety of emotional regrets. He steeled himself to the point where he told her such plans must be put aside as long as the seriously ill Duchess was still alive. "Nan, darling," he pleaded, "you must help me; our secret must not come out. Why, I would rather die than disappoint my party."[6]

Harding's desire to protect the party, a moral defect shared by most presidents, affected his handling of the serious allegations surfacing against Forbes. In January 1923, proof of Forbes' crimes were taken directly to Daugherty, since the attorney general was a personal enemy of the director of the Veterans' Bureau. He hastened to Harding, and sanctimoniously explained why it was a crime for Forbes to do what he and Jess Smith were doing. Harding's red-faced retort was: "That can't be!"[7]

With a wave of his hand he refused to hear anything further about his favorite poker player and court jester. Within two days, he contritely confessed to the ruffled Daugherty that *he* had been investigating Forbes and was now convinced the charges were accurate.

How does a president act in such a situation? The government had been robbed of millions. There had been a breach of trust in the care of scarred and maimed veterans, men who had given unselfishly of themselves and who would pay for this patriotic act in pain for the rest of their lives. Harding's first thought seemed to have been to suppress the scandal—to protect the party.

He sent Forbes off to Europe, advertising that he was to inspect facilities for disabled veterans. On February 1, Cramer handed in his resignation, and shortly thereafter committed suicide in Harding's former residence. On February 15, the Senate began to investigate the Veterans' Bureau and three days later, while consoling himself in Paris, Forbes announced his resignation.

After the conclusion of the Harding administration, Forbes was brought to the dock; he was charged with conspiracy and found guilty, eventually serving a year and nine months in Leavenworth Penitentiary.

Forbes was an old-fashioned crook—stealing with both hands. However, Jess Smith, Daugherty's inseparable companion, quickly established himself as Washington's chief influence peddler, a subtle form of larceny that depended on the cooperation of insiders. Everyone doing business with the government knew of Jess's entrée to the president's office. He was one of fifteen or so intimates Harding routinely invited to White House stag parties. He helped run "The Little House on H Street," which Daugherty paid $24,000 each year to maintain, twice his salary as attorney general.[8] This was a sultan's quarter in which Harding and his buddies enjoyed themselves in a fashion normally associated with frolicking Chicago gangsters.

The tie between the administration and the underworld went beyond a similarity in tastes. Prohibition had cut into one of the most lucrative sources of illegal profit: bars and liquor stores, often the front for gambling and prostitution, had been out of business since January 1920, when the Eighteenth Amendment had gone into effect. At first national statistics on the salutary benefits of prohibition fulfilled the promise of the Temperance League: crime went down, automobile accidents decreased, suicides and commitments to mental institutions declined. The noble experiment seemed to be a success.

However, the widespread depravity of the Harding administration was not likely to end at the doorway of the Prohibition Bureau. The members of this agency were extremely low paid, and their willingness to be misled has seldom been matched by a group of this size, ostensibly pledged to protect those they were intent on pillaging.

Commissioner Roy A. Haynes, a member in good standing of the Ohio gang, felt his main duty was to make sure that liquor deliveries, shepherded by Internal Revenue agents, were delivered by Wells

Fargo express[9] to 1625 K Street, where Howard Mannington, Harding's campaign manager, maintained the administration's roost for poker parties, drinking, and call girls.

Haynes had the authority to issue "B" permits; these permits allowed legitimate users of alcohol to purchase it, a practice outlawed for all other Americans. He soon began to grant these valuable exemptions to anyone recommended to him by Jess Smith; a criminal record did not bar one from favorable treatment by the enterprising Haynes. It was not surprising that under his guidance the Prohibition Bureau was commonly referred to as "the training school for bootleggers."[10] Those agents who tired of accepting bribes often resigned and went directly into rum-running.

Jess Smith was the bagman of the Ohio gang; he was the fixer to whom desperate businessmen came when in need. Criminals, seeking favorable endorsement from Daugherty for their pardon appeals, petitioned Smith. His hand was always out, and there was always someone anxious to fill it. Although Harding had originally planned to appoint him commissioner of Indian affairs, an office in which malefaction seldom aroused a public objection, the protests of Western senators made him think rather of selecting him to be treasurer of the United States. It was only Smith's modesty that kept Harding from that error. All Jess wanted was unlimited access to the White House and all federal agencies, and a desk near Daugherty's Justice Department office from which he would place his calls and be close to his friend.

Daugherty wrote of him: "Smith was not a man of great mentality, but was always jolly, a good mixer and a faithful friend. . . . He was popular with everyone who knew him." After describing him as a "simple, loyal friend," he confessed, "It became absolutely necessary to take Jess Smith with me wherever I went."[11]

Perhaps the greatest service Smith performed for the attorney general involved a swindle that cost the taxpayers $7 million. In September 1921, only months after Harding had taken office, but soon enough for the administration's lack of rectitude to be widely known in circles where such information was of value, Richard Merton, a German with pronounced Prussian mannerisms, arrived in New York. He was representing his family in a matter involving the confiscation of the American Metal Company by the United States during the First World War, 49 percent of which was owned by Metallgesellschaft & Metall Bank, a Merton enterprise.

The young Merton's story was that his family had sold their interest in the German Metall Bank one month *before* America had entered the war. The sale had been made to a Swiss enterprise, also owned by the Mertons. He was unable to produce proof of the sale, he explained apologetically, because the transaction had been consummated verbally.

Prepared to peddle this transparently bogus story, Merton went in search of someone who might buy it. He queried Wall Street associates about anyone "who could pave the way"[12] to someone in the Alien Property Bureau, the agency controlling the bank accounts in which money realized from the government's sale of the American Metal Company had been deposited. Republican National Committeeman John King was recommended. As one of the Eastern leaders of the party, King knew his way around; he contacted Jess Smith. Smith arranged for a September 20 meeting in New York attended by himself, King, Colonel Thomas Miller, custodian of alien property (later to go to prison for his role in this matter), and the dazzled, fantasizing Merton.

The details of that conversation were not recorded, but its results were clear; the next day, Merton received word from the Alien Property Bureau that his preposterous concoction was found fully plausible. Two days later, Daugherty's office endorsed this consummate example of gullibility.

Once Daugherty had given the green light, Miller moved to dispose of government money with uncharacteristic bureaucratic swiftness. He wrote out Treasury checks totalling $6,453,979.97, and authorized the collection of $514,350 in Liberty Bonds. With this little bundle he made his way to a "celebration dinner," which Merton had the presence of mind to organize in New York. Smiling his delight, as the fortune was placed in his hands, Merton expressed his gratitude symbolically with a two-hundred dollar silver cigarette case for each of his guests: Jess Smith, Colonel Miller, and Committeeman King (who died, while under indictment, as his trial over matters concerning this dinner approached).

A sentimental gesture in silver, however, was not sufficient for such assistance and the final accounting, made by Merton to King, consisted of $391,300 in bonds and $50,000 in cash. He distributed $224,000 to Jess, $50,000 to Miller, kept $112,000 for himself, and was not given sufficient time on this earth to explain what happened to the remaining $55,300.

It was the bonds that caused problems for this conspiratorial consortium, since they did not have the anonymity of cash. Certificates worth $50,000 were eventually traced to a joint account held by Jess and Daugherty in an Ohio bank.[13] Daugherty had all sorts of explanations about this account. It was necessary to rely on his word, since just prior to going on trial for crimes associated with it, Daugherty burned all his bank records.

Jess Smith, who handled Daugherty's personal correspondence and paid his bills, would have been able to explain had he survived until the attorney general's trial; however, once again fate intervened on Daugherty's behalf. Emotionally dependent on Daugherty, Smith was purported to be depressed when the attorney general rebuffed him. According to Daugherty, Harding had informed him Jess was "running with a gay crowd, attending all sorts of parties . . ." and he was no longer to be welcomed to the White House.[14]

Dejected past the point of recovery, Smith cleared out his Justice Department office, collected his accounts and Daugherty's private correspondence, and burnt them in a wastepaper basket in their Wardman Park Hotel apartment. He then placed his head in the wastepaper basket and blew out his brains.

Years later, when Daugherty finally went on trial for failing to prosecute the American Metal Company fraud, he refused to take the stand in his own defense, and explained his reluctance by implicating Harding. He first tied himself in with the former president:

"Having been personal attorney for Warren G. Harding before he was Senator from Ohio and while he was Senator, and thereafter until his death . . . and having been Attorney General of the United States during the time that President Harding served as President . . ."

After basing his plea of silence on this association with the president, he went on to write to the judge, "I refuse to testify and answer questions put to me, because: The answer I might give or make and the testimony I might give might tend to incriminate me."[15]

Daugherty had claimed Fifth Amendment privileges against self-incrimination. Understandable as this might be in the case of an ordinary felon, it seemed a strange line of defense for a man who had served as attorney general to be pleading on behalf of himself and, in effect, the former president of the United States.

The jury deadlocked after sixty-five hours, three men stubbornly refusing to be argued out of their suspicion that Daugherty might be an honest man. At his second trial only one man could be found with this mental aberration and he was thought to have been bribed.

Daugherty was not the only Harding Cabinet member to come afoul of the law. Albert B. Fall, secretary of the interior, and Edwin N. Denby, secretary of the Navy, managed to accomplish that distinction in an even more spectacular fashion.

Fall had been a senator from New Mexico when Harding reached out for his services. He owned the huge Three Rivers Ranch in that desert state. When the land and resources of the government came under his control, he was $140,500 in debt and owed eight years in property taxes. In bad health, he seemed to have viewed his appointment to the Harding Cabinet as a last opportunity to recoup his fortunes.

Coming quickly to his aid were two of the grandest oil plungers in that field of plungers, Harry Sinclair and Edward Doheny. Both men had their predatory eyes on government-owned oil lands, two sectors in particular: Teapot Dome, about fifty miles north of Casper, Wyoming; and approximately 100 square miles of California containing Elk Hills and Buena Vista Hills.

These areas had been set aside in the previous decade as wartime reserves for the navy. Doheny and Sinclair had been trying to obtain leases to drill into these known pools before Harding came to office, but without success. Doheny, in particular, understood the importance of politics in the ultimate determination of who was going to exploit those huge reservoirs. As a signal to all susceptible government employees, he had on his payroll four members of Wilson's former cabinet: Fall's predecessor as secretary of the interior, Franklin K. Lane, Attorney General Thomas W. Gregory, Treasury's William McAdoo, and Secretary of War Lindley Garrison.

Although previously committed to retain control of these naval reserves, Denby quickly changed his mind, and with a speed that did not allow for ceremony, endorsed Fall's request for jurisdiction.

Harding agreed with similar alacrity, and did not cavil over the clause written into the transfer, at Fall's request, which gave the secretary permission to grant leases for drilling without competitive bidding. From the first, it was a plan drawn up by pirates.

Fall borrowed $100,000 from Doheny without any collateral and he later admitted, under no obligation to pay interest. Over a period of two years, Sinclair also gave Fall in excess of $300,000; Sinclair had not even bothered to formally record his donation as a spurious loan.

On April 7, 1922, Fall secretly leased Teapot Dome to Sinclair; on the 25th, he turned over the California reserves to Doheny. When word of the deal was leaked by competitors at Standard Oil of New Jersey, Albert Lasker went to tell the president.

"This isn't the first time that this rumor has come to me," Harding responded with an assurance that was hard to question, "but if Albert Fall isn't an honest man, I'm not fit to be President of the United States."[16]

Eventually the Supreme Court invalidated the leases. By that time, however, Fall was convicted of accepting bribes, fined $100,000, and sent to prison for a year. He was the first Cabinet officer in history to achieve that distinction.

The outlines of the scandal were filled in by a Senate investigation and by the various trials that stretched out over a period of six years. During all that time a day seldom passed without a newspaper headline about Teapot Dome.

Harding did not live through the shame of this exposure. He died on August 2, 1923, in San Francisco's Palace Hotel, from what was officially recorded as an embolism, as he lay in bed listening to his wife reading a *Saturday Evening Post* article favorable to him.[17]

Forbes' crimes had been exposed and, despite the *Post*'s support, Harding's popularity was on the decline. Still, the more imposing oil scandals were not yet common knowledge, although *he* was aware of the dimensions of the disgrace. He was also aware of the corruption in the Prohibition Bureau, although the public thought this to be a mark of the times, not a specific failing of a specific president and his criminal associates.

There was about this most regular of partymen enough tragedy to wet the eyes of the most cynical. His secretary, Judson Welliver, spoke to William Allen White about this aspect of Harding while waiting patiently to see the weary president in the Oval Office anteroom.

"Lord, Lord, man!" Welliver told his old friend, "you can't know what the President is going through. You see he doesn't understand it; he just doesn't know a thousand things that he ought to know. And he realizes his ignorance, and he is afraid. He has no idea where to turn."

Welliver then went on to quote Harding during a recent moment of torment:

" 'Jud,' he cried, 'you have a college education, haven't you? I don't know what to do or where to turn in this taxation matter. Somewhere there must be a book that tells all about it, where I could go to straighten it out in my mind. But I don't know where the book is, and maybe I couldn't read it if I found it! There must be a man in the country somewhere who could weigh both sides and know the truth. Probably he is in some college or other. But I don't know who he is, and I don't know how to get him. My God, but this is a hell of a place for a man like me to be!' "[18]

There was a flash of insight that momentarily cracked through all that folly. How could a man like Harding get to such a place? That was really the key question about the multitude of crimes which historians have labelled "Teapot Dome."

No one bothered to notice that Teapot Dome was the inevitable result of the degenerate process used to select the president. Given the fact that Boies Penrose, George Harvey, and Harry Daugherty were going to choose the Republican nominee, the possibility he might be a decent, intelligent man, interested in the general welfare, and with the capacity to contribute to that welfare, was remote.

Teapot Dome was a warning rumble from the center of the earth, and yet, the wise men of the day spent their time wondering only how much Harding knew about Albert Fall.

15

The Institutionalizing of Presidential Incapacity

There is little to be expected from political parties. They are prone to subordinate everything to party success or to party expediency.

Senator William Edgar Borah[1]

"The business of the United States is business."[2] With this proclamation of his philosophy Calvin Coolidge went on to prove that an honest occupant of the White House could be as dangerous for the nation as a man addicted to fraud.

Born in Plymouth Notch, Vermont, he grew up to value the frugal, upright traits of his pious parents. He had one other characteristic of the North country: He was taciturn to an extreme. He did not believe in wasting a word and struggled, with frequent success, to repress the impulse to talk.

Republican bosses found "Silent Cal" appealing. He was utterly loyal to the party, conformist in every thought, and incapable of proposing any form of action that might discomfort the business community. Such men are moved ahead by party leaders, and beginning in 1906, he was successively a member of the Massachusetts House of Representatives, two-term mayor of Northampton, state senator in 1911, lieutenant-governor in 1915, and governor, finally, in 1918.

He was nominated in 1920 as Harding's vice-presidential partner on the whim of an exhausted convention. When he succeeded to the presidency on August 3, 1923, the popular impression was that a man

181

completely different from Harding was now in office. Their personal characteristics were worlds apart, but the party chiefs had chosen too carefully to be surprised by an ideological antagonist.

He mouthed support of laissez-faire economics, which should have led him to avoid any government intervention in the marketplace. Yet he lost no opportunity actively to further the interests of the business community; he advocated legislation to raise the protective tariff and further pleased his sponsors by urging the lowering of the inheritance taxes.[3] Addicted to inactivity, he nevertheless encouraged stock market speculation, lending moral support to those ticker-tape gamblers who kept tossing loaded margin dice in Wall Street alleys.

With aluminum millionaire Andrew Mellon advising him from the Treasury Department—a function Mellon performed with as little success for the other two members of that 1920s Republican presidential triumvirate—the possibility that some new idea might be entertained was slight. His major economic move was to grant refunds to corporations in excess of $3.5 billion, and to help struggling millionaires by reducing them from a 60-percent tax bracket to a more comfortable 20-percent liability.

He showed no such consideration for bankrupt farmers. Congressional attempts to pass a farm subsidy law, specifically the McNary-Haugen Act, were discouraged, and finally vetoed by him.

The indifference displayed by Coolidge toward the plight of the millions of destitute farmers was particularly grim. Farmers had entered a depression soon after the end of the war. They did not have any respite during the Roaring Twenties, as did some sectors of the economy before the Great Depression; yet he refused to view them as victims in need of aid, and chose instead the old moralist's stance: Their lack of success was an indication they were not worthy of success. While coddling the rich, he condemned the poor, advising them that if they would only start saving their pennies, they would soon be as rich as Rockefeller.

He viewed the struggling industrial worker in much the same fashion, and encouraged employers to keep them in their place by means of the open shop. Total union membership, which was 5.1 million in 1920, had fallen off to 3.6 million by the end of his administration.[4]

Law-breaking by the rich and influential did not arouse in him a similar sense of indignation. He let Daugherty remain as his attorney general despite pressure to discharge him, responding to Senator William Borah's demand that he do so with partisan wisdom: Party leaders liked the favor-selling Daugherty, Coolidge opined, and would be offended if he were discharged. "Daugherty was Harding's friend. He stands high with the Republican organization. I do not see how I can do it."[5]

Fall and Denby were parted from the Cabinet only when they were considerate enough to submit their unsolicited resignations. Daugherty held on until his bold refusal to allow Justice Department files to be inspected by congressional investigators left the president no excuse to avoid asking for his resignation.

Coolidge made absolutely no effort to pursue the truth of the scandals. Although apparently personally honest, he did not view it as a duty of an honest president to prosecute the crimes of his party predecessor. Such conventional loyalty deserved a conventional reward, and in Cleveland on June 10, 1924, the Republicans met to nominate Coolidge on the first ballot.

One would have thought that, after the recent Republican humiliations in 1924, the Democrats would have won the presidency with ease. That might have been the result had the electorate concluded there was a significant difference between the two parties. But two facts made such a perception difficult. William McAdoo, Wilson's son-in-law, was the leading Democratic candidate at the June 24 New York convention, and McAdoo's reputation had been irreparably sullied by the tar-baby of Teapot Dome. He had been on Doheny's payroll to the tune of $50,000 per annum. Even with this glaring liability, enough Democratic bosses wanted him to be president to prolong the selection of a nominee through 103 *opéra bouffe* ballots.

The second factor dissipating any Democratic Teapot Dome advantage was their final choice of a nominee. He was the ultra-conservative John W. Davis, prominent Wall Street lawyer. "I have a fine list of clients," Davis bragged. "What lawyer wouldn't want them? I have J. P. Morgan and Company, the Erie Railroad, the Guaranty Trust Company, the Standard Oil Company, and other foremost American concerns on my list."[6]

In short, the same men who were bankrolling the Republican party were bankrolling him. His extensive list, however, did not include the less affluent, who normally cast the bulk of Democratic votes. There was scarcely a raised eyebrow, therefore, when the left wing of the party combined with the Socialists, the American Federation of Labor, and the remnant of T.R.'s 1912 Bull Moosers to form the Progressive party. With popular "Fighting Bob" LaFollette, Wisconsin's straight-arrow champion of the underdog, in the field, Davis's defeat was hardly unexpected. Coolidge was elected with an edge of 54 to 29 percent, the worst percentage defeat ever suffered by a Democrat. LaFollette received 4,822,856 votes, over 16 percent of the total.[7] Had he not died the following year, this respectable showing, reinforced by continued rank-and-file dissatisfaction, might have led to the emergence of a new left-of-center party.

The lesson that might have been learned from this post-Teapot Dome, rather illogical Republican victory was that party politics had disenchanted the mass of citizens from whom the Democrats could reasonably expect their votes; the voters really said, "A pox on both your houses."

Coolidge revealed in retirement that he would have liked to run for a second elected term; however, as the 1928 convention season approached, his Yankee pride and speech did him in. On vacation in the Black Hills he briefly announced, "I do not choose to run for President in 1928."[8]

Apparently he dreamed, not even fully consciously, that the mere publication of such a horrific idea would call forth a chorus of pleas for him to volunteer once again to save the nation; instead, his disavowal was taken at face value. Party leaders had, in Herbert Hoover, a more appealing candidate readily available.

Hoover had gained an impressive reputation for his war-time relief efforts in Belgium, and similar postwar humanitarian efforts in Russia and the Mississippi Valley. He was universally admired for his organizational ability, partially the result of his training as a mining engineer.

These early efforts were made as an agent of the Wilson administration, and at that time technician Hoover projected an apolitical image. In January 1920, Democrat Franklin Delano Roosevelt had written of Hoover to the American ambassador in Poland, "He certainly is a wonder, and I wish we could make him President of the United States. There could not be a better one."[9]

By 1928, however, Hoover's party label was firmly affixed to his brow. He had, in fact, established Republican policy throughout the decade, exercising, in his role as secretary of commerce, the function of party seer. His philosophy was of the sort that would appeal to an engineer's practical mind: The government must balance its budget, as any storekeeper would, and protect its native industries by raising barriers to foreign businessmen; the richest men in America had gained their wealth by closing out competitors—why should the rules for foreign commerce be any different?

A man with this viewpoint could be nominated by the party of business without a qualm, and so he was, on June 14, in Kansas City, Missouri. The Democrats met later in the month in Houston and committed themselves to New York's governor, Alfred E. Smith, also on the first ballot.

Smith was the most unique candidate ever nominated for the presidency: He was the first Catholic given that distinction; he was also the first city-born-and-bred candidate. But it was in his appearance that he really stood out as an isolate. Al Smith came from the malodorous slums of the Lower East Side of New York, from the heart of Boss Tweed's old 7th Ward; in his brown derby and spats, he looked and talked like a street hustler.

Southern Democrats—at this time under the sway of revived Ku Klux Klan bigotry—suspicious of papist influence to the point of paranoia, critical of anything that came from Northern cities, tending to bristle at the mere sound of a Yankee accent, were being asked to vote for a man who irritated each of those prejudices; it was a defeatist act by a party that had little hope of victory.

Yet Smith had been a contender since 1920, and Cox and Davis had done so poorly that a flyer with Smith appealed to many party bosses. As head of the Tammany machine Smith resembled no one more closely than the men who were going to nominate him. "Wet" to his hair roots, Smith made sure he would not even carry the "dry" Solid South, when he called for the repeal of the Eighteenth Amendment. Moreover, party leaders weakened him in the North and West by proposing a platform almost as favorable to big business as the one on which Herbert Hoover ran.

Hoover won with 444 electoral votes to Smith's 87; for the first time since the Civil War the Republicans broke into the South, capturing five states. Congress, as it had been throughout the 1920s, was dominated by the Republicans. The day after the results were announced, the stock market had a "victory boom," and traders showed their confidence in Hoover by boosting volume to 4,894,670 shares, just under the all-time record.[10] Businessmen were blissful; during 1928 the Dow Jones industrial average climbed from 245 to 331.

But the future that Hoover envisioned was far from an Adam Smith's utopia, where the mobile forces of an unrestrained marketplace would allow a hard-working grocer to optimistically compete with Huntington Hartford's A & P. It was rather a future dominated by fat cats. His sense of efficiency was disturbed by the sight of tycoons wastefully competing with each other. Under his leadership the Department of Commerce had encouraged trade associations to pool much of their activity—insurance, purchasing, advertising: More than two hundred "codes of fair practice" were drawn up under his guidance, each of which had the effect of cutting down on the individual enterprise of America's free enterprisers. "We are passing," he forecast, "from a period of extreme individualistic action into a period of associational activities."[11] He was not as enthusiastic about encouraging the associational activities of labor unions.

As proof that the ability to add up a column of figures does not demonstrate your ability to conduct a sensible national economic policy, Hoover's first significant act was to call Congress into special session to legislate "limited changes in the tariff."[12] Given the fact that control of Congress was in the hands of protectionists, and that he had nothing in mind but upward revisions in tariff rates, his first act was a catastrophe for the world's economy; tariff barriers were already too high.

The United States had become a creditor nation as a result of loans to allies during the war. The ability of those allies to pay off their debts depended on their continued solvency. If they found American markets closed to them, the inevitable result had to be their bankruptcy, and then the decline of the American economy, which could not continue to be even moderately prosperous without worldwide outlets for the abundance of goods its factories produced.

Despite these considerations, Congress passed the Hawley-Smoot tariff, the highest in our history, effectively shutting off much of the world's commerce in minerals, chemicals, dyes, and textiles. The

American Bankers Association had joined with 1,028 academic economists and industrialists around the world, to plead the cause of economic sanity to Hoover.[13] Nevertheless, he signed the bill June 17, 1930, with every indication he was convinced the tariff wall around the American shoreline would protect the domestic economy from the disasters that were bound to overtake Europe. The results of such shortsighted selfishness were readily predictable; in less than two years twenty-five countries reciprocated with acts of similar madness and the world's economic system found itself massively disrupted.

Within six months of Hoover's ascension to power, the frost was on the bloom. Although some indexes had been declining for months—freight-car loadings, for example—and the officers of the Federal Reserve System were discussing the possibility they had been too liberal in allowing easy credit for stock market speculation, inertia, and the normal unwillingness to tamper with something which seemed to be pleasing so many powerful people, effectively restrained responsible action.

On October 24, 1929, Black Thursday, thirteen million shares changed hands, and the brokerage houses, which had earlier seemed to know with certainty how to make any shoeshine boy a millionaire, suddenly knew only that their margin accounts were overextended. The next five days were devastating, culminating in the sale of 16,410,030 shares on October 29,[14] in one day wiping out all the gains made during the previous boom year.

John J. Raskob, chairman of the Democratic National Committee, demonstrated anew the fundamental unity of the leaders of both parties. Himself a millionaire deeply enmeshed in the stock market, he issued a statement: "Prudent investors are now buying stocks in huge quantities and will profit handsomely when this hysteria is over and our people have opportunity in calmer moments to appreciate the great stability of business."[15]

He was joined in this attempt at reassurance by aged John D. Rockefeller, publicly silent for several decades, who had the following news: "Believing that fundamental conditions of the country are sound . . . my son and I have for some days been purchasing sound common stocks."[16]

Hoover's reaction to the hysteria was an admirable personal coolness. He gave little indication he thought there was an important role in this matter for himself. In his closing speech of the campaign, delivered in New York on October 22, 1928, he had explained his philosophy of "rugged individualism," which froze him into a position of inaction at this point. Forcefully he had insisted that the American system was "founded upon a particular conception of self-government in which decentralized local responsibility is the very base. . . . When the Republican Party came into full power it went at once resolutely back to that concept. Thereby it restored confidence and hope in the American people, it freed and stimulated enterprise, it restored the government to its position as an umpire instead of a player in the economic game."[17]

As any good umpire, he was now going to watch the game carefully, taking no part in it himself; at the most, occasionally blowing a warning whistle.

Throughout the crisis, he remained philosophically consistent: Something more was needed; it was not forthcoming. Instead, Hoover began to imitate the ostrich. Despite the collapse of the economy, he acted as if only psychotic worriers were complaining. Indeed, he seemed convinced that if only people would realize how good things were, everything would get even better.

Simeon D. Fess, chairman of the Republican National Committee, listened to his leader guarantee business would be normal by October, and when it did not happen, could only assume the entire crash was a conspiracy to discredit the Republican president. "Persons high in Republican circles are beginning to believe that there is some concerted effort on foot to utilize the stock market as a method of discrediting the Administration. Every time an Administration official gives out an optimistic statement about business conditions, the market immediately drops."[18]

It was so much easier for a party priest to explain the continuing decline in terms of Venetian intrigue than to face the difficult truth that the organization had chosen three presidents in a row who had, once in office, led the country, with the greatest self-assurance, into a disaster.

John Kenneth Galbraith, in his delightful book, *The Great Crash*, suggests several reasons for the mess, an understanding of which might have resulted in more productive thinking by Chairman Fess.

Most important, Professor Galbraith felt, was "the bad distribution of income," followed closely by the fact that "American enterprise in the twenties had opened its hospitable arms to an exceptional number of promoters, grafters, swindlers, imposters, and frauds. This, in the long history of such activities, was a kind of flood tide of corporate larceny."[19]

Another contributing factor was the party system, which, after all, controlled the apparatus of government. For partymen the major objective remained electoral victory. Economic recovery, for the prosperous politician, was merely one means—and perhaps too difficult a means—of achieving that objective. On election day the votes of the poor could still be bought with smiles, a wagon load of speeches with vaguely worded promises, and some judiciously spent money.

It was a much greater, indeed, uncalled for, extravagance to try to deal with problems about which you knew very little, whose solution was more safely left in traditional hands—namely, those of the businessman.

The Republican party had become an extension of the business community. The honest members of its congregation believed, as sincerely as any group of pilgrims believes in its mission, that what was good for business was good for the country. Its dishonest practitioners knew who had the largest honeypot, and did not concern themselves about the saving of souls.

It was this party mechanism, dedicated to the narrow interests of the rich, which chose Hoover and praised his wisdom long after his incapacity had been repeatedly demonstrated. A clue to their impressive loyalty was supplied by a congressional investigation which revealed the House of Morgan, apparently so many light-years away from Jay Gould, had a "preferred list" of partymen able to buy stocks below market value.[20] That the relationship between the party and the wealthy was mutually advantageous becomes apparent in a survey of the distorted tax laws; in the years 1930 and 1931 no Morgan partner paid a cent in income taxes.[21]

No doubt many wealthy people suffered because of the Depression; yet as matters worsened, and "Hoovervilles," occupied by the hungry, began to appear in the garbage dumps of America, the president pursued policies aimed primarily at supporting the interests of the rich. It was as though he were drawing up government wagons in a tight circle around a privileged few to protect them from the howling band circling threateningly in the gloom.

Hoover attributed virtue to wealth and assumed that if the owners of industry could be made more solvent by a loan from the Reconstruction Finance Corporation, the salutary effects of that governmental generosity would inevitably trickle down to the mass of the unfortunate. On the other hand, money given directly to the poor would be misspent, as it always was. Although an engineer trained to rely on verifiable facts, Hoover spent four years closing his eyes to every reality that confounded his nineteenth century prejudices.

He appeared to be a man of principle, who would not compromise his view of life merely because babies were hungry and distraught mothers held out their hands in supplication. Seemingly this practical man's mind saw nothing incongruous about the fact that millions went to sleep each night wondering if there would be food for them the next day, while unharvested fruit trees bent under the burden of their yield, and granaries had exhausted their capacity to store unsold crops.

To him, and his party of business bondmen, the major problems appeared to be balancing the budget, preventing competition from foreigners—for whom the American president had no responsibility—and somehow making sure the temporary inconvenience, which was the Great Depression, did not become an issue which could be successfully exploited by the opposition party.

Political morality, under the weight of a party in servitude to the interests of the business community, had ceased to have any conventional meaning: Concern for the weak and helpless was viewed as a personal weakness. To do good, have mercy, forgive your enemy— each precept upon which civilized morality, and civilization itself, depended—were considered by party leaders as debilitating qualities that slowed life's race. The party was an instrument of resolute men to accomplish ends which would otherwise be denied them.

For these party sentinels, posted, so the citizenry thought, to light the passage through a dark night, the most serious consequence of the Depression was that they would probably lose the next election.

16

The Accident of Ability

If all voters were enrolled party members and took as much care in selecting the candidates for party position as they do in selecting the candidates for whom they vote in the general elections (by which time they are usually reduced to a choice between two men chosen by others), office-holders would be uniformly exceptional men and women.

Boss Ed Flynn[1]

Franklin Delano Roosevelt became president in the classic manner, making his way through the maze of machine politics by means of deals and blind luck; for by the time he became interested in that destiny, there was no other way to achieve it.

This is not to say that he was without ability—far from it. He is the preeminent example, after Wilson, of the man prepared by family tradition, education, temperament, and talent for the office other men regularly sought equipped mainly with desire. American historians have listed him among the three or four greatest presidents—only Washington and Lincoln consistently place ahead of him.[2]

Handome enough to qualify as a matinée idol, his most obvious original asset was his popular distant cousin, the former president, who had personally given his niece, Eleanor, in marriage to the Hudson Valley squire. In addition, there was a vibrance about this beaming, Democratic Roosevelt which in 1911 caught the eye of Louis Howe. The study of Howe reveals a good deal about the election of modern presidents, since he was the prototype of that indispensable staff member for which each successful presidential aspirant yearns, the right-hand man, occasionally called, by enemies, the power behind the throne. He is a man fundamentally

191

indifferent to the nature of the person who pays his salary; for whom politics is a profession, essentially in the sales field, which engages his talents because it pays well, he's good at it, and a roll of the dice placed him in it.

Howe was a curious figure. Sickly from birth, he had an oversized head, most often described as gnomelike, which was topped with thinning, wispy hair. His face was narrow and pockmarked, but dominated by immense, expressive eyes.[3] He had a frail physique and chronically suffered with attacks of asthma, bronchitis, and emphysema.

Mrs. Roosevelt discussed an important aspect of Howe with his biographer, Lela Stiles, some years after F.D.R.'s death: "There has seldom been a story of greater devotion to another man's success but at the same time one realizes that this was not due to any lack of ambition on the part of Louis McHenry Howe. He loved power, but he also recognized realities and he decided that in the end he would exercise more power through someone else and he prided himself on the judgment he used in choosing the individual with whom and for whom he was going to work."[4]

Before choosing young Roosevelt as the politician for whom he was going to work, Howe tied his fortunes to Thomas Mott Osborne, reform mayor of Auburn, New York. He was one of the state's leading anti-Tammany figures, who pursued the governorship unsuccessfully for a decade. Howe worked for him from 1906 as a covert informant and strategist until Osborne's patience with his pleadings for money ran out in 1912.

That he knew how political power was really exercised is apparent in an article he wrote as part-time Albany reporter for the *New York Herald* in 1907, three years before he laid eyes on Roosevelt:

"No legislative correspondent in forecasting the vote on a measure of public interest asks 'How will this Senator vote?' but how does Senator so and so's boss stand on the matter? To find this out he then ascertains how the particular group of corporations, which in turn control the boss, regards the measure. Then he knows.

"Nothing so amuses the experienced corporation lobbyist as to see a well meaning but inexperienced citizen, anxious for the fate of some reform bill, pore over the roll call of the upper house and gravely speculate upon what this or that Senator thinks about it; for the lobbyist knows that the Senators, with the exception of possibly a dozen 'freelancers,' are the male chessmen of the great financial interests that move them at will upon the board in the game of legislation."[5]

Young Franklin, quickly labelled by Howe as "a freelancer," was elected to the New York Senate in 1910 from Dutchess County. Shortly thereafter, the exuberant neophyte took on the machine. This is a standard method, even when it is used in complete sincerity in the service of a worthy cause. It signals serious political intent to those who might otherwise ignore you.

The fight centered around the selection of a U.S. senatorial nominee. Tammany Boss Charles F. Murphy, a direct descendent of Tweed in appetite, but slightly more sedate in technique, had chosen the man he wanted; he was to be William F. Sheehan, known as "Blue-eyed Billy,"[6] party leader in Buffalo, a plodder for the utility companies and whichever monied interest was willing to pay his price. Since the direct election of United States senators was about to go into effect, this was the last time Murphy was going to be able to personally pick that officeholder. He was determined to have his way, and was outraged to discover the freshman from Hyde Park was equally determined he would not.

Roosevelt quickly displayed his charismatic qualities. He convinced twenty of his Democratic colleagues to join in opposing Murphy, a formidable task among these politicians, most of whom had accepted the boss's favors or could easily imagine themselves some day seeking them.

As the struggle continued for weeks, and then months, the young senator's effort to block the Tammany choice began to draw national attention. Howe was assigned by his editor to find out what made the Young Turk tick. Roosevelt invited him to his Albany home. That evening the misanthropic Howe decided he had finally found a winner; years later he spoke of that night: "I was so impressed with Franklin Roosevelt, his seriousness, his earnestness, his firm dedication to his cause, that from that moment we became friends—and almost at that very first meeting I made up my mind that he was Presidential timber and that nothing but an accident could keep him from becoming President of the United States."[7]

Roosevelt swiftly saw the value of Howe's dedication; he consulted with him constantly, including him in on insurgent caucus meetings, much in the manner that Osborne had. After eleven weeks in this hopeless fight, Tammany was forced to retreat and Roosevelt's career had been launched on the proper, successful reform note.

At the start of the 1912 presidential campaign, Roosevelt became chairman of the Executive Committee of the New York State Wilson Conference, an organization of independent Democrats supporting the New Jersey governor. Roosevelt asked Howe to do the committee's publicity and the disciple immediately took a leave of absence from his job.

Howe's zealousness burned with such an apparent fever that anyone exposed to similar adoration, with the possible exception of someone as supremely confident as Roosevelt, might have reasonably felt embarrassed. In June, 1912, Howe penned a note to young Franklin which revealed the intensity of his devotion. It begins, "Beloved and Revered Future President," and after a good deal of uncharacteristic gushing, concluded with, "Yours, Howe."[8]

Roosevelt came down with typhoid and was bedridden for weeks, at the height of his 1912 reelection campaign. He turned to Howe for help, contacting him by phone at Wilson headquarters. "Louis," he said with the authority of a future president, "you have so many ideas on how to run a campaign I'm going to give you a chance to put them into practice. I'm flat on my back and the doctors say I have to stay here. You run the campaign. You'll have a check-book and a free hand. Now, go to it."[9]

Howe raced around the district, promising Hudson River shad fishermen lower license fees and apple growers legislation to standardize the size of their barrels,[10] all the time peppering the indisposed incumbent with progress reports, one of which was signed "Your slave and servant, Louis Howe."[11]

That described the relationship between the two men to perfection. For many years Mrs. Roosevelt treated Howe with polite coolness, finding herself much more in sympathy with Louis's frequently deserted wife.

When Wilson won, Roosevelt was summoned to Washington to assume the office of assistant secretary of the Navy, a position once occupied by cousin Teddy and clearly meant as a showcase for the

attractive New Yorker. Howe was commissioned to come on board as
F.D.R.'s private secretary, a position he had unsuccessfully sought
with Osborne, and, with perseverance that would have shamed a
Sherpa guide spent the next eight years at his master's side, blotting
his signature and sticking his finger in any political dike that sprang a
leak.

Whatever task Howe performed, his true intention was to prepare
for the day when his beloved Franklin would ascend to the presidency.
Secretary of the Navy Josephus Daniels, F.D.R.'s boss and friend
during those years, commented on this obsession: "Louis Howe
would have side-tracked both President Wilson and myself to get
Franklin Roosevelt to the White House."[12]

That Howe's mission was motivated by personal loyalty and not
principle is shown by his role in New York State politics. Soon after
F.D.R. went to Washington, a struggle for power broke out between
Democratic Governor William Sulzer and Tammany Hall. During
his 1914 reelection campaign Sulzer petitioned Roosevelt for support
in a fight which he felt he was continuing for the anti-Tammany
former Dutchess County senator. Howe urged caution, warning
F.D.R. to avoid the "whole mess," and making it easy for him to do so
by writing Sulzer, what he described as "pussy-footed answers."[13]
Sulzer went down to defeat, but did not drag Howe's man down with
him.

Within a year Roosevelt was being pressed to run in the first New
York primary for the new popularly elected office of federal senator.
After committing himself to the race, he began to contemplate a new
position toward the party organization, controlled by his former
opponents in Tammany Hall. While Boss Murphy took his usual
stance of listening to all offers before making up his mind, Howe
wrote to the worried Roosevelt, advising, "I think this is the right time
to show you don't hate all Tammany."[14]

But the Tammany tiger was, finally, too stirred up by the sting of
previous lashes to be soothed by friendly sounds. A suitably popular
figure, James Gerard, ambassador to Germany, was pressed into the
primary fight, and F.D.R. tasted his first impressive political defeat.

This experience seemed to have convinced him that Howe's practical advice was worth taking. Despite his humiliating rebuke the year

before, in the fall of 1915, he sought the opportunity to address a Tammany-sponsored meeting in Greenwich Village, where he extolled Al Smith, Murphy's candidate for sheriff.[15]

In the summer of 1916 he accepted a Tammany invitation to address the state Democratic convention in Howe's home town, Saratoga Springs. The reconciliation had gone so far that by the following summer F.D.R. and Boss Murphy were posing together happily at Tammany Hall's Fourth of July slambang.[16]

So convinced was Murphy of Roosevelt's conversion to regularity that by the time the 1918 spring primary approached, he was making a strenuous effort to persuade the assistant secretary of the Navy to run for governor. Howe's advice was to sit this one out; the war was on and it was hardly the time for a young man still of fighting age to be advancing his political career while other patriots were "over there."

This was pragmatism of the sort the boss could understand, and F.D.R. made his refusal more palatable to Tammany by his subsequent behavior. His friend and political ally, William Church Osborn, now sought the nomination. After originally encouraging him, F.D.R. devoted his full energies to winning the nomination for Tammany's candidate, once again Al Smith. At this time Smith was president of the organization-controlled New York City Board of Aldermen, a group still commonly referred to as "The Forty Thieves."[17]

Osborn had worked hard for F.D.R. in 1912, during his siege of typhoid. He now wrote his friend to ask for a public declaration of his support. Howe responded that F.D.R. would "be away a long time"[18] on a tour for the Navy Department and therefore could do nothing for him.

Smith won the primary, and the election, and Murphy was in debt to the man whose decapitated head he would have relished viewing as recently as 1914. The public, however, seeing only what was on display, had an image of a stalwart, successful Roosevelt, obviously ready for bigger things.

His time seemed to have come in the summer of 1920 when the Democrats assembled in San Francisco to pick a candidate to oppose Harding. The Democratic pattern during the previous seventy-five years had been to nominate a presidential candidate from New York and then pick a vice-presidential nominee from Ohio, or some adjacent Midwestern state. The Republicans tended to reverse the order. This year, however, the Democrats chose a resident of Ohio for the top spot and then went searching for their second man in the Empire State.

Roosevelt had come to the convention as a vociferous supporter of Al Smith, but when Smith was defeated, the national organization attempted to placate Tammany and simultaneously exploit a popular political name by selecting F.D.R. as its vice-presidential nominee.[19] He was now considered a dependable partyman.

It was during this campaign that Eleanor Roosevelt first became active in politics. Shy by nature, she had filled her life with the duties of a mother raising four boys and a girl in a household from which her husband was frequently absent.

Joseph Lash, the companion of her later years, and admiring biographer, wrote of that time: "She disciplined herself to treat his flirtations as summer shadows. . . . She could treat Franklin's dalliances lightly so long as she was sure of his love, sure that she came first with him."[20]

However, in September 1918, while nursing him back to health from a siege of pneumonia, she discovered Lucy Page Mercer's love letters. Filled with dismay, she confronted him, offering him the choice, divorce or an end to the affair.

Franklin pledged to break off with Lucy; Lash was suspicious of his reasons. "If Franklin was in any doubt about what a divorce might do to his political career, Howe was there to enlighten him."[21]

Mortified by her discovery, her shaky self-confidence further undermined, Eleanor held few illusions about why their marriage continued. "For years," Lash related, "Eleanor believed that the decisive factor with Franklin had been his realization that a divorce would end his political career."[22]

In an endeavor to give the appearance of marital harmony so helpful in political campaigns, Franklin invited Eleanor to join his campaign train. It was 1920 and women, more important than ever to politicians, had received the vote in time to be offered the opportunity to cast it for Warren Harding.

Mrs. Roosevelt felt completely out of place. Franklin preferred to spend his spare time playing poker with reporters. Since she resented Louis Howe's influence with her husband, his constant presence was of little comfort. This pivotal trip of her life began poorly and its prospects were dismal. Nevertheless, Howe was determined that her eight years of enmity toward him would end. Lash described the metamorphosis:

> Howe was a sensitive, perceptive man who refused to be deterred by her coolness; he knew the blow she had been dealt by the Lucy Mercer business. She was the only woman on the *Westboro,* and he saw that many things bewildered or irritated her. . . . Louis sensed all this: her loneliness, her great sadness, her lack of self-confidence, her need of appreciation. He was aware also of her abilities—her good judgment, remarkable vitality, and organizational gifts. He saw the way people responded to her warmth and courtesy. He began to tell her, and she desperately needed to hear such words, that she had a real contribution to make to her husband's campaign. He brought drafts of speeches to discuss with her. He explained the ways of newspapermen and encouraged her to meet them as friends. . . . She was grateful to Louis for that. Together they discussed the issues of the campaign and the politics of the towns through which they traveled. Eleanor discovered that Louis had a wide range of knowledge, a nice sense of humor, a feeling for poetry and the countryside. Louis knew when to be silent and when to speak up. By the end of the trip they had become fast friends.[23]

Eleanor's role in her husband's political life now took on greater importance; nevertheless, her contact with the party was almost nonexistent. She was always interested in things the party ignored: issues, causes, the reasons for doing things. Her major political role for the rest of her life seemed to be as a lobbyist, a spokesman for the people, with whom the leaders of her husband's party were often at odds.

It was Howe's devotion to Franklin's political destiny, as much as his humanity, that led him to act as Eleanor's tutor. Most of his effort on the campaign train was devoted to furthering Franklin's ambitions. Foreseeing the likelihood of defeat, he spent his time preparing for his champion's more important campaign, now more than ever a certainty in Howe's mind; he assiduously collected the names of local leaders attending the eight hundred speeches made by F.D.R., who might some day be of service. After Cox took the ticket down to defeat, Howe embarked on a letter-writing campaign. The letters, signed with a flourish by Roosevelt, were always inspirational, with numerous suggestions about how the off-year congressional elections might be won.[24]

Perhaps Louis Howe's greatest service to his friend came in the summer of 1921, when he received a telegram from Campobello Island, off the coast of Maine, saying he must come quickly since F.D.R. had just been stricken with an undiagnosable illness.

Upon arriving, he discovered Roosevelt could not move his feet. Howe stayed with him constantly; massaging his back, gently flexing and rubbing his inert legs. A consultation with a Bar Harbor doctor suggested the probability of infantile paralysis.

Howe's reaction was instant; no one must know. "There is even a possibility," he told Eleanor, "that if the public heard the words 'infantile paralysis' it might think that Franklin's mind had been affected. . . . It's a thing that will plague him the rest of his life, but later he will be better able to meet it. The public must not see him again until they can see him cheerful and smiling. The wrong thing at this time might wreck his political career."[25]

Howe informed the press Roosevelt was suffering from a heavy cold and then sequestered him. When it came time to leave the island, he devised elaborate diversions, so that newspapermen were waiting at the wrong dock; meanwhile Howe took the stretcher containing F.D.R. to the train by a circuitous route. Only when he was propped up at a window, and the train was ready to pull out of the station, did he summon the photographers. They rushed to the window where the paralyzed Roosevelt managed a smile and a jaunty wave of his cigarette holder as Howe signalled the conductor to get the train rolling.

Howe now moved into the Roosevelt household, where he remained until his death. His importance to his chief was symbolized by the fact that this necessitated, in New York, shunting the children next door to their grandmother's. Since Eleanor had ceased cohabitating with Franklin during the war, when she became aware of his infidelity (an infidelity which continued with Lucy Mercer to the day of his death), Howe's residency at Hyde Park, or in the White House, provided her with a platonic companion. She had accommodated herself to Howe's presence since the 1921 campaign, now that he was allowing his relentless gaze at Franklin, occasionally, to include her.

Mrs. Howe had to settle for weekends; she bought a home in Poughkeepsie, where she was close to her Vassar daughter, and contented herself with nursing an exhausted Louis when he could spare a day away from Franklin. Years later Mrs. Roosevelt spoke of Howe's dedication: "From that time on Louis Howe put his whole heart into working for my husband's future."[26]

For this strange little man, living his life vicariously, Roosevelt's calamity seemed almost a blessing, Shortly before his death, in 1935, he spoke of his feelings during the year after Campobello:

"And there are times when I doubt if Franklin might ever have been President if he had not been stricken, tragic though it was. You see, he had a thousand interests. You couldn't pin him down. He rode, he swam, he played golf, tennis, he sailed, he collected stamps, he politicked, he did about every damn thing under the sun a man could think of doing. Then suddenly there he was flat on his back, with nothing to do but think. He began to read, he began to think, he talked, he gathered people around him—his thoughts expanded, his horizon widened. He began to see the other fellow's point of view. He thought of others who were ill and afflicted and in want. He dwelt on many things which had not bothered him much before. Lying there, he grew bigger day by day."[27]

It was Howe who was his constant companion; reading to him when he was tired, telling him of the other fellow's point of view, pointing him constantly in one direction: recovery to the best possible extent, and then a siege of the party organization, which would be lifted only when the presidential nomination was won.

F.D.R.'s mother, Sara Delano, wanted to shelter him; she urged him to retire to Hyde Park where he could spend his time managing the estate, and she recognized Howe as the chief obstacle to the reasonable organization of her son's life. "You have good common sense, Louis," she argued. "Can't you see that a political future is now out of the question for my son?"

Howe's response was unyielding. "I expect him to be President," he said to the usually unopposed dowager. "Anyway he is going to have his chance."[28]

By February 1922, F.D.R. was able to briefly leave his wheelchair and stand with the aid of crutches. Howe insisted his ward must not step into the public spotlight too soon; potential voters must never see him being carried.

Therefore, when the New York organization began to look for a candidate in 1922 who might oppose William Randolph Hearst for governor, and Roosevelt's name was prominently mentioned, Howe made it clear he was not available. Instead, F.D.R. was active in persuading Al Smith to run; he then had to withstand Smith's request that he strengthen the ticket by running for the Senate.

As his health improved, with bulletins going out regularly under Howe's careful supervision, his standing with the party increased. Tammany's aging leader, Charles Murphy, came to him in the spring of 1924, confident he would not be rejected, and asked his help in rounding up convention delegates for Smith's presidential drive. Roosevelt was enthusiastic, accepting, in May, the chairmanship of "Citizens for Al Smith."[29]

Smith's demands on him did not end; he insisted F.D.R. must place his name in nomination at the June convention. When the moment arrived, twenty thousand people, jammed into every corner of Madison Square Garden, stared in silence as Roosevelt, dramatically struggling on crutches, supported by his seventeen-year-old son, James, made his way to the podium. After steadying himself, he delivered his electrifying "Happy Warrior" speech, which—although it did not succeed in winning the nomination for Smith—did establish F.D.R. as a leader of the party.[30]

It was a party, despite his incessant wooing of its leaders, about which he had great doubts. In 1925 he wrote, "In the minds of the average voter the Democratic Party has today no definite constructive aims."[31]

Nevertheless, these doubts were muted as he sought the good will of the party's leaders.

By 1928 Smith could no longer be denied the party's presidential designation. To strengthen the ticket in New York, he insisted Roosevelt had to accept the nomination for governor; Howe was against it. His schedule had Roosevelt running for office only when he could appear in public without crutches, and besides, his time would come in 1936. As for now, it was only other men's ambitions which would be served by his nomination.

On October 1, 1928, as the state Democrats met in Rochester, Howe got off a message to Roosevelt: "At 10:30 *World* man reported Al still hoped to draft you. Jim [Farley] tells me confidentially that real pressure comes from leaders and job holders who feel you will be elected and patronage made secure and that the Governor does not really consider your nomination vital to his personal success."[32]

In short, it was the party hacks who wanted Roosevelt most; he had their confidence. Jim Farley, a contractor and state boxing commissioner, and, as secretary of the State Democratic Committee, already a power in the party, was demonstrating his esteem by whispering confidences in Howe's receptive ear. The most important single boss in the state, Edward J. Flynn, head of the Bronx machine, now joined Farley in calling for F.D.R.'s nomination.[33] This time the pressure was too great, but when he yielded, there was no sign of regret.

Roosevelt campaigned vigorously, accompanied by Farley and Flynn, who between them knew every reasonably important party figure in the state. Howe stayed at the Biltmore Hotel headquarters playing his standard role of schemer and coordinator. Jim Farley accepted Howe's role although he found it difficult to warm up to him. "When we first became acquainted, Howe seemed about the oddest little duck I had ever known and for some time he had me completely puzzled. I like to meet people and to be friendly with them, but Louis made no effort to be friendly and quite often didn't even bother to be polite."[34]

Farley believed that Howe's one purpose was to make Roosevelt president. "Howe thought of nothing else during his waking hours. He was a man of intense loyalty and devotion, rebuffs never discouraged him, and he was grim as a little bulldog in hanging onto what he wanted. He looked over all visitors with a coldly critical eye, wondering where they would fit into the great scheme he had in mind. . . . That was all he cared about, and he had no other test for any man."[35]

Flynn viewed him in much the same light. "Louis Howe was extremely jealous and suspicious of anyone who appeared to become too friendly with Roosevelt. I think it is only fair to say that Howe felt that in order to protect Roosevelt he had to be careful to supervise whatever relations Roosevelt had with other people."[36]

This uneasy triumvirate of advisors was skillfully orchestrated by

Roosevelt, who recognized their strengths and defended himself against their weaknesses.

On election night Smith and F.D.R. listened to the returns in a national guard armory. By midnight it was apparent Smith had lost, but the New York race was still in doubt. Roosevelt squeaked through with a 25,564 margin, out of 4,234,822 votes cast,[37] although Smith suffered the humiliation of losing even in his home state. There is no doubt that Roosevelt's narrow victory can be attributed to the success of his efforts to treat Tammany with respect.

Howe had to revise his schedule; Roosevelt should be the presidential candidate in 1932. Smith, his New York senior, had obviously been eliminated. In a telegram to the vacationing governor-elect at Warm Springs, Georgia, Howe began with the significant: "Six hundred letters came in this morning of which 400 out-of-state refer to national affairs. Want to send the following letter to them and also to selected list of 2,000. . . ."[38]

He then went on to suggest the most important aspect of F.D.R.'s 1928 victory was that he would now have the opportunity to devote himself to winning the 1932 presidential nomination.

F.D.R. wired back a corrected copy which read, "I am of course convinced that had we kept our national organization going in between elections we should have done better and I hope that steps will be taken to have this carried out during the next three years. This is no time to discuss candidates but it is time for putting into effect a permanent working organization. I hope you will write me your views."[39]

That note of encouragement went to all members of the national committee, each state chairman, every delegate to the previous national convention and all Democrats who had run for Congress, regardless of whether they had won. In short, every conceivable individual who might have some influence in deciding who might be the 1932 nominee.

Although F.D.R. was now the most popular figure in the party, his nomination was far from certain. Placing the matter in doubt was the "two-thirds" rule, stubbornly maintained through the years by party bosses, as a guarantee that the most powerful of them would always have the ability to block any candidate. A man who wanted that nomination—and with the stock market collapse in the fall of 1929 it looked quite valuable—had to accept the fact he must go hat in hand to the Democratic power brokers.

F.D.R.'s immediate problem was in his home state, for as the end of his first term approached a developing scandal in New York City made Tammany's support problematic. The city's mayor, debonaire James J. Walker, was looting the public treasury with abandon, scarcely bothering to conceal his largess—at the taxpayer's expense— to his Tammany brethren.[40]

New York papers, and Republican politicians, were demanding the governor use his special powers of investigation to determine the truth of the charges. Not wanting to offend the organization on which he must soon depend, and perhaps send it scampering in the direction of the still popular, although tentatively retired Smith, Roosevelt sought every possible way to avoid a confrontation.[41] He wrote to Howe, proposing a possible foot-dragging tactic: "In regard to the Mayoralty fight, I am keeping in reserve the thought of having both LaGuardia and Enright (the police commissioner) come before me and demanding, in the presence of a stenographer, that they back up their demands for an investigation with definite facts. If they have the facts I will start the investigation; if not they will look silly. Think it over. FDR."[42]

Roosevelt's Republican opponent in 1930 was Charles Tuttle, U.S. Attorney in New York. Tuttle had developed a reputation as a remorseless prosecutor. He accused the incumbent governor of deliberately failing to pursue an investigation whose need was obvious to any casual reader of the daily press. He also berated Roosevelt for clearing his appointments to the state courts with Tammany, and specifically of placing a judge on the General Sessions bench who had allegedly paid Tammany $30,000 for the job.[43]

By the time Roosevelt finally commissioned Judge Samuel Seabury to probe "Gentleman Jim," Tammany had every reason to appreciate the effort he had made on its behalf.[44]

Since Howe's declining health prohibited him from travelling about the state during the 1930 campaign, F.D.R. decided to use Farley's talents as a hail-fellow-well-met. With an effort at tact, which was not up to its requirements, Roosevelt eased Al Smith's state chairman out and replaced him with the pink-faced, gregarious backslapper.

Farley was indefatigable, travelling everywhere, speaking to everyone; yet his greatest conquest was the charming of Howe, normally on his guard against anyone who might challenge his place in Roosevelt's affections. In an interview in December 1974, Farley, still vigorous, spoke of Howe with reverence, as one does of a superior.[45]

The results of Farley's campaign vindicated Howe's and Roosevelt's decision to placate Tammany with a fence-straddling position on corruption: F.D.R. won by a 725,001 margin out of a total vote of 2,815,683. The organization provided 500,000 of that plurality within New York City. It was, nevertheless, a personal victory, since the party was unable to gain control of either house of the state legislature.

Scarcely had the count been completed than Howe instructed Farley to start beating the drum for Roosevelt's presidential nomination. In a victory statement written by Howe, Farley enthused, "I do not see how Mr. Roosevelt can escape becoming the next presidential nominee of his party, even if no one should raise a finger to bring it about."[46]

Farley said that when he asked the jubilant governor for his reaction, he was answered jovially, "Whatever you said, Jim, is all right with me."[47]

The fact that an organization wheelhorse like Farley was new on the F.D.R. team is confirmed by Farley's declaration that this was the first time he had ever discussed the possibility of the presidency with Roosevelt.[48] Howe had been talking to him about it since 1912.

The next week Roosevelt wrote in gratitude to Farley. "When I think of the difficulties of former State Chairmen with former Governors and vice verse(!), I have an idea that you and I make a combination which has not existed since Cleveland and Lamont. . . ."[49]

F.D.R. was increasingly becoming an avowed candidate for the nomination. Two weeks after the election he invited Ed Flynn to Albany, where, during an Executive Mansion dinner, at which the only other guest was Howe, he revealed his intentions. "Eddie, my reason for asking you to stay overnight is that I believe I can be nominated for the Presidency in 1932 on the Democratic ticket."[50]

Farley and Flynn became Roosevelt's strongest links to the local organizations across the country. Both had been Smith partisans and had only come to work for Roosevelt when Smith assured them he was no longer interested in the nomination. However, relations between Roosevelt and Smith deteriorated as Roosevelt charted his own course, largely ignoring the former Governor.

The matter came to a head at election time in 1931 when Smith allowed his nettled feelings to show at a Tammany rally; he blasted Roosevelt's sponsorship of a $20 million reforestation referendum. F.D.R. described his reaction in mildly disappointed terms in a letter to a friend: "What a queer thing that was for Al to fight so bitterly on No. 3! I cannot help remembering the fact that while he was Governor I agreed with almost all the policies he recommended but I was against one or two during those eight years. However, for the sake of party solidarity, I kept my mouth shut. . . ."[51]

In the cause of regularity, he was willing to stifle any impulse to protest. This attitude was not lost on party leaders. In order to make sure they were paying attention, within days after the 1930 election, Howe had completed a study of how Roosevelt had done in normally rural upstate Republican areas, and sent the message off to those much courted leaders.

By early 1931 he had opened presidential headquarters for F.D.R. at 331 Madison Avenue, euphemistically called "Friends of Roosevelt"; in June he had decided on who the key figures in the Roosevelt campaign would be in thirty-seven states. Later that month he commissioned Farley to contact as many of these leaders as possible in a preliminary eighteen-state survey. This so-called Elks Tour, so named because Farley ostensibly was on his way to address the Seattle Elks convention, was Howe's effort to gain an accurate nose count.[52]

Farley came back full of overblown enthusiasm; nothing, he opined, could stop Roosevelt; he would win on the first ballot. The state chairman's lack of experience in national politics had betrayed him. Promises had been made by leaders who could not deliver votes at the convention. Colonel Edward House, who had been Wilson's closest advisor, and aspired to a similar status in the new Roosevelt administration, warned Howe of Farley's callow exuberance. Howe wrote the Colonel on August 17, 1931, trying to calm his fears "about the possible danger of using Mr. Farley as our representative in the field."[53]

He had no intention of using him in the South or anywhere his "breeziness of manner" might offend. Still there was a place for such a hawker. "We need exactly this type of man; one who will impress the politicians with whom he talks with the fact that he is a politician of experience and that the Governor's affairs are being handled by real political experts."

Colonel House must understand presidential nominations are made by professional politicians and Farley was a man they would find appealing. "Should we unfortunately come in conflict with the regular organization machinery in any state," he continued, conjuring up a nightmare, "it will be necessary to appeal to the electorate on high economic and moral grounds and we will need someone decidedly more of the intelligentsia to enlist prominent men in such states who are not ordinary political workers. For this purpose Farley is utterly unsuited."

But prominent men and representatives of the intelligentsia were to be approached only as a last resort. It was the likes of Joe Guffey, soon to be U.S. senator, whom he wanted in Roosevelt's camp.

When Guffey finally announced for Roosevelt, Howe was ecstatic. His secretary, noting his unusual display of glee, asked who he was. "He's the Democratic leader of Pennsylvania, has been for years, and his uncle Jim Guffey was leader for years before that," Howe explained with uncharacteristic patience. "Joe has a knack of reading the political barometer and he's for Franklin because he knows Franklin is a winner. Catch on?"[54]

Was good ol' Joe interested in knowing where Roosevelt stood on any of the issues? Of course not. He was interested in being with the winner, regardless of what the winner stood for, because only the winner could hand out jobs. Catch on?

In terms of logic, it was an extraordinary situation. A man of outstanding ability was forced to accept the fact that his success in achieving an office, for which he was eminently suited, must depend on men noted mostly for their lack of intelligence and character. In the process, he was made to appear less than he was: a tragic, rarely discussed, demoralizing aspect of the party system.

Roosevelt was smoked out of the pose of traditional coyness on January 23, 1932, when he found it necessary to authorize, in writing, the entrance of his name on the North Dakota preferential primary ballot, as state law insisted. The alternative was to lose, by default, a delegation solidly in his camp. With the two-thirds rule in effect, he could not afford to be that careless.

A phalanx now formed about him, led by Harvard friends, millionaires, conservative Midwesterners (who could recognize a winner as quickly as Guffey), Ku Kluxers, pro- and anti-League of Nations advocates, high- and low-tariff men. Out front were the names of reputable senators: Cordell Hull of Tennessee, soon to be secretary of state; Alben Barkley, future vice-president from Kentucky; and Thomas Walsh, the Montana scourge of Teapot Dome villainy. But behind the scenes Howe was dealing with a less savory group: William Randolph Hearst, who was motivated not by love for Roosevelt, but rather, by pathological hatred for Smith; Huey Long, the persuasive Louisiana demagogue, who aspired to nothing more than being the first American dictator; Tom Pendergast, Missouri's answer to Tweed; and James Curley, mayor of Boston or occupant of a Boston jailhouse, depending on which portion of his career was being inspected at any given moment.[55]

Within two weeks of Roosevelt's North Dakota declaration, Smith let it be known he would be happy to accept the nomination if it were offered to him. Tammany now saw its opportunity. The stories of Sheriff Thomas Farley's "little tin cup" had been setting Boss Plunkitt's teeth on edge for months, and Roosevelt was allowing the investigative zealots to be loosed on him. It was time for the tiger to have a little fun.

The convention delegation was to be made up equally of delegates-at-large, chosen exclusively by the state committee controlled by Tammany, and district delegates, approximately half of whom were elected in Tammany-controlled localities. Therefore it came as no surprise when Governor Roosevelt discovered he was going to the convention without the support of his own state delegation. Plunkitt, who believed the worst liability a politician could have was a college education, advertised that New York was uninstructed, but in reality his men were committed to Smith.

By April, little more than two months before the convention, Farley's predictions were coming back to haunt him. Smith, worshipped in the Catholic Democratic wards of Massachusetts, won that state's bloc of thirty-six votes by a three-to-one majority. Within a month F.D.R.'s prospects became gloomier as the Speaker of the

House, Texas's John Nance Garner, unexpectedly defeated him and Smith in the California primary. With the backing of a sizeable Texas delegation, Garner looked as if he might well be the dark horse nominee, now that a deadlocked convention seemed likely.

As the convention opened in Chicago on June 27, Howe established headquarters in Room 1702 of the Congress Hotel, and began programming Farley to greet delegates. He had a complete history and convention itinerary for each delegate, neatly typed out on index cards, and received hourly reports on all who displayed a trace of indecision.

The first fight came over the choice of convention chairman. John Raskob, as conservative as Andrew Mellon, but national chairman of the supposedly liberal Democratic party, was determined to block Roosevelt. To this end he engineered a drive to make his executive committee head, Jouett Shouse, permanent convention chairman. After a vicious fight, in which charges of deceit were hurled against Howe, Farley, and Roosevelt for going back on their commitments earlier in the year to support Shouse, Senator Walsh was elected.[56] Ominously for Roosevelt, the vote was 626 to 528, an indication he was nowhere near the needed two-thirds tally.

The nomination speeches were completed at 4 A.M., July 1, and that condition of exhaustion, which so pleases the professionals, had gripped the moilers sweating on the floor. Deafened by ten hours of blasts from numerous brass bands, they numbly waited for the signal from their delegation chief as to who should receive their cherished vote.

When New York's turn came, Farley found the Tammany delegates so hostile he had difficulty locating a seat. Smith sat surrounded by cronies, chomping away at his stogie, as the roll was called. When his name was sounded from the podium, Jimmy Walker walked gracefully to the delegation microphone; the area fell into an unaccustomed silence.

The Seabury investigation was at its height and New York newspapers were insisting, even as Walker clutched the microphone, that Roosevelt exercise his power to suspend the playboy mayor. Spotlights shone on him from every corner of Convention Hall, and for an instant this handsome scoundrel was the center of the universe. Then in a defiant voice he announced, "I vote for Alfred E. Smith!"[57]

At the end of the first roll call Roosevelt had 666½ votes to Smith's

201¾ and Garner's 90¼, with a large cluster of votes scattered among favorite sons.[58] Roosevelt was 100 votes short, with no convincing sign of where he might dredge for the rest. Farley raced around the floor trying to barter the vice-presidential nomination for the switch of a key delegation.[59] Democratic pros were accustomed to these pressured moments and had learned in 1920 and '24 that wonderful things might be theirs if they would only be patient and allow worried petitioners to come to them.

Farley forced a second rollcall, hoping not to have to face Howe until the nomination had been secured. Roosevelt picked up only 11½ votes, still far from the winning number. Farley later wrote, "Missouri gave most of the votes we picked up because Tom Pendergast, boss of Kansas City, was friendly."[60]

Farley would have settled for adjournment at this point, but Smith and Garner were sure they had stopped Roosevelt and were determined to prove it on the next ballot.

The results of the third ballot satisfied no one. Roosevelt crept five votes closer to the needed total, but his opponents held fast; adjournment finally came at 9 A.M. Farley rushed back to the Congress Hotel, where he closeted with Flynn, Joe Guffey, and Frank Walker in an effort to concoct some strategy which could be presented to the asthmatic[61] and heat-oppressed occupant of Room 1702. A glum Farley told them, "I have no authority to do anything until I see Louis Howe and hear what he has to say."[62]

Lela Stiles, then working as Howe's secretary, described the scene: "They went hurriedly to Room 1702. There on the floor, just as he had lain all night, was Louis Howe. His shirt was open, his tie was off, his head rested on a pillow, and his harsh breathing filled the room. They looked at each other in silence. Then, as the others quietly withdrew, Jim Farley laid his great bulk down beside Louis' wasted form and there the strategy was outlined, Louis' voice barely audible as he whispered in Farley's ear. When Farley lifted himself from the floor and joined the others, Joe Guffey said gravely, 'This is the end for Louis, isn't it, Jim?' "[63]

It was an outrageous thought to Farley, whose single-minded purpose was political. "Of course he'll last," he shot back, "Anything else is nonsense. You know he's not going to die until he sees Roosevelt nominated."[64]

Soon after Farley left, Howe vindicated his faith in him. He sent for Harry Flood Byrd, boss of the Virginia machine once guided by Jefferson and Madison. What would convince him to throw his state's votes to Roosevelt? Howe demanded pragmatically. Byrd responded he merely wanted to be one of Virginia's senators; but the venerable Carter Glass, author of the Federal Reserve Act, and Claude Swanson were content to fill Virginia's two seats. Byrd's desire, which all his powers as boss of his state's party had not been sufficient to fulfill, seemed beyond Howe's ability to gratify.

Howe gazed at him coolly and then asked, "Is that your price?" When Byrd answered affirmatively, Howe, far from being indignant at being asked for a nonmonetary bribe, busied himself thinking only how best to deliver. "Very well," he pledged as his part of the deal, "We'll put either Glass or Swanson in Franklin's Cabinet."[65] Swanson subsequently became secretary of the Navy.

Armed with this new ammunition, Farley went to see Sam Rayburn, Garner's campaign manager. He conjured up memories of the 1924 deadlock between Smith and William Gibbs McAdoo, which had destroyed both men and condemned the party to defeat even before the campaign began. Was that what a party loyalist like Rayburn wanted? How much better a union of their interests with an unbeatable Roosevelt-Garner ticket!

Finally convinced, the always practical Rayburn reached Garner in Washington, where he was accepting calls from no one else, and obtained his agreement to the bargain. He had greater difficulty with the Texas delegation. The forty-six members of that group had waged a hard fight against a Roosevelt slate in the spring primary, and defeated it. A majority was convinced Roosevelt was a demon more to be shunned than Satan himself. Nevertheless, the crack of Rayburn's whip in the caucus quickly converted them to a new religion, although only by a slender 54-51 margin[66]

McAdoo, having received word from Rayburn, was chosen, in his role as party leader and head of the large California delegation, to announce the nominee's name to the groggy Convention Hall crowd. It was a duty Wilson's son-in-law relished, since Smith had blocked his nomination in 1924.

"California came here to nominate a President of the United States," he began innocuously to universal cheers. "It did not come here to deadlock this convention—" Since there was only one way to undeadlock a convention in which Roosevelt held such a predominant lead, his intention was suddenly clear, and he was now interrupted by boos from galleries packed with Smith partisans.

Chicago's Mayor Anton Cermak, a Smith supporter, who was assassinated in Miami, February 15, 1933, by a bullet meant for F.D.R., was called to the platform to calm those same men he had previously placed in the galleries to bellow at any reference to Roosevelt. Only with great determination was McAdoo able to conclude his statement with the declaration that California would not "engage in another devastating contest like that of 1924. California casts forty-four votes for Franklin D. Roosevelt."[67]

The fight was over. Roosevelt immediately told Howe to hold the convention in session, while he flew out to address the delegates. All previous nominees had been ritualistically informed of their good luck by a committee of delegates, sometimes weeks after the conventions. Convinced the country needed strong leadership, Roosevelt felt his flight from New York would dramatize the difference between him and the inert Hoover, who had been nominated on the first ballot in Chicago two weeks earlier.

"Let it also be symbolic," he told the cheering partymen, "that in so doing I broke traditions. Let it be from now on the task of our Party to break foolish traditions and leave it to the Republican leadership . . to break promises."[68]

The speech was a call for centrist experimentation; more than that, it was a rallying cry to the party, the mechanism of the bosses, to go out and win for the usual reasons. He pledged "100 percent" support of the party platform, which called for a "25 percent cut in the costs of government," and "a balanced budget."[69]

Farley was designated, at Roosevelt's insistence, chairman of the Democratic National Committee, and proceeded to conduct the campaign as a party function. He spent much of his time cajoling the leaders and maintaining contact with the 140,000 local party workers on Howe's list.

Back in New York Roosevelt had to deal with Tammany's darling, Mayor Walker. The Seabury investigation had been timed by F.D.R.'s opponents so that it reached its climax in August, just as the election campaign was about to get started. During the latter part of August

Roosevelt was forced to sit in personal judgment over a harried Walker, questioning him directly about his debauched administration. As this spectacle drew to its climax, Walker broke, submitted his resignation[70], and bolted for European exile, where he spent most of his remaining years, luxuriating in bitterness over the "unfair, un-American"[71] manner in which the New York governor had allowed him to be pursued.

More important to Roosevelt than Walker's pique was the fact that he had been relieved of the perilous responsibility to deal with the organization's idol. The city had been rid of its criminal mayor, but F.D.R. had escaped the need to personally act, thereby avoiding the Sachem's wrath.

With the nomination struggle and the Walker investigation behind him, with a united party, which was satisfied it had a winner, and was, therefore, working hard for his election, Roosevelt began to express himself more forcefully on behalf of "the forgotten man." During the rest of his campaign he outlined the revolutionary New Deal policies of the next six years.

The confidence Democratic leaders had in Roosevelt was justified on election night when it became apparent he had inflicted on Hoover the worst defeat a Republican nominee had ever suffered. More important to them than Roosevelt's margin of 27,821,857 to 15,761,841 was the enormous majorities run up in Congress, and the state houses across the country, by their confederates swept into office on F.D.R.'s coattails.

Howe was both pleased and disconcerted by the results. True, his Franklin had finally won that prize for which he had so long labored. Still, a reckoning had to be made with all those political types he had so sternly appraised years earlier when, as a reporter, he had surveyed their soiled ways. He spoke to the students at the Columbia University School of Journalism about professional politicians shortly after the election. In response to a question as to whether politics would be a good career for a young man, he said, "You can't adopt politics as a profession and remain honest. If you are going to make your living out of politics you can't do it honestly."[72] The *Times* screamed that revelation across its front page.

Close to the end of his life, his mission accomplished, Howe had summed up his experience with the breed. Although he did not like them, and never pretended to, he had spent thirty years cultivating them; for he understood with perfect clarity that if his purpose was to be achieved these dishonest men would be his instruments.

He had, from the first, shown no interest in reform and no tendency to cavil over the niceties of moral issues. He was a professional politician, like a professional plumber, not attached to the persona or tools of his trade, except for their utilitarian purpose. Like a plumber unstuffing a clogged drain, he was not squeamish about the filth that coated his hands; he could work with a crooked politician or damn him, cozy up to a bitter opponent or conspire to destroy him even as he was negotiating a truce. And, although his affinity for trickery, his contempt for the ordinary voter, was always in service to his boss the suspicion does not arise that if his own fortunes were associated with another candidate he would have applied himself with any less vigor.

Whether Roosevelt would have become president without Louis Howe is extremely doubtful. Franklin Delano Roosevelt was a great leader: brilliant, charming, persuasive, capable of enlisting the enthusiasm of a resplendent group of subordinates. He was audacious, persistent, courageous, especially in his personal life, an opportunist of rare skill. Roosevelt had a flair for dramatics which was essential in mobilizing his countrymen to follow him along uncharted paths. Yet these were only peripheral reasons why he was selected as the presidential nominee of the Democratic party.

His ability to perform in office was an accident as random as any collision between cars on an icy road. The fact that he was one of our greatest presidents, and managed, with the aid of Louis Howe's skill and grit, to navigate the crumbling, perilous channels of party politics, should not disguise the central fact that in order to do this he had to overcome his party leaders' inbred apathy toward men of independence and quality. Franklin Roosevelt was the last such president to accomplish this feat. His election underscores the hazardous nature of the process now used to select our chief magistrate.

17

The Decline of
the Presidency

*The fact remains that the institution [the Presidency]
provides camouflage for all that is petty and nasty in
human beings, and enables a clown or a knave to pose as
Galahad and be treated with deference.*

George E. Reedy[1]

Harry S Truman was a normal product of party politics. Delivered
to the nation by Tom Pendergast's ignominious Missouri machine,
he was every bit as inadequate for the job as might have been expected.
That we survived him, and many historians have come to think of
him nostalgically as one of our better presidents, is less a tribute to
him, than a measure of America's innate strength at the end of the
Second World War, and the deficiencies of the men who succeeded
him.

Adding to his appeal is the curiosity that he was a plain-speaking
man in the field of politics, where doubletalk is the usual language.
The average American, and especially those too young to have witnessed his generally lackluster performances, find his occasionally
earthy candor refreshing.

Yet he does not appear to have deceived himself. In her 1972 book
about her father, Margaret Truman described his self-evaluation: "To
this day Dad cannot picture himself as a great man, or a great
President."[2]

He resembled Harding in that respect; both wondered aloud
whether they were up to the job. If he had had his way, Truman would
have been a haberdasher in Kansas City, checking inventory instead of

215

concentrating on budget figures for the Marshall Plan; but, fate intervened. Truman's business lasted only from 1919 until 1922 when, he felt, it failed because Harding and Mellon had "started a 'wringing-out' process"[3] which forced the little man to the wall.

At age thirty-eight, married scarcely three years, deeply in debt, and with no prospects during the postwar recession, Truman turned to politics. He had been in local politics before the war, as road overseer in Washington Township, Missouri, an office he inherited in 1914 from his deceased father. He had also served as postmaster of Grandview, and in addition, had been Democratic clerk in every election since 1906. All of these jobs were patronage plums handed out by the clubhouse to the obedient.

Truman, in his memoirs, described his entrance into elective politics in this manner: "When the time came for the Pendergast organization to endorse someone as candidate for eastern judge in 1922 . . . Mike Pendergast (the boss's brother) informed the gentlemen there that he thought it would be a good thing for them to support me as that candidate."[4]

Truman wanted to be an administrative judge; in that capacity he would be involved with levying taxes: He would also determine who received contracts to build roads, homes for the aged, schools for delinquent children, and asylums for the insane. It was the one aspect of government in which the Pendergast machine was always most interested, since that was where the possibilities for profit existed.

The "busted merchant,"[5] as he referred to himself, won easily along with another Pendergast man, giving the organization control of the three-man court. Whereupon, Truman declared, "we promptly took all the jobs."[6]

He lost his bid for reelection but was quickly "able to make a connection with the Automobile Club of Kansas City."[7] A man who had spent two years handing out contracts to build roads was clearly of interest to those trying to encourage the use of the gas buggy. "It gave me a substantial income,"[8] Truman commented without guile.

By this time, he was interested in a political career, and, having performed to the satisfaction of Pendergast, awaited his reward with equanimity. "In 1926, when the election machinery was being oiled up by the party leaders, I was slated to run for presiding judge of the county court."[9]

It is clear from his references, and the listing of his patronage jobs going back to 1906, that every political job he sought in those days interested him primarily as a source of income. He never aspired to high office, having nothing more grandiose in mind than earning a county paycheck.

"Mike Pendergast had suggested that I run for county collector of Jackson County," he recalled candidly, "and I was in a willing frame of mind to do this because it was a good public office with a substantial income."[10]

Truman, with years of experience in petty politics, knew how these matters were settled. "Mike and I went to see his brother Tom and discussed the matter with him. He said he had already promised to support someone else for that job, but he thought, because of my experience as eastern judge, I ought to be a candidate for presiding judge."[11]

Tom Pendergast seldom advanced a man unless he saw in that gesture a possibility for self-advancement. Truman, habituated to the realities of machine politics, quickly showed his grasp of that fact. "Although I was to become very well acquainted with Tom Pendergast, I barely knew him when I was first elected presiding judge of the Jackson County Court. He was a power in local politics, of course, and when the bond issues for Kansas City were up for consideration I went to see him."[12]

For ten years Pendergast had been trying to get the voters of Kansas to approve bond issues that would provide him with the source of lucrative road contracts with which to reward his contributors. Suddenly he had a grateful Truman, who would be in charge of dispensing the contracts, willing to campaign hard to get the suspect bond issues approved. He accepted without hesitation, for, although accused of many crimes, he was never accused of being stupid; he watched with growing appreciation as the peripatetic judge beat the bushes for votes.

After the bond issue passed, Truman was not startled to discover the boss wanted part of the action. "When the first contracts were to be let, I got a telephone call from Tom Pendergast saying that he and some of his friends were very anxious to see me about those contracts. I knew very well what was in the wind, but I went to their meeting."[13]

Truman maintained he told the boss the contracts were going to go to the lowest bidder, regardless of the source of the bid, and further-more, Pendergast raised no objection to that proviso. Pendergast had little reason to complain; with Truman's indispensable help he had finally gotten the bond issue past the barrier of the polling booth. There was now more than enough millions available to "oil up" the party machinery, even if some of it slopped over onto the machinery of some unaffiliated road contractor.

In an earlier passage in his autobiography Truman underscored the insignificance of his stipulation that contracts would only go to the lowest bidder. He had remarked that a specific contractor was honest, "very unusual for a contractor of county business in Jackson County at that time."[14] Obviously he had only to decide which thief was to receive his approval. It was, perhaps, a mark of his character that he was determined that that thief would be the lowest bidder.

Having to deal with these dishonest contractors did not necessarily make the uncomplicated Truman dishonest. Nor did his giving "all the jobs" to the clubhouse boys necessarily mean conventional bribes were being offered to the stolid judge; nevertheless, it made him no enemies in the party.

By 1934 he was thinking it might be time to run for Congress, but the organization had someone else in mind. A loyalist such as Tru-man, however, was not to be left out in the cold; he was encouraged to make a primary run for the Senate nomination.

"Two fine and very experienced congressmen opposed me for the nomination," he remarked. But, he had been around long enough to realize, character and experience were hardly determining factors in the selection of United States senators. "Each of them had been in Congress for many years and they had wonderful reputations. Fortu-nately for my prospects, however, I had become acquainted with all the county judges and county clerks in the state of Missouri and was very familiar with the operations of the so-called 'courthouse gangs' in all the counties."[15]

The result was predictable, and Truman settled down to ten years in the Senate, convinced no man could have a better friend than Tom Pendergast. Since Truman also was convinced loyalty to friends was one of man's most positive characteristics, Pendergast, despite hard times which befell him, was never heard to utter a word of criticism about his Washington connection.

Truman's rise to the presidency was, as it always is, a result of the random effect of chance and the more direct impact of party politics. Roosevelt had retired John Nance Garner as vice-president, in 1940, after the Texan had served two terms in that holding position. He had taken as his third-term ticket-sharer Secretary of Agriculture Henry A. Wallace. Wallace's radicalism and independence had won him the enmity of party leaders, so that the 1944 national convention assembled in Chicago not to debate a fourth-term nomination for F.D.R., but rather to settle on who should be his vice-president. The choice was particularly important since Roosevelt was obviously in declining health.

Truman had received excellent publicity for the job he had done as chairman of the Senate Committee to Investigate the National Defense Program. More important, he had the support of professional partymen, and since the 1944 convention was one of those occasions when an ideological struggle was going on between conservative professionals and radical idealists, he was the rallying symbol of party regulars in their brawl with the newcomers, many of them intellectuals, who had been unaccustomedly drawn into politics during the 1930s by their fervor for Roosevelt's New Deal.

Men like Harry Hopkins, Rexford Tugwell, and Felix Frankfurter were typical of a genre of energetic, unaffiliated individuals who enter politics during periods of crises. Desperate to discover a method of improving conditions, they race into organized political activity, recognizing that the party system at least offers them a structure within which they can operate. Disillusionment comes with the realization that party leaders have no interest in ideals, and little interest in, or concern about, people.

As events reached their climax, Roosevelt wearied of the fight and, in a delicately worded letter to the convention's chairman, which was quickly circulated[16], he abandoned Wallace, acquiescing to what the *Times* called "the new Missouri Compromise."[17] The Missourian replaced Wallace. Within little more than three months after his inauguration, Roosevelt was dead in Warm Springs of a stroke, and Truman was president.

An impulsive man, who acted as soon as the thought took shape, he spoke without pretense in the vernacular of a small-town boy. The day after he had been sworn in, he chatted with a group of reporters in the Senate Office Building. "Boys," he said, a tremor in his voice, "if you ever pray, pray for me now. I don't know whether you fellows ever had a load of hay fall on you, but when they told me yesterday what had happened, I felt like the moon, the stars, and all the planets had fallen on me. I've got the most terribly responsible job a man ever had."[18]

The responsibilities of his great office did something to Truman; he became decisive in all things big and small. Without judging the merits of his acts, a mere listing of some of them numbs the mind at their audacity: he ordered the dropping of two atomic bombs on Japan and thereby opened up the possibility of total human annihilation in some future war; he took over America's steel mills when their owners disagreed with him and relinquished them only when the Supreme Court said he had violated the Constitution; he scrapped price controls in the face of runaway inflation; asked Congress to draft striking railroad workers into the Army; and, without a moment's hesitation, took the country into the Korean War.

The diffident manner he displayed for the first six months of his presidency finally disappeared and Americans became accustomed to, if not enraptured with, the self-confidence with which Truman approached even the most complex matters. There was an appeal in his directness which won the approval of many Americans.

Given Truman's earthy personality, the Republican convention in 1948 selected the one man he would have preferred as an opponent. Thomas Dewey was his exact opposite, an elitist without personality,[19] whose cautious instincts led him to fill his innocuous campaign speeches with sentences like: "Our future lies before us."

The Democrats, convinced they could not win with Truman, wanted Dwight David Eisenhower, a certified military hero, as their candidate. Since he had never voted in an election, nor declared any party preference, they had as much right as the Republicans to bid for his services.[20]

In this enormous country, crammed with thousands of talented citizens, the party selection system had become so restricting, the field of potential candidates so narrowed, that party bosses could only think in terms of a general or, if forced to it, an unpopular Missouri politician.

Those who argue that parties provide a needed structure, by means of which the orderly selection of a president is achieved, should ponder the disorderly and disoriented approach party leaders took that year in choosing between these two men.

The most powerful leaders in the Democratic party wanted Eisenhower. William O'Dwyer, mayor of a disreputable New York regime, from which he was soon to flee into Mexican exile, had asserted the general was just the man to clean up the country; Jersey City's Mayor Frank Hague, the epitome of the party dictator, liked Ike; Jake Arvey, Chicago's Democratic boss, reflected the common thought of the professionals when he revealed why he would support Eisenhower: "Come convention time I will vote for the man who comes closest to personifying the principles of our party and who can put them into effect. And by that I mean a man who can be elected."[21]

Even Truman seemed to be convinced Eisenhower should have the party nomination; during a friendly interlude in Berlin in 1945, he had confided to him, "General, there is nothing that you may want that I won't try to help you get. That definitely and specifically includes the Presidency in 1948."[22]

The Democratic leaders were thwarted, however, by a tradition that had held sway since World War I. Professional military men were expected to resist the temptation to seek the presidency. Aside from Leonard Wood's unsuccessful endeavor in 1920, World War I had produced no serious martial contender for the White House. General George Marshall, Eisenhower's commander during World War II, had repulsed many attempts to convince him to run. Eisenhower himself had summarized the arguments for the "wise subordination of the military to civil power" in a letter to New Hampshire publisher Leonard Finder while slamming the door on efforts to draft him in 1948.

"In the American scene I see no dearth of men fitted by training, talent and integrity for national leadership. On the other hand, nothing in the international or domestic situation qualifies for the most important office in the world a man whose adult years have been spent in the country's military forces. At least this is true in my case."[23]

Left with no alternative, the party leaders nominated Truman and resigned themselves to defeat; Dewey, they were convinced, would shatter their nominee. The pollsters reinforced their gloom. On Election Day Truman astounded the soothsayers, and the savvy leaders of his party.

Although Truman had every personal reason to be overjoyed, proponents of democracy cannot view the 1948 election with the same emotions. The total vote for the two major parties had declined dramatically, reversing a trend of several decades; it was necessary to go back to the 1936 Roosevelt-Landon contest to find a lower total. The voters did not appear to be enchanted with the choice party bosses had given them. In that situation, the party machines flourish, since their coterie comes out in dependable numbers regardless of the nominee, concerned not so much with personalities as with prospects.

By the end of his second term, Truman, although the last president eligible to seek a third term, had no taste for the fight. His decision was based on at least two portents of defeat so dismal they were impossible to ignore. His ratings in the Gallup poll had fallen to an all-time low for any president; only 23 percent of the people questioned thought he was doing a good job. During the week he handed in his resignation, Richard Nixon finally descended to a similar standing with Gallup's cross section. Jimmy Carter reached the floor of that pit in July 1979, when his indecisiveness in the face of astronomical OPEC oil price increases and double-digit inflation was impoverishing large numbers of Americans, while his fiscal policies were deliberately plunging the nation into what his advisors described as a corrective recession.

Much more foreboding for Truman than his low standing in the polls was the prospect his opponent would be General Eisenhower. The General was the most popular man in America. Republican leaders were pressing him to accept their gift to themselves, his nomination. With Eisenhower, they would defeat any Democrat; without him, the majority fashioned by Roosevelt, in the absence of Truman, would reassert itself.

Free to choose from the heart, the Republican organization would have given the nomination to Ohio's Senator Robert Taft, William Howard Taft's son; he was genuinely conservative, the party's leader in the Senate, and a contender at the previous three national conventions.

Even though it was obvious Eisenhower was a much stronger candidate, Taft came close to defeating him in that pivotal 1952 convention. The vote at the end of the first ballot, before Minnesota's switch started a stampede for the General, was 595 for Ike and 500 for Taft.

After twenty years of defeats, the Republican convention should not have come that close to exchanging sure victory with charismatic Ike for sure defeat with dour Taft; however, the mechanics of party politics almost brought about this fiasco. Taft, following the example of his father in 1912, had courted the graveyard districts of the South. With the support of these paper organizations, whose vote was as good at the national convention as the vote of any viable Northern Republican district, Taft was a much too serious contender in Chicago, where the board of directors of the party, not its stockholders, was meeting.

That other techniques were used by the Taft forces to narrow the distance between their hero and the hero of Normandy was explained to me by Harold Burton, a delegate to the 1952 convention.

Burton was the black Republican leader in preponderantly Democratic Harlem. He greeted me, one wintry night in 1953, at the door of his 137th Street Square Deal clubhouse; a snub-nosed gun was strapped to his hip. The chain blocking the door was not released until I produced his latter authorizing the interview, a clearance gained only as a result of my meeting, in Chicago, with some of his fellow delegates at the convention.

Soon after he welcomed me in out of the cold we were chatting amiably in a room cluttered with rows of dust-covered folding chairs, at the front of which was his battered desk. The genial, graying Burton assured me he had behaved with honor at the convention that nominated the first Eisenhower-Nixon ticket, and illustrated his contention with a story about an attempt to buy his vote. "The Taft people offered me $10,000," he said, rightfully proud that he had rejected this deal, but neglecting to mention the far better one Governor Dewey had been giving him for years.

What Burton was never able to explain was why he continued to man this lonely outpost of Republicanism, since everyone along Lenox Avenue knew this was Democratic territory. Burton understood, better than most, that the chances of Harlem electing a Republican to any office were not nearly as good as his chance of being mugged on his way home that night; yet he was not in the least discouraged. The explanation, at first obscure, becomes apparent when proper weight is given to the fact that the state and national organization recognized him as the authentic party representative in that section of Manhattan. When nomination season came, he packed his valise and along with the other, more successful, leaders of the party went off to convention city to pick mayors, congressmen, governors, and presidents. In the lifelong performance of this duty, he had never been known to disappoint the genuine leaders of New York Republicanism, though the observance of this demanding code might even occasionally call on him to reject a $10,000 bribe.

Ike's lines held and it became a season of success for the Republicans; they managed to overcome their scruples and nominate a winner. The Democrats, disappointed that Everett McKinley Dirksen, the point man for Taft, had not had his way, anointed the contemplative, nimble-witted Adlai Stevenson as a sacrificial offering to the General.

The fact that Stevenson, then governor of Illinois, gave the General such a good race can be attributed to a disenchantment with Ike's philosophy, which was revealed to the voters only after the campaign began. All those opinions of his that had never seen the light of day were now public knowledge. During the campaign he deserted his old friend General Marshall solely to placate Senator Joseph McCarthy. That desertion showed Ike to have a moral weakness that had never previously been ascribed to him. Finally, Richard Nixon's designation as the Republican vice-presidential nominee, at age thirty-nine, weakened the ticket. The secret fund scandal, which erupted in the middle of the campaign, reenforced the negative opinion many Americans had of the young senator.

Nevertheless, in terms of democratic participation, the election was a smashing success: Eisenhower's 33.9 million and Stevenson's 27.3 million represented the highest vote total for both winner and loser in a national election. The grand total exceeded by more than 15 million the sum of the prosaic 1948 campaign; Stevenson actually outpolled the victorious Truman by 3 million votes.

Despite his personal victory, Eisenhower spent the next eight years demonstrating his unwavering party regularity. Within weeks after the convention he had humbled himself enough to Taft, at their "Morningside Heights reunion," so that the Ohio senator consented to use his influence, on the General's behalf, with the party organization.

Eisenhower was a remarkable figure in terms of party politics. His overwhelming popularity should have made him independent of the machine politicians; they needed him; it was that simple. With a few deft gestures he could have easily put them in their place and performed his duties in a manner rarely possible for presidents since the advent of the party system.

Instead, he seemed to underestimate his ability to dominate their greedy impulses. Perhaps it was the old Army habit of team effort that did him in: They were, after all, on his team; didn't that obligate him to cooperate with them? Moreover, how could men who professed to like him be untrustworthy? General Grant, when it came to dealing with party figures, displayed the same naiveté.

In addition, when it was necessary for Eisenhower to assert control over the party apparatus, there seemed to be a loss of energy, in fact, a failure of will. Leaders who should have reacted to each of his words with the sensitivity that litmus paper reacts to a drop of acid, found it easy, and safe, to ignore him. Believing he needed the party more than he did, but unwilling to devote himself to its management, he sought surrogates who would wear themselves out in this effort; Richard Nixon was an eager volunteer.

The 1954 congressional elections offered Eisenhower the first opportunity to demonstrate his indispensability to the machine. Instead, he turned the campaign over to Nixon, maintaining his golf schedule and relaxed pace, as Nixon raced around the country speaking at party gatherings and cementing ties with party chiefs.

Although Nixon was to remain outside the circle of Eisenhower's trusted advisors to the end of his administration, the indifferent president allowed the party machinery to come under his control. The party, unconcerned with issues, discovered that it had a titular leader who was unconcerned with the party; as a consequence, Nixon's attentiveness was more than flattering, and his reward not long in coming. In 1956, when Eisenhower privately asked Nixon to withdraw as a candidate for renomination as vice-president, it was the firm support of the professionals on the Republican National Committee that allowed him to stand up to the most popular man of his generation.

During his second term in office, the ailing Eisenhower was scarcely a factor in the party's blueprints. Nixon was the campaign chief year after year, and the General was used mostly as the American flag was used at party functions: Glimpses of him brightened the moment and rallied the guileless.

Eisenhower proved to be an inept, self-indulgent president, often more intent on practicing his putting than minding the store. During his administration, McKinley economic policies, pursued with his sanction by his secretary of the Treasury, George Humphrey, plunged the nation into three recessions. Hoover, a busy Taft supporter at the '52 convention, was quickly won to his side.

No doubt his heart attack in 1955 left him less able to deal with the burdens of his office; yet, this did not dampen the enthusiasm of the partymen for his renomination. Although an invalid for the rest of his life, they saw in him the glorious dispenser of patronage, whose partisan vigor had not been impaired. His own sense of responsibility led him only to warn prospective voters in 1956 that he would have to take more frequent vacations, and work for shorter periods of time if reelected.

Even in foreign policy, where one might have expected him to be most perceptive, awkwardness seemed to keynote his actions. He was the first president to commit American advisors to the Vietnam War; and as the French were on the verge of defeat at Dien Bien Phu in 1954, he seriously considered recommendations from Nixon, and Secretary of State John Foster Dulles, that atomic bombs be dropped on the North Vietnamese. American economic and military involvement in that country escalated at a steady rate during the remaining years he was in office.

His effect on Middle East affairs was negative; its full impact was still being absorbed as the decade of the 1980s dawned. At the time of the 1956 joint British-French-Israeli expedition into Suez, which quickly met with success, and promised to neutralize potential difficulties with Arab oil producers of that area, Eisenhower, vexed over not being informed of the operation in advance, demanded the removal of the joint force. Many of the subsequent problems plaguing the energy-starved industrial world could be traced to the unrealistic position adopted by Eisenhower during that Suez War.

On the eve of his retirement, the country was deep in an economic decline whose bottom had not yet been reached. A sense of indifference, and lack of purpose, had settled over the Eisenhower decade.

The moral resolve that had infused the Roosevelt era had dissipated. In its stead was the morality of the clubhouse, homogenized through society, with each splendid striver wondering whether some day he would be able to tee-up at Burning Tree.

Eisenhower represented the replacement of substance with image—the president as a symbol, the presidency as a reward. The party philosophy of winning at any cost had resulted in mere popularity becoming a qualification for nomination.

18

The Honcho Presidents: One in Style, the Other in Substance

American Presidents drift into trouble . . . because they are never quite sure whether they are primarily the Chief Magistrates of the Republic or the leaders of their party.

Walter Lippmann[1]

The 1960 election removed the Eisenhower anomaly from the political scene and placed the selection of the presidential nominees back in the hands of the party bosses. John Fitzgerald Kennedy, junior senator from Massachusetts, a lean six-footer, with a matinee idol's smile and a teenager's rumpled chestnut hair, was the product of their schemes.

Grandson of Boston's celebrated politician Honey Fitz, son of millionaire shipbuilder, realtor, movie, and booze financier Joseph P., who was one of F.D.R.'s original backers and his ambassador to Britain, young Kennedy was nurtured on party tactics. His older brother, Joseph Jr., had been confidently told by his father that some day he would be president. When Joseph's bomber was lost on a mission over the English Channel during World War II, young John, who had been prepared only to serve his brother's ambitions, became his surrogate.

At the end of the war, in which he took part heroically as a South Pacific PT boat commander, Kennedy returned to civilian life. In 1946, responding to the wishes of his father and grandfather, he ran for Congress in Massachusetts' 11th District. He was only twenty-nine, but the voters of Irish and Italian heritage, who comprised most of the district's electorate, saw him as a reincarnation of the beloved Honey Fitz, and he had no difficulty winning.

Kennedy's mildly liberal voting record conformed to the opinions of his section and party. Only once in these early days did he split away from the leadership of the Massachusetts's machine, at that time under the control of House Democratic Leader John McCormack. The issue concerned Mayor Curley, then serving as Boston's chief magistrate, while simultaneously serving a six-to-eighteen-month sentence for mail fraud in the Danbury federal prison.

McCormack thought there was something unbecoming about the mayor of Boston wearing jailhouse gray, and had circulated a petition, among Massachusetts' congressmen, which urged Truman to grant him presidential clemency. To his credit, Kennedy was the only one who refused to place his name on that petition.[2] Truman sided with McCormack and Mayor Curley was no longer forced to conduct Boston's business in a cramped cell.

In the midst of his third term in the House, Kennedy decided to challenge the apparently invincible Henry Cabot Lodge, Jr., for his Senate seat. Lodge had been the focal point of Republican effort to convince Eisenhower that he should accept the 1952 nomination; in the process, he had neglected his own political fences, and young Kennedy found gaping holes in them.

While Lodge spent the better part of 1951 talking to party leaders and flying to Paris NATO headquarters to confer with Ike, Kennedy crisscrossed the Bay State. Even before the start of the 1952 election year he had visited three hundred cities and villages familiarizing himself with the names and preferences of every party leader. Almost 150,000 Democrats signed his nominating petitions, and each of them received a letter requesting the names of ten persons to whom the congressman might write.

Kennedy money played a substantial role in this victory: The six major Kennedy committees eventually claimed they had spent $350,000; but the massive television/radio/newspaper advertising campaign, plus the enormous letter and telephone canvass, might well have cost substantially more.[3]

Kennedy entered the Senate in 1953 as Nixon became its presiding officer. Both men had their eyes fastened on the White House. Even at this early date, Nixon had every reason to believe his expectations were reasonable; he was already vice-president. Kennedy, a practicing Catholic in a country that had displayed the strength of its prejudice as recently as 1928, had only money and determination to encourage him.

Continuing his practice of voting carefully enough to avoid contention, Kennedy, now in his thirty-seventh year, began to draw attention. With his new photogenic bride, Jacqueline Lee Bouvier, he became a popular subject of Sunday supplements. His political rating climbed when he wrote a best seller: a series of short biographies on American statesmen, entitled *Profiles in Courage*. He was awarded the Pulitzer Prize for it, the only member of Congress to be the recipient of that honor.

By the spring of 1956 he was being mentioned as a vice-presidential possibility. Connecticut's Governor Abraham Ribicoff and Rhode Island's Governor Dennis Roberts both announced they would go to the convention to work for his nomination. *Look* magazine published a survey that claimed to show that a Catholic candidate would help the Democratic ticket.

As a result of his excellent showing in 1952, Stevenson quickly won redesignation to the top spot. Kennedy had delivered Stevenson's nominating speech and made a smashing impression; delegates previously committed to Tennessee's Estes Kefauver for the vice-presidential nomination began to waver. On the night of August 16, Stevenson confounded party tradition by refusing to select a running mate. He told this gathering of yes-men they were going to have a free hand in choosing the candidate.

Kennedy was not confused by this show of faith in majority rule. He quickly attempted to contact the men who controlled the delegations: Mayor Richard Daley, always a Kennedy stalwart, pledged Illinois; Harry Byrd, Jr., son of Louis Howe's bartering partner, brought Virginia into his camp; Carmine DeSapio, Tammany's boss, who was soon to go to jail, thought he might go for Kennedy after a first-ballot vote for New York's favorite son, Mayor Robert Wagner. Even his brother-in-law, actor Peter Lawford, was enlisted in the cause; he called his Las Vegas friend Wilbur Clark,[4] the guardian of the gaming tables at the Desert Inn, and, not surprisingly, a delegate to this Chicago stakes race, to see whether his fellow gamblers might be willing to place a bet on Kennedy's prospects. It was all to no avail; Kefauver was chosen.

Kefauver's victory, however, was merely a prelude to the punishing November defeat of the ticket by incumbent Eisenhower. Kennedy took his convention loss in sportsman-like fashion, and escaped the stigma of that Election Day rout, which might have put an end to his aspirations; after that debacle he emerged as the leading contender for the 1960 presidential nomination.

For the three years before that convention, Kennedy travelled the country, much as he had toured Massachusetts when running for the Senate. He spoke in every state in the union, amassing a list of thousands of persons who might be of help to him.

Eleanor Roosevelt was perhaps the most influential member of the party who openly showed her distaste for him. She had been disenchanted by his unwillingness to express any opinion on Joe McCarthy's excesses. When brother Robert sought a job with McCarthy's Senate Permanent Investigating Committee as minority counsel, she took this as a sign of familial sympathy for the Wisconsin demagogue.

Their disagreement came to a head after the Army-McCarthy hearings, in the spring of 1954, when the freshman senator managed to maintain complete silence on the subject of McCarthy's outrageous conduct. This no-comment stance continued, and became more galling to Mrs. Roosevelt toward the end of the year, when McCarthy's fellow senators moved to censure him, without the slightest encouragement from Kennedy. He, in fact, chose this time to undergo surgery to correct a spinal injury incurred in the service ten years earlier.

Voicing her distress over what she interpreted as cowardly behavior, F.D.R.'s widow stated that she could not support Kennedy's candidacy, since he was "someone who understands what courage is and admires it, but has not quite the independence to have it."[5]

An older political sore may have been irritated by his candidacy: in 1940, Joseph Jr. had been delegate to the "third-term convention," and had cast the family vote for Jim Farley, F.D.R.'s former retainer, who then viewed himself as presidential material. On a television program in December 1958, as the Gallup Poll had Kennedy leading Nixon by the startling percentage of 61 to 39, Mrs. Roosevelt indicated her continued disapproval, saying she had been informed the senior Kennedy "has been spending oodles of money all over the country"[6] in an apparent attempt to buy the presidency for his son.

A month earlier he had won a second term in the Senate with an astonishing majority of 869,000. As a result, Mrs. Roosevelt's caveats about money and independence influenced few party leaders hungry for federal patronage after eight lean Republican years. His ties to Chicago's Mayor Richard Daley—the leader of the strongest party machine in the country—were as tight as ever.

Kennedy's primary victory over Hubert Humphrey in West Virginia, in the early months of 1960, added to the strength he had amassed among big-city bosses. The addition of Senate Majority Leader Lyndon Johnson to the ticket gave him some hope of holding the Southern states, which had been provoked enough by Smith's Catholicism to vote for Hoover.[7]

On July 27, Richard Nixon, almost overcome with "the fatigue I had felt as a result of three days with almost no sleep . . ."[8] appeared before the Republican convention to accept the nomination which had been his, beyond serious challenge, for four years. Eisenhower's distaste for, and distrust of, his vice-president, often privately expressed, could not steel him to the task of publicly opposing his selection as the 1960 presidential nominee.

The election battle was close. Two relatively young men, with approximately the same political experience, and many of the same perceptions of what politics was all about, sparred cautiously for position. Kennedy finally succeeded in goading a reluctant Nixon into accepting a challenge to four televised debates. The nervous, seemingly unshaved vice-president showed to poor advantage in their first meeting on September 26. This may well have been the deciding factor in the campaign, since 80 million people viewed this spectacular—the largest television audience since the Checkers speech. In Nixon's "post-mortem" he remarked he had "looked pale and tired," and concluded that since he "knew that appearance may at times count more than substance . . . I recognized the basic mistake I had made. I had concentrated too much on substance and not enough on appearance."[9]

Kennedy became president by a remarkably close division: a scant

113,000 out of 68,800,000 votes cast. A shift of 4,000 votes in Illinois, which Nixon lost when Mayor Daley produced the needed margin in late-reporting Cook County wards, plus 9,000 other votes in a handful of closely divided states, would have made him president in 1960. Nixon never tired of suggesting the election had been stolen from him.[10]

Kennedy quickly reversed Eisenhower's tight-money policies, and within the first year of his administration the country had snapped out of its severe economic recession. America now experienced eight years of unparalleled prosperity. The inflation rate during Kennedy's three years in office was held to 1.2 percent, while unemployment fell from over 6 million to less than 3 million.

This was most likely his greatest accomplishment, although more attention is given to his behavior during the Cuba missile crisis. The Kennedy recovery was substantial and meaningful, and affected the lives of hundreds of millions of people around the world. His hand, however, was not steady at the helm; he was habituated to approach national problems on a political level and the new view from the presidential heights did not alter that practice.

Kennedy cast light on this aspect of his thinking when speaking of a president he admired. "Franklin Roosevelt would phone a senator at two o'clock in the morning. No hour was too late, no chore too hard, if it helped accomplish his objective. A President must 'play politics' in the best meaning of the phrase. He must be trained for it and he must love it."[11]

The love of it caused him to hesitate when the possibility existed of congressional opposition. As a result two years of his precious few as president went by before he publicly committed himself to a legislative program, and death at an assassin's hand overcame him before a single measure was enacted.

In terms of foreign policy, he was president just long enough to get the country deeply committed to the defense of South Vietnam. His social impact was greater than most presidents'. This handsome man, with his eloquent voice and graceful manner, made the Camelot regal image acceptable in a society taught to worship democratic institutions. Louis XIV would have admired the abandon with which he spent $400,000 of the taxpayers' money to take his entourage to Newport to view the regatta.

*   *   *

His successor, Lyndon Baines Johnson, although a poor boy at birth, quickly learned to pamper himself. With the aid of his Texas oil sponsors, he managed to rise to the status of millionaire by the time he retired—after a lifetime of collecting moderate paychecks from the federal government. His patrons were never heard to complain, since it could scarcely be maintained that they would have done as well without him.

Johnson's political career, deprived of the kind of financial backing given to his son by Joseph Kennedy, never floundered because of needed campaign funds. Bobby Baker, his right hand in matters political, before he was sent to jail, found there was always enough money in the checking account to pay for the hulking Texan's campaigns.

Assistance from Texas oil interests was essential; it made possible the lavish publicity drives which accompanied his rise to power. Originally a New Dealer, spoken of as a protégé of F.D.R. while he was in the House of Representatives, his voting grew more conservative after his successful Senate campaign in 1948. In a primary where 988,295 Texans marked their ballots, he won by eighty-seven votes, making gestures of appreciation to his financial backers not only a matter of politeness, but the wisest sort of primitive political wisdom. Texas newspapers henceforth referred to him as "Landslide Lyndon,"[12] and, as might have been expected in so close an election, charges of voting irregularities were voiced from one end of the state to the other.

Johnson's ascension to power depended finally on John F. Kennedy; it was his decision in 1960 that he needed a right-of-center Southerner to balance his ticket; that placed the hardly popular Senate Majority Leader in the line of succession.[13] On November 22, 1963, Lyndon Johnson became the thirty-sixth president of the United States because a fury-driven person in Dallas decided to alter history.

As president, Johnson proved to have more strength of purpose and more determination to achieve his objectives than any man since Franklin Roosevelt; that this had some sad results for the American people has been proved by the legacy of the Vietnam War. A less assertive man would have avoided the waste of lives and money spent with such self-assurance by this machismo president with a taste for cowboy hats.

George Reedy, Johnson's press secretary, shrewdly observed that "In the White House, character and personality are extremely important because there are no other limitations which govern a man's conduct. Restraint must come from within the presidential soul and prudence from within the presidential mind."[14]

Yet restraint was exactly what Lyndon Johnson lacked; he was the quintessence of the arrogant ruler, intent mainly on giving scope to his whims. He had a reputation for being the most adroit legislative tactician of his generation; that reputation was not based on concern about other opinions, but rather on his ability to pressure and cajole until his view prevailed.

The quality of his arrogance is reflected in an anecdote told by George Higgins in a 1974 article in the *Atlantic* magazine:

"Lyndon Johnson's Lincoln Continental sorties through the ranch on the Pedernales necessitated disposal not only of the beer cans, but also of the contents processed through the Presidential kidneys. Procedure called for a Secret Service Agent—one was named Henderson—to stand at the Connie door and shield the Presidential anatomy from vulgar view. One day Henderson, disbelievingly, felt at his station something warm and wet on his trousers. 'Mr. President,' he said, when continued sensations precluded further disbelief, 'you're pissing on my leg.' 'Henderson,' the President said, 'ah *know* ah am. That's mah prerogative.' "[15]

Johnson's overblown estimate of his self-importance was mixed with a conviction people were conspiring against him. He once remarked, "I don't trust anybody but Lady Bird [his wife], and sometimes I'm not sure about her."[16]

This fear led him to use the F.B.I. as a personal spying service. J. Edgar Hoover supplied him with reports on the activities of his political opponents, many of which dealt with their private sexual lives. The two had a symbiotic relationship; the aging G-man— masterful in his handling of both party's leading politicians— protected himself from rumored dismissal by catering to Johnson's appetite for erotic gossip.[17] When two of Johnson's friends complained Hoover was a threat to civil liberties, the president explained his patience in characteristically earthy terms. "I would rather have him inside the tent pissing out than outside the tent pissing in."[18]

In terms of his domestic policy, he returned to his earlier liberal tendencies; his "Great Society" program, passed by a pliant Congress within months after Kennedy's death, was a model of social legislation. But even as he was proposing projects such as the domestic peace corps, job programs for school dropouts, preschool training for ghetto children, and college-bound programs for the educationally deprived, his nature led him to express his intentions in fundamentally militaristic terms. On January 8, 1964, he announced to Congress, "This Administration today, here and now, declares unconditional war on poverty in America."[19]

He was soon waging a much more bloody war; yet each step in his effort to intensify the conflict in Southeast Asia was accompanied by declarations that he would never think of increased American involvement.

During his reelection campaign against Barry Goldwater in 1964, he posed as the "peace" candidate. While Goldwater bluntly told the electorate he wanted to be president so that he could order the Air Force to defoliate Vietnam forests, and bomb the pants off Ho Chi Minh, Johnson affected the mien of a smiling Buddha. Yet once his landslide victory was safely tabulated, Johnson grimly engaged in every tactic the Arizonan suggested, and many that he had not had the imagination to conjure up.

There was about this party-oriented president an aura of autocratic disregard for democratic procedures. By March 1965, he sent the first American combat troops to Vietnam; these two marine battalions were the vanguards of hundreds of thousands of Americans who fought in Vietnam over the next seven years. During this period Lyndon Johnson lied to believing Americans with a regularity that could not have been accidental.[20]

When he unexpectedly announced in a nationwide television speech on March 31, 1968, that "I shall not seek and I will not accept the nomination of my party as your President,"[21] few tears were shed. Senator Eugene McCarthy's 40 percent tally in the New Hampshire primary two week's earlier had proved to Johnson that opposition within the party was substantial.

By this time the party role in such matters had become institutionalized and strengthened: During recent years the party chairman had become a full-time, paid official, no longer brought on board to pilot the ship during the last months before the campaign; the permanent staff in Washington was enlarged; huge treasuries were accumulated. Furthermore, the national party apparatus was exerting greater influence over state organizations. The party was being nationalized as loyalty oaths and prior commitments were extracted from formerly free-wheeling state delegations. In fact, the national party apparatus, through credential and rules committees appointed by its leaders, often determined which of two challenged delegate slates would be seated, and, therefore, which of two candidates would receive its most valued blessing. Precisely as the mass of voters were losing their sense of allegiance to the parties, the national organization's grip on the selection process was tightening.[22]

Troubled with a severe heart ailment, which caused his death within four years, and faced with increased party opposition, Johnson chose to pass the burden.

A sense of lost opportunity marked Lyndon Johnson's term of office; it was begun on a high note, the country prosperous and at peace with itself. Yet less than four years later, with our armed forces besieged in Vietnam, his reputation lay in ruins. His bad choice of alternatives in foreign policy was largely due to a failure of character, a flawed aspect of temperament shared by many of his predecessors; it led him to conclude that running the United States was like running a county caucus: All that was needed was a bright smile, a plausible line of patter, and enough control of your nerves to get you past the next vote. The party system—with its frequently bogus contests (often fought on bogus issues) whose outcome was determined by men he valued much more than the artless voter—had taught him to hold people in contempt with a conviction which even he did not appear to consciously recognize.

There were some people with short memories still willing to believe, as the 1968 election approached, that Lyndon Johnson was an unusual sort of president. The melancholy fact was that he was only too typical. The party system, in its tireless search for the supple and the safe, had made the selection of an outstanding leader unlikely. That it might some day select a mental defective, a moral deficient— perhaps even a criminal—as president seemed reasonably certain; it had, in fact, already done it several times. The best that could be hoped for was that if every eligible voter crossed his fingers, the gods of chance might be prevailed on to occasionally select an occupant of that office who was worthy of it.

19

How a Criminal
Became President

*I have never had much sympathy for the point of view,
"it isn't whether you win or lose that counts, but how
you play the game."*

Candidate Richard Nixon[1]

*I let down my friends. I let down the country. I let down
our system of government and the dreams of all those
young people that ought to get into government, but
think it's all too corrupt.*

Former President Richard Nixon[2]

When twenty-four-year-old Richard Nixon graduated from Duke
University Law School in June 1937, he had no intention of entering
politics; he wanted to be a corporation lawyer, hopefully working for
some New York house with sturdy ties to Wall Street accounts. One of
the biggest disappointments in his young life was to discover that
John Foster Dulles's partners were not interested in a tense, inexperienced lawyer from Whittier, California; a wider search, in the
sanctums of less prestigious pettifoggers, produced no better results.

He reluctantly returned home and was quickly placed, with family
influence, on the staff of the town's only law firm. Had the Second
World War not intervened, there is every indication he would have
permanently farmed his law library for a comfortable living.

His political career began after the war, in a most unusual manner.
Leaders of the Republican party in his district, which is to say the
bankers, the insurance executives, and the uncategorized rich of all

239

occupations, were at their wits' end to find someone who could put up a respectable showing against the popular Democratic congressman, Jerry Voorhis.

So bleak did their prospects seem that they were forced to radical extremes. Calling themselves the "Committee of One Hundred," they submitted a classified ad to twenty-six local newspapers. It was published in August 1945, over a year before the election, and read in part:

> "WANTED: Congressman candidate with no previous political experience to defeat a man who has represented the district in the House for ten years. Any young man resident of district, preferably a veteran, fair education . . . may apply for the job. Applicants will be reviewed by 100 interested citizens. . . ."[3]

That their standards were not high is apparent in their own choice of words: they wanted a *young, inexperienced* applicant with only a *fair education*. Nevertheless, the response was poor; eight aspirants were interviewed; none pleased.

The quest continued and inquiries turned up Nixon's name. Since Herman Perry, a Whittier banker, knew the Nixon family, he was chosen to broach the topic; Nixon was still in the Navy, stationed in Baltimore. In response to Perry's telegram, he placed a collect call to the town bank. Perry brusquely stated his associates were looking for a candidate to oppose Voorhis; all he had to know at this point was whether the willing Nixon was a Republican.

"I guess I'm a Republican," Nixon responded, "I voted for Dewey in 1944."[4]

Perry felt that was qualification enough; he sent him air fare and on September 29, 1945, the lieutenant commander, decked out in uniform, appeared before the Committee of One Hundred: seventy-seven were present. They were not particularly impressed by Nixon's pastiche of banalities, nor the staccato manner of his delivery; but what was the alternative? The final tally was no overwhelming show of confidence: fifty-five were for him, twenty-two favored continuing their mission.

This incident taught Nixon a lesson about Republican politics that he did not forget for the remainder of his tumultuous career. One hundred self-appointed businessmen had been responsible for selecting him; the only cross-section of society they represented could be found at any Chamber of Commerce meeting. They had not submitted their choice to the voters for confirmation; and yet, theirs had been the significant act in selecting the nominee.

Good fortune, machinations, maneuvering, hard work, all played a role in his progress, but the one indisputable fact, at every crisis point in his career, was that small numbers of men with the proper clout were frequently in the position to stimulate, or put an end to his dreams. Having digested this piece of wisdom, at the age of thirty-three, Congressman Nixon made it the theme of his politics.

His appeal, henceforth, was always to the party organization, and to those powerful men in the business community whose money brought them great influence in that organization. His stand on issues was conservative: anti-Red China, pro-McCarthy, anti-economic controls, pro-lower taxes for upper income brackets, and a free hand for businessmen, especially oilmen. But this was merely a minimum requirement, at that time, for membership in the Republican party. What marked him, and other successful members of his party, was the singleminded manner in which he attempted to tie himself to the leaders, and to recognize that often the most important leaders of the party were unaffiliated millionaires.

Years later, Helen Gahagan Douglas spoke of this aspect of her 1950 opponent in the race for the Senate. "He was acceptable to the oil people. He was always against regulating oil drilling. The techniques used [Nixon's red-baiting and smear tactics against her] were the least of it. Oil was the big issue. The issue was resources. How were recources going to be used? He had all the money he needed because he favored vested interests of every sort."[5]

Immediately after entering the Senate, Nixon started his pursuit of the 1952 vice-presidential nomination. In the middle of May 1950, scarcely five months after taking his seat, the thirty-six-year-old contender flew to Paris to visit with Eisenhower; he had already travelled around the country to contact party groups which might be of help.

Equally important were the unannounced efforts on his behalf. Murray Chotiner, his campaign manager, and soon to be one of Washington's most active influence peddlers, helped set up a slush fund to cover expenses that might arise in his effort to secure the nomination. The seventy-six contributors, a large percentage of them connected with the oil industry, turned their money over to Chotiner, or Dana Smith, Nixon's finance manager, in whose name the Pasadena bank account was kept.[6]

Smith explained the contributor's motivation: "Here we had a fine salesman," his quaint way of describing a United States senator, "who didn't have enough money to do the kind of selling job we wanted, so we got together and took care of some of those things . . . and we put a limit of five hundred dollars per person on the amount anyone could give in a single year . . . just so no one could say that we were buying a senator."[7]

When the scandal became public knowledge, at the height of Eisenhower's 1952 campaign for the White House—a campaign keynoted by the slogan "The Crusade Against Corruption"—Nixon denied he had done anything wrong, while admitting all the accusations were true: Yes, such a fund had been collected; furthermore, it had been kept in a secret account under someone else's name, although the money was solely for his use.

It was six weeks before Election Day and Eisenhower wanted him to resign from the ticket; he sent Dewey to him with that message, but the beleaguered senator wasn't listening; he had one ace left, and, before it was played, he had no intention of throwing in his hand. That ace was the party professionals, who could not understand what all the fuss was about. Didn't Ike know that was the way the game was played?

After five days of negotiating for his resignation, while the campaign came to a halt, Eisenhower agreed to let Nixon face the television cameras and give his version of the secret fund. He made it clear, however, that Nixon must let everyone know the final decision was going to be Ike's: Nixon agreed, although, he later confessed, he had no intention of living up to his promise, for he knew that if he did, the General already had the firing squad lined up at the side of his freshly dug political grave.

On the evening of September 22, 1952, Nixon delivered his "Checkers" speech. In tone, it was maudlin, concerning itself largely with matters having nothing to do with accepting bribes. He simply did not discuss the facts involved in his illegal behavior; instead, he told a story about his dog, and made a reference to his wife's cloth coat.

Audaciously, at the end of what might well have been his last public speech, he pulled a coup by means of which he rescued himself. At the point where he was supposed to ask General Eisenhower to render his decision, he altered the script.

"But the decision, my friends, is not mine," he said, looking directly into the camera. "I would do nothing that would harm the possibilities of Dwight Eisenhower to become President of the United States; and for that reason I am submitting to the Republican National Committee tonight, through this television broadcast, the decision which is theirs to make."[8]

This was one of the greatest displays of calculated arrogance in American political history. Nixon knew that a majority of the National Committee were in favor of keeping him on the ticket; he was handing Eisenhower a pair of loaded dice. Without a moment's hesitation, he continued: "Let them decide whether my position on the ticket will help or hurt. [Not whether it was *right* or *wrong*.] And I am going to ask you to help them decide. Wire and write the Republican National Committee whether you think I should stay on or whether I should get off. And whatever their decision is, I will abide by it."[9]

Within a few hours the National Committee announced that more than two million people had voted 350-1 in favor of Nixon. The politicians' contempt for human reason was never more clearly demonstrated; they were asking Americans to believe that in a matter of a few hundred minutes an emergency staff had not only read, but tabulated more than two million telegrams.

The National Committee, acting on its own intelligence, voted that same night 107-0 to keep Nixon on the ticket.

Ike squirmed before he swallowed, but swallow he did, and Nixon had proof positive that if the machine was on your side, even the Supreme Commander of the Allied Forces might be brought to heel; it was a lesson whose traumatic impact could never be forgotten. Partisan Nixon now became the superpartisan: besmirching innuendo, which he had practiced during the Voorhis and Douglas campaigns, became his chief tool; anticommunism, the heritage of the Hiss affair, became his program.

On October 27, as election day neared, he made a speech in Texarkana, Texas, which bore the characteristics of much of his future political pronouncements. "President Truman and Adlai Stevenson are traitors to the high principles of the Democratic party," he declared, going on to assert that they "tolerated and defended Communists in the government."[10]

Truman raged over that remark, convinced that Nixon had implied he was a traitor. Years later, when Merle Miller was interviewing the former president for what was to become his biography, *Plain Speaking,* he had not yet cooled down. "I've told you, all the time I've been in politics there's only two people I hate, and he's one. He not only doesn't give a damn about the people; he doesn't know how to tell the truth. I don't think the son of a bitch knows the difference between telling the truth and lying."[11]

During the mid-fifties Nixon was hardly concerned about what a retired president thought of him; he was too busy trying to decide how he could overcome the sitting president's distaste. His old friend, newspaperman Ralph de Toledano, spoke of those days: "He worked for a man [Eisenhower] who in my book was just a complete sadist, and who really cut Nixon to pieces. He would cut him up almost just for the fun of it and I don't think Nixon ever really survived that. I don't think I am talking out of school and I say that when he was Vice-President and I saw him frequently, he would come back from the White House and as much as he ever showed emotion you'd think he was on the verge of tears."[12]

Searching that stormy pinnacle for some rock on which to anchor himself, Nixon's experience told him the party might be his salvation. He spent much of his time cultivating fledgling congressmen, holding seminars, where he would pontificate on administration policies, and nourishing political friendships, which might some day be helpful.

Eisenhower's offhanded delegation to Nixon of the responsibility for the 1954 congressional elections, as already noted, further placed partymen in the vice-president's debt. He made hundreds of speeches across the country, and, although the results in terms of victories were a distinct disappointment, the results in terms of his personal prestige, within the party, were not.

Before the year was over, he once again desperately needed that party support. Eisenhower called him to the White House in mid-January 1956, and cautiously told him he thought his ambitions to be president would be strengthened if he decided not to run for vice-president again. Didn't Nixon know, he asked coyly, that the vice-presidency was considered a dead end? Think how he could advance himself in the esteem of the voters if he took a Cabinet post and got all that valuable executive experience. The reasons proliferated as the convalescing heart patient tried to persuade his supernumerary to step aside. Herbert Hoover, a man Nixon professed to admire, had become president on the basis of his work as Coolidge's secretary of commerce, a persistent Eisenhower offered, attempting to prove the unprovable—that being vice-president was not a good job for a man who wanted to become president.

Eisenhower told him to ponder what he had said and bid him goodbye. Years later Chotiner, a grimace on his puffy face, recalled those terrible days. Nixon had been "very hurt. How would you feel if you were asked to step off the ticket?"[13]

Months dragged on, while the vice-president visited with party friends, few of whom had enjoyed such moments with Eisenhower. The General found himself under increasing pressure; his weekly press conferences focused largely on the question of whether he, now committed to run for reelection, would commit himself to the re-designation of Nixon.

Finally, on April 27, Eisenhower answered a reporter's query about Nixon's plans, almost plaintively, "Well, he hasn't reported back in the terms in which I used the expression that morning, no. He hasn't given me any authority to quote him, any answer that I would consider final and definite."[14]

Within minutes Nixon was on the phone with presidential assistant Sherman Adams, arranging for an appointment with the harried chief-of-state. He was determined, after four years of obsequious behavior, to show Ike his flintier aspect. The secret-fund scandal had convinced him Ike would yield to an opponent, when not to yield might cause him public discomfort.

In an aggressive mood, he strode into the Oval Office and informed his leader he was content to follow him for another four years. Not only was he available, he said confidently, ready to show him that party ace, which by now he had permanently tacked to his sleeve lining, but he was sure the president would be happy to know he had the near-unanimous support of the National Committee.

Sherman Adams commented in his memoirs: "It was one of those times when the President was pressured out of a previously prepared position by political clamor and harassment."[15]

Once renominated for vice-president, the road to the presidential nomination in 1960 was unobstructed; the Twenty-second Amendment had removed the charismatic Ike from his path. Nixon spoke of him as being devious, and breathed easier now that the publicly affable, privately irascible General was a lame duck.

He paid his dues again in the 1958 off-year elections, travelling 25,000 miles and visiting twenty-five states; it was essentially a fence-mending mission, an effort to show the flag in distant provinces. The results, for many of the candidates Nixon was attempting to aid, were disastrous; the Democrats again swept to control of Congress.

Within three days after the election Nixon was made to understand the party leaders did not hold his failings against him. Leonard Hall, chief political representative of the old Dewey machine, called to invite himself and Clifford Folger, former National Finance Chairman, to dinner. His message was simple: "You must start now."[16]

Their vote of confidence on November 7, 1958, was incomparably more important than anything that might happen until Election Day, 1960. As authentic party kingmakers, they were intent on narrowing the people's choice to Richard Nixon, and whomever their Democratic counterparts would choose.

Nelson Rockefeller made a half-hearted attempt to challenge him. The list of delegates was, however, so heavily weighed in favor of the party's darling that "Rocky" did not have the will to pursue his effort to the floor of the convention. Nixon was nominated on the first ballot: he garnered 1,321 votes to 10 for Goldwater.

Nevertheless, Eisenhower held back. Nixon, in a desperate fight with Kennedy, urged the president to a greater campaign effort, only to be rebuffed. Suppressing his disappointment, he tried, in *Six Crises*, to explain why Ike had refused: "He felt it was important for me to establish my own identity as the new leader of the party. He also expressed the conviction that his great influence with the American people was due in substantial part to his image of being President of all the people, and not just a partisan as Truman had been."[17]

Eisenhower's attempt to hold himself above the battle was a serious blow to Nixon, however, the president's flip remark at his August 24 news conference may have cost the embarrassed vice-president the election. Asked by a reporter, "What major decisions of your Administration has the Vice-President participated in?", he responded, "If you give me a week, I might think of one."[18]

This was hardly the image of indispensabilitv Nixon was trving to nurture.

He travelled around the country at a killing pace, in an effort to communicate a confidence that did not exist and a competence of which motion was no proof. Finally he was able to brag that since the party placed its blessing on his brow, he "had travelled over 65,000 miles and visited all the fifty states."[19] Nevertheless, on November 8 Nixon lost.

Between 1960 and 1962, he turned his hand to law, signing on with Adams, Duque and Hazeltine of Los Angeles. Again party considerations were paramount in his mind. Although his close race against Kennedy had made likely his nomination for a second try in 1964, Nixon's chronic raw nerves would not allow him to idle his time away in the interval; against the advice of his closest advisors, he entered the race for governor of California. Herb Klein, his press agent for many years, explained why Nixon would not let well-enough alone. "There were a lot of pressures on him from all sides. He was trving to keep the party together in California."[20]

The party had been good to him; it had, in fact, been the source of all that was good in his public life. What possible harm could there be to answering the call of homestate Republicans?

The answer was provided during the campaign, when a scandal involving his brother Donald and himself became the central issue of the race. In 1956, just after Nixon's reelection as vice-president, millionaire Howard Hughes had lent his brother, whom the Las Vegas hermit had never met, $205,000. Nixon's mother, Hannah, had put up a vacant lot, worth a fraction of that sum, as collateral.

Why, Democrat Pat Brown, Sr., wanted to know, did Howard Hughes, the country's tenth largest government contractor, suddenly decide to be so generous to the brother of the vice-president?

It was eventually revealed the loan money had been laundered through front men so that its connection to the drug-addicted Hughes was concealed. As the California campaign was in progress,

Attorney General Robert Kennedy was considering the wisdom of indicting members of the Nixon family for income tax evasion, and Hughes for offering a bribe.

Although Kennedy's ruminations were not current knowledge at the time of the election, the simple fact that Hughes had given the Nixon family such a large sum of money, all of which had been defaulted within six months, was enough to once again raise substantial doubts in the press about the former vice-president's honesty.

In a desperate attempt to salvage his fortunes, Nixon and his campaign manager, H. R. Haldeman, Louis Howe's political clone, devised a "dirty tricks" scheme. Taking $70,000 out of the swollen kitty collected for the Republican campaign, they created a cover organization called the Committee for the Preservation of the Democratic Party (CPDP).

This paper group, passing itself off as an organ of the Democratic party, conducted a "postcard poll"; it was aimed at some of the 900,000 conservative Democrats. When this sampling of the right wing of the party was finally tallied, and the carefully fragmented results released, the distortion was represented as the "voice of the rank and file Democrats." Nixon's pollsters concluded that California Democrats were fearful for the future of their party unless Nixon was elected.

The Democratic State Committee did not consider this normal campaign tactics, and with an unusual show of moral indignation, took Nixon and Haldeman to court. For the next two years a San Francisco judge, Byron Arnold, languished over the facts, finally signing a stipulation judgment declaring the poll was fraudulently conceived and executed, since the CPDP had concealed that its mailing was paid for by the Nixon for Governor Finance Committee. Judge Arnold ruled the poll had been revised, amended, and finally approved by Mr. Nixon personally.

Clearly laws had been violated: Nixon and Haldeman had conspired to obstruct the honest conduct of an election. No doubt this was still far from the massive sabotage and espionage efforts of the 1972 campaign. However, one wonders whether, if Judge Arnold had not been so lenient in sentencing (he ordered Nixon to pay a wrist-slapping $100 to the Democratic State Committee and $268.50 in court costs), the greater crimes of Watergate, committed by the same cast of characters, might not have been avoided.

After his defeat in the race for the governorship, Nixon left the scene of his disgrace; he headed for New York and a profitable law practice with Mudge, Rose, Guthrie and Alexander. John Mitchell was one of the firm's senior partners; they joined hands in a relationship that passed for friendship.

Within weeks after Nixon's California debacle, Barry Goldwater had wrapped up the 1964 presidential nomination. He used the same strategy employed by his philosophic mentor, Robert Taft, in the 1952 preconvention campaign, collecting the votes of the infirmed Southern organizations and clinching matters with the backing of the conservative Midwestern sector of the party.

Goldwater was confronted with an insoluble problem: The party organization was for him, but some of the most glamorous individuals in the party were not. Henry Cabot Lodge, Nixon's 1960 running mate, who was serving as Johnson's ambassador to Vietnam, tendered his resignation and returned to America where he openly took a stand against Goldwater; and Nelson Rockefeller, short on delegates but not without his constituency, opposed him as he would the lowering of interest rates. Without support from the Eastern liberal wing of the party, represented by those GOP mavericks, and with no prospect that any number of Democrats would cross party lines to vote for him, Goldwater had a worthless nomination.

Despite the hopelessness of the effort, Nixon made his most strenuous electioneering foray in years; with no apparent personal stake in the outcome, he devoted himself to Goldwater's interests. Chotiner attempted to explain: "Once the party picked the man, he had to support him."[21]

The more probable reason for the extent of his exertions was not long in revealing itself; the party professionals, nursing a permanent grudge against the men who had done in their conscientious conservative, had eyes only for the man who had kept the faith. As soon as the results were in, Nixon held a press conference and stripped the epaulets from Rockefeller's Republican uniform. No one who sat "on the sidelines"[22] during the election could expect future party consideration. So much for Nelson Aldrich's grandson.

Within a month of the '64 disaster, Nixon had summoned Goldwater to a parley in a New York hotel.[23] Wasting no time on the myth of titular leadership, he informed him that Dean Burch, the Arizonan's choice for National Chairman, had to go; he was to be accompanied to a leaking lifeboat by the entire staff of the National Committee. Nixon was too familiar with the pivotal nature of that citadel to allow it to remain in anyone else's hands.

Through 1965 and '66, as Nixon exploited popular approval of the war in dozens of speeches, in which he declared that there was no substitute for victory in South Vietnam, the party regulars fell in behind him. As the popularity of the war declined in the national polls, he retreated into silence on the subject, explaining his vagueness with the excuse that he did not want to criticize the president during a time of national crisis.

The campaign against Hubert Humphrey was waged on that level of cleverness: Rationalizations took the place of reasons, slogans replaced explanations; in short, it was an ordinary campaign, conducted in a conventionally unilluminating manner, notable mainly for the fact that Nixon's fund-raisers collected $35,000,000, by far the most money accumulated for an election. Most of it was devoted to a monster television operation consisting of canned commercials. They were filmed after extensive rehearsals and aimed at maximum impact, if not enlightenment.[24]

Despite a slow start, Humphrey came on in a rush, which had Nixon reliving his narrow loss to Kennedy. Nevertheless, the final count had him ahead of the Democratic party's wheelhorse 43.4 to 42.7 percent. Money and deception had done for him what he had been unable to do for himself in any election since the 1950 campaign against Helen Douglas.

As soon as the election was out of the way, the public promises, which had secured it, were jettisoned; his plan to end the war within weeks after being inaugurated, was replaced by a blueprint for its escalation. During his first year in office, the quantity of guns and men sent to Vietnam rose sharply, as did the casualty figures.

It was in the field of domestic economics, however, that Nixon failed most grievously; on Election Day, 1968, the inflation rate was a moderate 2.5 percent per annum. It had remained at that level for the previous three years, despite the increasing amounts of money Johnson was spending on the war. As soon as he took office, Nixon accepted the advice of conservatives, such as Arthur Burns, and allowed interest rates to be forced up in a semihysterical effort to lower this acceptable inflation figure. Instead, by the end of his first year in office, that rate had gone up to 5 percent. By the time he resigned, the country was experiencing a Weimar inflation rate in excess of 12 percent.

Unemployment, which had been at 3.3 percent of the work force when he was elected, was 8 percent when he moved out of the White House. During his five and a half years in office, the country experienced four years of economic decline. There was only one short upturn during the 1972 election year, as the need to win his last campaign drove him to extremes which included not only Watergate, but a sharp dose of Keynesian pump-priming economics. Arthur Burns, then head of the all-powerful Federal Reserve System, gulped down his lower-interest medicine, knowing full well that the day after election he would be allowed to administer another dose of Hoover snake oil to the ailing economy.

As the 1972 election approached, Nixon, firmly in control of the party machinery, could think only of himself; his lack of real dedication to the party was shown by his near-total neglect of every other Republican running that year. Under his uninterested leadership the Republicans had failed to secure control of Congress in 1968 and again in 1970; by 1972 any effort was too great. The Republican party, his inaction suggested, was Richard Nixon, his victory was its reason for existing; in order to win that victory, any act was justified.

It was under this guidance that criminal behavior in the Oval Office became the norm: Secret agents of the president, under his direction, felt free to break into private offices and rifle files; illegal wiretapping of newspapermen became an asserted presidential prerogative; refusal to comply with court orders was suddenly a new form of executive privilege; the president's deputies pleased him by bribing apprehended felons and lying before grand juries; he used government funds to increase the value of his San Clemente and Key Biscayne villas, and compounded his frauds by filing personal income tax returns that would have sent a Capone to the rock pile.

His agents solicited illegal corporation campaign contributions, while promising the donors favors of greater value. William S.

Powell, president of Mid-America Dairymen, was brazen enough to publicly admit, "Whether we like it or not, this is the way the system works."[25]

Other corporate executives, when pleading guilty to charges of illegally giving hundreds of thousands of dollars to Herbert Kalmbach, Nixon's personal attorney, claimed they had been victims of presidential extortion.[26] Alexander Hamilton would have understood the real nature of the transaction. He once said, "Those who pay are the masters of those who are paid."[27]

In the midst of the growing assaults on his reputation, Spiro Agnew, his personal selection for vice-president, was disclosed to be under investigation by the U.S. Attorney in Baltimore on charges of bribery, conspiracy, extortion and tax evasion. While governor of Maryland he had set up an organization, run by his political sidekicks, to collect a percentage of every contract let by the state. This money was disgorged to him over a period of years, payments finally becoming so routine that favored contractors personally handed him the envelopes with the crisp anonymous cash. He had discovered what American politicians had known for over a century, that control of a party was a more effective way to relieve his fellow citizens of cash than by assaulting them with a deadly weapon.

Even after he became vice-president, he solicited bribes, beguiling his contributors with thoughts about grander opportunities for larceny now that he was playing on the national stage.

After adroit plea bargaining with Attorney General Eliot Richardson, Agnew admitted his guilt to a charge of income tax evasion on October 10, 1973, and that same day became the first vice-president to resign from office.[28]

As Agnew's agony drew to an end, knowledge of the Watergate crimes—the break-in took place on June 17, 1972—was becoming more widespread. Nevertheless, as the documented criminal behavior of the president was revealed to the public, most often in his own statements, and finally in his own words on altered tape recordings, the men of party came forward to defend their own.

John Ehrlichman, the president's confidant, testifying before Senator Sam Ervin's Watergate investigating committee, on July 24, 1973, in clear view of millions watching on television, insisted that Richard Nixon was above the law; if he felt so inclined, he might commit criminal acts, and could be found accountable in no court in the land. He was, after all, Ehrlichman proclaimed, leader of his party with responsibilities to that party, and as such he had a need to obtain "political information."[29]

The president himself refused to turn over evidence to the courts, misplacing two tapes that he had previously sworn to protect and, finally, reluctantly submitting the rest of them only after the most potentially damaging 18½ minutes of it had been clumsily erased.

The man who had sworn to uphold the Constitution and defend the law ended by refusing to cooperate with Congress and threatening to disobey the Supreme Court. To all of this, Melvin Laird, a nine term Congressman dedicated to party loyalty, averred that if his political leader was indeed guilty of all the crimes of Watergate, he did not want to know about it.

As pleas of guilty were registered by his closest subordinates, who admitted to having committed a staggering number of felonies, the leaders of his party came forward to insist that while in office the president could not be indicted; the only recourse they held out to Americans seeking an end to Nixon's clear acts of criminality, was impeachment. Yet, the move to impeach depended on the strength of character of party politicians, and it was clear that long after most of them were fully convinced of Nixon's guilt, they were still working to rescue their fallen leader.

Although James Madison, George Mason, and Benjamin Franklin believed impeachment would check the power of tyrants, it proved to be a slender protection against the type of man thrust forward by party. Before Nixon's time it had already proved no protection against numerous cases of incompetence, and in the instance of Wilson, no remedy for incapacity.

Watergate was an unusual crime; it was, among other things, an attempt to insure what was an apparent victory in the national election. Such a felony could not be taken seriously by party leaders; they had spent too much of their energy executing similar felonies. After the break-in, in which few of them were involved, they willingly took on the onus of their chief's criminality by excusing the greater series of crimes committed in an attempt to eradicate any trace of his complicity.[30]

Nixon's major defense, most often expressed for him by Barry

Goldwater and Ronald Reagan, was that other presidents had lied and cheated as frequently;[31] it was a call for moral irresponsibility at the summit of political power. Taken on a more common level, it would allow any criminal to offer in his defense that others regularly robbed and raped.

Richard Milhous Nixon, conditioned by an arduous career to seek salvation through the agency of party support, toughed it out until all the members of the House Judiciary Committee indicated they would recommend his impeachment to the full House. On August 9, 1974, he became the first president of the United States to resign.

He was succeeded by Gerald Ford, a man who during twenty-five years in Congress had never expressed an unorthodox thought, and prided himself most on never once having deserted Nixon or his party.

The major lesson he took away from the Watergate tragedy was expressed to a gathering of Midwestern Republican leaders in Chicago four months before he became president. "Never again must Americans allow an arrogant, elite guard of political adolescents like CREEP [The Committee for Re-election of the President] to by-pass the regular party organization and dictate the terms of a national election."[32]

To describe John Mitchell and Maurice Stans as political adolescents, was to prepare his audience of approving partymen for the larger joke that political corruption would end if only all future national elections were placed exclusively in the hands of the regular party organization.

Ford's views on party politics were as predictable as his rush to pardon the disgraced former president, even before he could be brought before a grand jury and offer testimony under oath. Within weeks after taking office, this party gladiator indicated how little he understood his role as leader of all Americans. In the face of rising unemployment and simultaneously ruinous inflation, he took time out to tour the country on behalf of Republican congressional candidates.

Speaking to a rally in Greenville, North Carolina, he told of what most weighted down his mind and tore at his heart. "I believe that the two-party system is in grave danger today," he warned. "If this heavy majority of spenders [usually called Democrats] is substantially increased in the 94th Congress, the two-party system of government established by our Founding Fathers will be in serious danger."[33]

The fact that he was misrepresenting the Founding Fathers may not have been deliberate; ignorance about the origin and function of political parties has been widespread. His concern for the welfare of the party system, however, was no inadvertency. Gerald Ford had been the first beneficiary of the latest extension of party power in American life. With the passage of the Twenty-fifth Amendment, it had become possible for the president, the chief official of a political party, to select his successor without any input by the electorate.

As a result, one of the worst presidents in American history, a man whose associates filled jails from one end of the country to the other, had nominated his successor; and the party grip on the political system tightened.

Ford was deemed a worthy successor to the presidency by a man who told David Frost on May 19, 1977, in a widely-viewed television interview: "When the President does it [commits a crime], that means that it is not illegal."

Richard Nixon had been allowed to choose the first president to assume that office without being elected to it. He was given the option, if it pleased him—and he could convince key party leaders—to replicate his own dissolute self.

The method of selecting a president had, in the hands of politicians, finally been completely debased. The choice of a king is determined by the accident of birth; it was now difficult to argue that dependence on that accident would not produce a better ruler than reliance on the discretion of those who had produced a Richard Nixon. Perhaps this is what Gouverneur Morris had in mind at the Constitutional Convention when, considering how the president should be chosen, he said, "It would be better than chance should decide than intrigue."[34]

20

A Timid Supposition
and A Simple Proposal

A scholar ... begins timidly, moderately, he begins by asking a most modest question. ... He immediately quotes such and such ancient writers, and as soon as he detects some kind of a hint or something that he believes to be a hint, he at once becomes emboldened and self-confident ... forgetting completely that he has begun with a timid supposition; he already believes that every-thing is clear and his argument is concluded with the words: ". . . so it is from this point of view that we look at the subject!" Then he proclaims it . . . for all to hear, and the newly discovered truth is sent travelling all over the world. . . .

Nikolai Gogol[1]

When the Constitutional Convention assembled in Philadelphia in 1787, its members were by no means certain that they could fashion a durable government. Clearly the Articles of Confederation, under which they had functioned for over six years, were inadequate; they had been fatally weakened by the unwillingness of the thirteen former British colonies to fashion a new government around a strong chief executive.

Yet the delegates to the convention could not overcome their distrust of any head of government who would mold policies and then issue the orders to implement those policies. A generation of suspicions about kings and cabals had shaped the writers of the Constitution; they had rebelled, seen their brothers slaughtered and endured privation, firmly convinced all of this had occurred because of a tyrannical leader, mad King George, and the small group of powerful aristocrats, who used Englishmen for their selfish purposes.

As they debated scores of issues, it became clear that their most sustained fears concerned the presidency. It was the first subject they discussed, and, four months later, it was the last question that divided them. They reasoned that it would always be difficult to obtain the approval of the mass of Americans to coordinate a blow against the state; Congress, mostly composed of affluent individuals divided by local interests, might be an even more intractable group to enlist in such an enterprise. But one man in a fit of irresponsible anger, or spasm of uncontrollable fear, might give the order that would protect his power and destroy popular rights. Furthermore, if political parties were allowed to exist and to dictate who would be president, the leader of the nation would be their lackey, concerned primarily with winning, and keeping, their approval.

In an endeavor to avoid this disaster they tried to invent a method for choosing a president that would at once free him from the heady demands of factional supporters (since they could detect no advantages to such party parasites and were only too well acquainted with their disadvantages) and simultaneously make him responsive to the accumulated wisdom and restraints, of a large well-informed group: namely, themselves and their successors assembled in Congress. Their original and most long lasting position, one which was only partly realized in the final version of the Constitution, was to have the president elected by Congress. After considering this idea, and at least twenty-seven other ingenious proposals, all of which excluded political parties from the process, the compromise at the last moment involved the creation of an Electoral College; the Electors were to be independent men of judgment protecting the presidency against capture by an unworthy man.

They were to reach their decision in widely scattered locations once every four years; there was to be no thought of personal advantage, which might be nurtured by their own continued term in a salaried career-oriented position; they were to approach their task motivated solely by the desire to find the best qualified man. Having performed that service, they were to return to the life which had led their neighbors to select them for this civic function. Only if the Electors could not muster a majority, which the Philadelphia philosophers thought would happen more frequently than it has, would Congress choose the president.

In the normal course of events, this pure vision was altered. The weakness in the concept was the omission of a practical nominating mechanism. Electors dispersed throughout the Republic could not easily conspire with each other, but they were likewise unable to benefit from each others counsel: it was not possible for them to discuss a group of candidates, their strengths, their promises, their weaknesses, and eliminate them one at a time as the process of consensus sculptured a winner. Since politics abhors a vacuum as much as any other natural phenomenon, a workman-like practice soon replaced the original idealistic concept; the Electors quickly lost their limitless independence and were given a helping hand, in determining who they could consider for president, by the most active political figures in the new country: the men who had been elected to Congress.

It was unreasonable to think that congressmen could be eliminated from the earliest decision-making regarding the selection of presidential nominees: on the average, they were the best informed about political matters, the most determined to make their opinions heard; and, more important, they formed an aristocracy of leadership, which, in the absence of a unified electorate, could not be denied.

The natural, almost inevitable, consequence was the emergence of the Congressional Caucus, an institution nowhere mentioned in the Constitution. By the end of the first decade under the new government, it was well established that two groups of congressmen would caucus separately every four years to pick nominees representing their viewpoint. The two men thus singled out would be the only candidates considered by the members of the Electoral College, although, theoretically, their discretion remained as unfettered as it had originally been intended it should be.

Free choice for the Electors, so fundamental in the final decision of the Philadelphia delegates, was gone. In its place was a process whereby Congress selected the president, although this reality was somewhat disguised by the largely meaningless pantomime in which the members of the college quickly, and contentedly, assumed their passive roles. During the next twenty-five years this symbiotic relationship between the Congressional Caucuses and the Electoral College flourished; the caucuses announced the nomination of their candidates and the college elected one of them president.

This arrangement, however, excited the distrust of many Americans, who were accustomed by the democratic philosophy which had inspired the Revolution, and by their own rugged sense of individualism, to think they should have an equal voice in the selection of their leader. It was an understandable distrust, in keeping with the national character, and with human nature; where does one find a person who, given a choice, would allow others to make mistakes he can make with as little effort?

By 1820 advocates for equality were heard more frequently. Their cry was to take the awesome power of nomination away from the congressional political elite. The times were ripe for such a protest, and, with no great effort to resist, Congress ceased to caucus on presidential nominations. Having gone that far, the imagination of the reformers failed them. The inspiration for their crusade had been a desire for equality; but how was that sentiment to be translated into a practical democratic nominating mechanism? The Constitution had placed the authority to elect a president in the hands of the Electoral College and Congress, and it remained in their frozen grip; but nomination, where did that majestic power lie?

The selection and functioning of the original Electors had been an approximation of egalitarianism; they had been chosen by a direct vote of the people who knew them in their home districts. Although they were expected to exercise their independent judgment, it was a judgment molded by a community consensus. Nominations, in some unspecified manner, were expected to come from that consensus. But by the 1820s the state legislatures had interceded in the process and made the Electors their captives. An aspiring Elector could no longer gain his franchise by the direct vote of his neighbors; he must now first be placed on a slate committed to a nominee picked by one of the legislative caucuses in his state; only then was he granted a merely ceremonial role in a script written by politicians. With the Congressional Caucuses out of favor, and, in fact, out of existence, the decisive remaining influence exercised on the acquiescing Electors was exerted by state legislators.

Was this any more democratic than nomination by the Congressional Caucuses? Obviously not; the nominees for the presidency, and the president himself, were still not being elected by a direct vote of the people. The new system had additional disadvantages: the men serving in the state legislatures had been placed in their seats by a small number of votes, since restrictions on granting the franchise were still formidable. As a result, many legislators, who were now drawing up the Electoral slates, were likely to be in thrall to some county grandee, who viewed them as a servant to his interests. In addition, although some states did not have parties, and, in others, parties had a phantom quality, several states had well-developed clubhouse organizations. In those states, legislators had already assumed the supine position required of them by party bosses; it was the party sachems who really picked the Electoral slates.

Matters were not to improve during the 1830s as the average citizen's desire for equality was focused on economic issues; and whatever sense of political grievance he had could be drained off in that greater, and more rewarding, migratory adventure, made possible by America's rich, undeveloped western territories.

Once again political activists saw an opportunity, since the impotence and indifference of the distracted voter was only too apparent to political professionals. With a swiftness whipped on by greed, party operators, like Martin Van Buren, created the national nominating convention, and, by legitimizing the monopoly of that apparatus to nominate presidential candidates—in effect, their own monopoly—further removed the average citizen from the process of selecting his leader.

During the period between the establishment of the Republic and the 1830s, national political parties, functioning the way they do today, did not exist. Yet it is not too much to say that, with rare exceptions, the men nominated by the Congressional Caucuses were our greatest presidents and that the system that placed the nomination process under the control of parties, after that time, has produced superior presidents only accidently.

Why is it that after 1840 the nominating apparatus, which should have operated as a filter that progressively removed faulted aspirants, so often advanced them? How is it possible that Van Buren, Harrison, Tyler, Taylor, Fillmore, Pierce, Buchanan, Andrew Johnson, Grant, Hayes, Garfield, Arthur, Harrison, McKinley, Harding, Coolidge, Eisenhower, Nixon, Ford, and Carter—men at best, of mediocre abilities—found the chancy road to the White House so open to them?

Some philosophers have maintained that it is the people's fault. The people, they insist, get the kind of president they deserve. Such cynicism cannot disguise the fact that since Van Buren refurbished the national convention and placed it in its ascendancy, giving it the power to nominate the president, the people seldom have had much of a role to play in deciding who would occupy the White House. Delegates to those conventions are now largely anonymous to all but the party leaders who control them. Having usurped the role of the Congressional Caucuses, they now, quadrennially, present the names of two men to the Electoral College, the members of which, as added insurance against independence, party leaders pick from among the most docile of the party regulars within their own states. The result is that the American voter, apparently left with the ability to elect, although even that function can only be indirectly and inaccurately recorded through the party-selected Electors, has been effectively deprived of the much more important power to nominate. Recognizing the vestigial nature of the Electoral College, Senator Birch Bayh had placed on the calendar of the Senate, April 10, 1979, a constitutional amendment (S.R. Res. 28) to eliminate the Electors and choose the president and vice-president solely on the basis of the nationwide popular vote—a reform long overdue.

Americans sought greater equality when they objected to the role of the Congressional Caucus; what they got was a presidential selection process controlled by partymen who are often oblivious, but always indifferent, to popular opinion.

No doubt the citizenry has had some benign influence; those party leaders who have actually selected our mayors, governors, legislators and presidents have had to glance over their shoulders to make sure that some excess was not arousing the slumbering giant. But the same is true of all governments, since a sudden burst of mass temper can topple a king or a president.

If only Van Buren, when manipulating those first national conventions, had provided the nation with a superior, or even an adequate, method of nominating candidates, even though the system is blatantly undemocratic, his contrivance might have served an interim purpose until a more democratic device could have been fashioned. We might have tolerated such a utilitarian system for nominating superior candidates. However, the national party system that emerged from Van Buren's scheming proved to be incapable of that kind of selfless, efficient act; its leaders insisted on ferreting out men of proven inadequacy; they demanded the advancement of the loyal dullard; they shackled him to their desires.

And there is every reason to think that this is a pattern as petrified as any primordial stone, since the objectives of most party bosses are not identical with those of most voters; they are men whose appetites are frequently appeased at the expense of national well-being. The languid observer who remarked that politics was no pastime for gentlemen had neglected to identify the much larger group for whom it was a living: the callous, the egotistical and the dishonest.

Since there is every reason to believe that the party system will continue to replicate a fair sample of its worst models, the time has surely come to regain the vision of the summer of 1787. Potential national leaders must be made to think of themselves not as Democrats or Republicans, but as their countrymen's guides and servants.

Candidates for office must be encouraged to make their appeal to the electorate on the basis of civic contributions; serious contenders for the presidency should not spend the two years prior to bogus national conventions ignoring their jobs as governors or congressmen, while bustling around the country hunting down party hacks who they might impress with promises of spoils.

Those who would be president must learn to value candor, rather than opportunism; they must be encouraged to display a dedication to the performance of their duties, rather than a subservience to the whims of their patrons; they must be urged to exercise reason and exhibit wisdom, qualities which carry no weight on the scales used in smoke-filled rooms.

In short, political parties must be recognized as a major weakness in our democratic system—a weakness that has not yet been fatal, at this point in our odyssey, but that continually debilitates and enfeebles our government.

The founders of this country constructed a national political system without parties. At our peril, in the middle of the last century, we were turned away from that system by party manipulators. The corruption and waste that resulted should, long ago, have led to a general rejection of this redundant institution, and a revulsion against the politician's self-serving sloganizing about the sanctity of the two-party system. The American voter was imposed on when he was muddled into revering that "two-party" nonsense, whose underlying philosophy insists it is unwise to let anyone but an oligarchy of grasping politicoes choose the nation's leaders.

Why should two small groups of connivers, who rarely expose themselves to popular judgment by running for office, be allowed to gain control of political power and use it for their own benefit? Why should some unscrupulous men of wealth, through bribery, have disproportionate access to that power?

So skewed has the political system become under the malignant pressure of party politics that victory for either party provides fruits mainly for those clustered about the boss's table, where little thought is given to the needs of those voters who made possible the feast.

It is, perhaps, worth noting that most modern tyrants have employed a party system as a means of oppressing their people. They recognize in the party machinery an instrument for organizing restless souls, giving them a method of channeling their energies, otherwise potentially dangerous, into acceptable authoritarian conduct. Leaders of the Soviet Union and The People's Republic of China would have much less control over their subjects if there were no Communist party. Indeed, it seems inconceivable that Hitler could have so completely dominated Germany without the ritualizing, self-subjecting apparatus of the Nazi party.

Someday a dictator of a major country, who is bolder, may well experiment with the two-party system as a method of prolonging his rule; some Latin American caudillos, with marked success, already have. Of course, both parties would accept his infallibility and be loyal to his cause; but our experience with two-partyism shows that this is not beyond a shrewd leader's expectations. There are few souls more conformist than those clubhouse tenants striving to win the boss's approval. Factionalism exists in both major parties, yet, finally, it is a clique of like-thinking chiefs in those parties who decided most issues. The dictator intent on solving his major political problem, the threat of rebellion from excluded dissenters, might consider the advantages of welcoming a competition between even a large number of parties whose leaders, despite their apparent differences, worship at his totem.

Americans believe in the values of democracy; we like to think we rule ourselves. We see many of our brothers, in other lands, crushed by dictators, living in fear of the results of any significant non-conformity and we are rightfully pleased that we do not share their fate. But we commit a potentially dangerous error if we conclude that our good fortune is owed, in any measure, to our two-party system. We flourish despite them, not because of them.

American political parties perform one major function; they nominate candidates for office. Between elections the minimal utility of parties is observable at casual glance. No longer pressed with the need to nominate, the organizations are largely dormant: national headquarters becomes a small office in Washington with a custodial staff to answer the phone; precinct headquarters around the country are converted to places where the boys gather for poker and beer.

It is the nomination dance that calls the political hoofers onto the floor; all the greasing and screeching of party loyalists—their patriotic posturing, their evocation of men long dead, with whom they have nothing in common except a label—comes from their desire to more effectively monopolize this central political rite. Talk about "principles" and "party purpose," although a factor in the thinking of many on the fringe of party activity, is saved for platform ceremonials by those in control of the party apparatus. It is the nomination of successful candidates at national conventions, and in the case of local candidates, at state and precinct conventions, that constantly absorbs the attention of partymen; for they know that those who gain office command vast wealth and dispense enormous numbers of jobs. Control of the nomination mechanism has given them this strangle hold on power: it is a power that partymen were never meant to have, do not deserve to possess, do not know how to exercise for the general good, and should be relieved of before they cause further harm.

That is my supposition.

Let us carry this supposition a step further; let us suppose that such people are the last to whom we should ever entrust anything of value. Let us cling to the thought that the nation's well-being is better entrusted to honest leaders, who have learned to curb their baser instincts.

It is time now for a simple proposal, one that is hardly original, since it was made by the delegates to the Philadelphia convention and written, with as much force as they could muster, into the Constitution. I propose that we adopt the sophisticated political approach to which they were committed; namely, a no-party system. Although some of the delegates were latent monarchists, and others were wedded to no thought beyond the need to establish the stability in which commerce flourishes, most of them were democrats; most of them trusted the people above the individual. They wanted the direction of the country placed in their hands, not the octopus hands of the party con men.

The aim must be to erase the sham from our elections. It is now time to make the process by which our free choice is exercised more capable of reflecting our opinions, and in so doing, make "the right to vote" as important as it always should have been; it is time to eliminate the blockade of party intervention and clear the channel between the people and the persons they select to represent them. In this way both voter and officeholder will be made more responsible.

Since political parties exercise their most significant role in the nomination of candidates (local and state governments, after all the hoopla, do control and conduct the actual elections), if parties are to be eliminated, a new nominating process must be created. The following simple procedure might be suitable, but is proposed only in the hope that it will provoke additional recommendations, which might lead to some worthwhile reform.

Let us begin by acknowledging that which has always been so apparent it has seldom been noticed: The people rarely have a genuine opportunity to elect the delegates to national party conventions. That is where the break in the democratic circuit occurs. The people do, however, elect their representatives to Congress, the state legislatures, and the various city councils. Furthermore, every voter has a chance to judge these legislators' performance and, if satisfied, to reward them with a new term in office. This creates a definite, if distant relationship between them. Although the voter has no control over a party boss, he does catch the eye of every office holder.

All of this reinforces the conviction that the early method of nominating presidential candidates, namely the Congressional Caucus, was essentially the correct one; it produced a generally fine group of candidates, it utilized an apparatus already in existence, and it was ultimately accountable to the electorate.

However, rather than having congressmen of like political persuasion retreat into private meetings where they would negotiate a caucus nominee, I propose that Congress exercise its power to nominate in the open. Every four years, at the end of the summer vacation, each member of the Senate and House would be given the opportunity to sign a petition for any American who they think should be president: any person receiving 5 percent of the signatures of the members of Congress would be considered nominated.

At this point there might be as many as twenty candidates, reflecting all shades of opinion. Most voters would find in this group a candidate whose opinions somewhat closely represented their viewpoint, a situation so rare in recent elections that a majority of citizens have been forced to cast their ballot for the one of two men they distrusted least—the 1980 Democratic party primaries between Jimmy Carter and Ted Kennedy provided a dramatic example of this phenomenon: Carter's administration was commonly viewed as a failure and Senator Kennedy was tarred with the residue of personal scandals which constant explanation could not eradicate. Yet their names were the only ones presented to the voters in most of that party's primaries.

The campaign, in which this multitude of nominees would run, would last six weeks, a week longer than the British elections. It would be conducted exclusively on television and radio, since almost everyone can be reached directly by those media. The exhausting tedium of frenetic travel, and the wastefulness of rote speeches to restless crowds, would be ended.

All campaign costs would be paid by the Treasury; private contributions would be outlawed. Rather than the present concept that the race belongs to the one who can buy it, and, therefore, the shrewd candidate is the one who can raise the largest amount of campaign money, regardless of whom he promises what, the new view would be that victory at the polls is to be won by good works. Gone would be the spot commercial, repetitiously flashing some politician's saccharine smile simply because he had the money to make possible such an intrusion into the family living room.

The election would take place, as is now customary, at the beginning of November. There would be no party labels camouflaging the names of this legion of candidates.

Central to this plan is the thought that each nominee is running for either the office of president or vice-president. Four of the last seven presidents have been vice-presidents; clearly both men must have the confidence of their compatriots.

In order to accomplish this, a simple technical adjustment in machine voting will have to be made so that two identical lists appear on the ballot board; those two duplicate lists would have the names of all the nominees. When the lever is pulled for a presidential candidate on List #1, his name would automatically be blocked on the vice-presidential list. The voter would then have to pick someone else on List #2, the vice-presidential list.

In this manner the majority would pick both the president and vice-president; no longer would the vice-president be an afterthought concocted by a tiring bunch of hucksters: an afterthought which, since the 1920s has filled that office with such men as Coolidge, Dawes, Garner, Truman, Nixon, Johnson, Agnew, and Ford.

Since voting would be exclusively by machine, there would be no difficulty in tallying for this swarm of candidates. This is important, since the likelihood that any candidate would achieve a majority on Election Day is reduced because of the fragmented vote, and a run-off election would frequently be needed.

In effect, this first election would be equivalent to a national primary; it would differ from the present presidential primaries, which take place in only thirty-seven states, because it would be held on one day, would involve all candidates and would not be dominated by parties. The present primary system frequently confuses the selection process by diffusing the impact of voters, and making the results of these contests, all of which are run under varying rules, so contradictory, as to render them useless. It also gives too much importance to the early maneuvering in Iowa and New Hampshire, states whose small population should not win them such power.

Should a majority be lacking after the first election, the run-off would take place the following week. At that time the top five candidates would face each other. Although the field would be narrowed, the likelihood remains that most citizens would find that the positions of one of those candidates still somewhat approximated their own. If this run-off proved inconclusive, a third and final election would be held the next week, involving only the top two candidates.

This repetitive, meaningful polling may conceivably go a long way toward revitalizing voter interest. The fact that recent presidential elections have resulted in dismally low turnouts suggests that such a revitalization is needed.

The new arrangement, with its persistent effort to determine the true sentiments of the voter, would enhance the individual's feeling he or she has an important role to play in elections; each succeeding election would become more engrossing as issues sharpen and the race quickens. The old political bosses, constantly striving to shut out the unaffiliated citizen, would be gone, and in their place would be the new political bosses, the engaged American voters.

On the state and local levels, governors and mayors would be elected in much the same manner. Nomination for governor would be by petition of 5 percent of the members of the state legislature; for mayor, by 5 percent of the city council. Private donations to the subsequent campaigns would not be allowed; and, in case of an indecisive result in the first multi-candidate popular balloting, run-off elections would decide the issue.

In this manner all elected executive officials in the United States would be nominated by legislative bodies and then finally chosen by the people. There would be no qualifying conventions or primaries controlled by party organizations, and there would be no party labels to provide inadequate factotums with an imprimatur of competency which they do not possess.

This nominating authority properly belongs to legislative bodies. There is every indication that the founders of our Republic felt that the legislature was the most dependable of all branches of government, the best representative of popular opinion, the most knowledgeable in its deliberations, and the most likely to render wise decisions.

The new electoral system, in effect, pivots on the proposal that legislative bodies should assume the power to nominate elected executives, a power that has been, in our time, seized by political parties. In order to insure that party bosses do not reenter the system, by exercising a decisive role in the selection of the individuals who will sit in these legislative bodies, I suggest that we employ much the same system that was used in the early days of the Republic, and that is so commonly employed in organizational elections. If any individual wants to run for city council, state legislature or Congress, he will circulate petitions, collect signatures of qualified voters, let us say, one thousand for city council, two thousand for state legislature, and three thousand for Congress. He will submit these to nonpartisan Boards of Election, which already exist throughout the country, during the second week in September, allowing approximately seven weeks for assembling ballots, and the actual campaign. The subsequent elections, which would not be held the same year as those in which presidents, governors, or mayors are to be elected, in order to reduce potential confusion, exactly in the style that elections for this variety of offices are now staggered, would provide the honest democratic consensus now so sadly lacking.

The people will retain the power to nominate and elect legislative candidates, who will then have the delegated responsibility, from the voters, to nominate the list of candidates for president and vice-president, governors and mayors. The legislator's sense of responsibility to the voter will be stronger, since the question of his own future will no longer be at the mercy of an interdicting party mechanism, but, rather, directly where it always should be in a democracy, with the people.

This is not a call for the end of politics; and it is not an outline for a country without a political system. Every social group must have its political arrangements. It is a plea for Americans to recognize that their political system has been taken over by two parties whose basic function is to exclude them from the process of selecting their leaders, while giving them the impression that the entire system pivots on them and exists only to respond to their wishes.

It is also a call for change, and, as such, it may disturb those who perceive of their existence as immutable, reliable and the product of natural laws with which man cannot tamper. But institutions do change; slavery, upon which an economic and social system depended, has disappeared; knighthood, once thought of as the defense of the weak by the chivalrous, when it was finally recognized as a bully's vocation, faded from the scene; female chatteldom, reenforced by the authority of milleniums, has lost its granite form.

Political parties are not the institutional fortresses that these mighty vanquished once represented. There are no priests sprinkling holy water on their brows; there are no poets singing of their pure purpose. They are acknowledged in the silent understandings of our minds to be petty structures, built of mud, that will wash away with the first heavy rain of reason.

The new partyless election, with its emphasis on issues, and its affinity for candidates who have performed services for their country over a period of time, would be directed at bringing the archaic, rural-oriented nineteenth century political system into synchronization with the technically proficient, densely populated society in which we live; it would supply us with a truly democratic voting instrument, free of the leeches who now drain its strength, which would be suitable for the advanced industrial age into which we have barely begun to venture. At the same time, it would help protect us against the totalitarian tendencies of such a society.

Many people feel unable to do anything that will significantly influence their destiny; they feel a similar helplessness in dealing with the state. This is a major problem in mechanized societies, where people are out of touch with the processes that produce their food, clothing, and shelter, where entertainment comes packaged on mesmerizing television, where unions, corporations, and government are so remote and uninterested that people with substantial insecurities feel overwhelmed: Their neuroses are fed by reality.

But man has always been a cipher in the universe; he has always been degraded by nature, a mere mouthful for ants in the food cycle. It is in society that man has attempted to achieve a dignity and meaning for his existence that is not provided by the indifferent and often hostile mechanisms of biology.

The trauma of detachment, which for many people results from living in oversized cities, where they perform depersonalized and highly specialized work while being serviced by apathetic government bureaucracies and profit-oriented business monoliths, is made worse by the operation of the party system; parties increase the individual's feeling of isolation and ineffectiveness. Their lack of morality, their lack of regard for the opinions of the citizenry, their determination to bamboozle and confuse, are additionally crushing factors enfeebling the inhabitants of all advanced industrial societies.

One does not assume an unreasonably high moral tone when insisting that the people who would be our leaders must be of good character. When undergoing the oath of office, one of the few oaths ever extracted from an American citizen, political leaders are swearing to a level of morality not expected of ordinary members of society. It is, therefore, disheartening to see that high level of morality given voluntarily by most citizens in our largely conformist society, and so rarely given, under any circumstances, by a discouragingly large number of their rulers.

It is not my intention to romanticize former days or make gods out of men who undoubtedly had our faults in equal profusion. I am not advocating that we go back to those supposedly carefree times when everyone was happy and everything went as it should.

My concern is the common tendency to conceive that we must always have parties merely because they have existed for some time. If partymen could claim that all the traditions of our system are connected to, and dependent on them, then they might appeal to our regard for custom: the sacredness of custom leads us to repeat many foolish rituals and waste a great deal of time that could be spent in innocent and subtle pleasures; but that does not appear to be the case. Change is mandated by life.

Recognizable man has been on this earth for hundreds of thousands of years, constantly tinkering with one or another governmental arrangements; his efforts have collapsed with the regularity of family feuds, plagues, and a myriad of disasters. Although civilization brought some semblance of order to the chaos that had previously been considered normal, wars and revolutions continued to interrupt the history of every nation. So ephemeral are nations that there is no instance of any surviving, even in somewhat altered form, in the six thousand years of recorded history: pharaonic Egypt, democratic Athens, the realm of medieval Christianity, even the mighty British Empire, are gone.

But we may have found a formula for survival: representative democracy. If we have, the formula might continue to be effective if we obey the mandate of life and rid it of the defects that have manifested themselves in our evolving system.

Simply because it is so promising, it deserves our most serious effort to make it better. Surely this twinkle of time since independence from Britain should not delude us into thinking we have shaped a system that cannot be improved; such fantasies dishonor the descendants of Franklin, Madison, Washington, Hamilton, Adams, and Jefferson.

The weakest element in our governmental structure is exactly that element our founders believed would give us the greatest trouble: a strong chief executive bound to partymen. They thought they had eliminated the threat inherent in that party bind, but that is a task that has been left to a later generation.

The party system has devoured much of the nation's wealth and energy, misdirected honest efforts, and begrimed the administration of government. Both Republican and Democratic bosses agree on one thing: Their parties are an essential component of our politics. The power to nominate, they maintain with an aggressiveness of style that is shared by desperadoes in all callings, must remain with them.

The rest of society does not have the financial or emotional stake that either of these cabals have in perpetuating that affront. Our common liberty, and good sense, must be allowed to mold the form of our political institutions. We are a free, responsible people who have proved we are capable of accomplishing wonders. Among these can be the construction of an election system that will honor reason and, hopefully, lead us further from the cave and the club toward a time when party taskmasters will no longer be in a position of determining to whom we give our precious gift of leadership.

Chapter Notes
and Sources

1. A Nightmare Vision

1. James Madison, *Notes of Debates in the Federal Convention of 1787* (Athens, Ohio: Ohio University Press, 1966), 52.
2. *The New York Times,* May 1-4, 1974. Subsequent versions of these transcripts released by the House Judiciary Committee, as a result of its impeachment hearings against the president, disclosed that the most damaging conversations between Nixon and his staff had been deleted. Cf. *Times,* June 21, 1974.
3. *Washington Post,* November 18, 1973. Before 400 Associated Press managing editors in Orlando, Florida, he prefaced this extraordinary remark with the observation, "People have got to know whether or not their President is a crook."
4. Only 38 percent of a disillusioned electorate was willing to expend the energy to cast their ballots in the 1974 congressional elections. Cited by John Herbers, *The New York Times,* Nov. 10, 1974, Associated Press analysis of election returns.
5. *The New York Times,* January 16, 1975.
6. Madison, op. cit., 52.
7. Samuel Johnson, "The Idler and the Adventurer," W. J. Bate, John M. Bullitt, and L. F. Powell, eds., *The Idler,* No. 10, June 17, 1958. In *The Works of Samuel Johnson* (New Haven, Conn.: Yale University Press, 1965), II, 32, 33.
8. Pope to E. Blount, August 27, 1714. In George Sherburn, ed., *The Correspondence of Alexander Pope* (Oxford: Clarendon Press, 1956), I, 247.
9. Madison, op. cit., 31.
10. Ibid., 46.
11. Ibid., 150. This was the revised Virginia Plan as amended by the convention's Committee of the Whole. It called for a seven-year presidential term.

275

12. Cited by Roy F. Nichols, *The Invention of the American Political Parties* (New York: Macmillan, 1967), 138.
13. Richard Hofstadter, *The Idea of a Party System* (Berkeley, Calif.: University of California Press, 1969), 48, 49.
14. Jefferson to Francis Hopkinson, March 13, 1789. In Julian P. Boyd, ed., *Papers of Thomas Jefferson* (Princeton, N.J.: University of Princeton Press, 1958), XIV, 650.
15. Cited in its full historical context by Clinton Rossiter, *1787—The Grand Convention* (New York: Macmillan, 1966), 304. The entire document is in John C. Fitzpatrick's *The Writings of George Washington* (Washington, D.C.: Government Printing Office, 1940), XXXI, 47, 48.
16. Resolution of Confederate Congress in the National Archives.
17. Nichols, op. cit., 158-161.

2. The Low Point of Party Influence

1. Hofstadter, *Idea of a Party System*, 53.
2. Noble E. Cunningham, Jr., *The Jeffersonian Republicans: The Formation of Party Organization*, 1789-1801 (Chapel Hill: University of North Carolina Press, 1957), 34.
3. John Taylor, *A Definition of Parties* (Philadelphia, 1794), 2, 15.
4. "The Farewell Address," March 30, 1796. In John C. Fitzpatrick, ed., op. cit., XXXV, 226.
5. Ibid., 227.
6. Cited by Cunningham, op. cit., 95.
7. Ibid., 96.
8. Ibid., 145.
9. Nichols, *Invention*, 205.
10. Madison, *Notes*, 427.
11. Harry R. Warfel, *Noah Webster, Schoolmaster to America* (New York: Macmillan, 1936), 267.
12. Burr had been given the responsibility of selecting a Rhode Island Elector who would vote for Jefferson but not for Burr. Unaccountably, he picked one who lost to a Federalist, so that he and Jefferson ended with identical electoral totals.
13. Samuel E. Morison, "The First Nominating Convention, 1808." *American Historical Review*, XVII, 4, (July 1912), 744-63. Morison comments: "In the eyes of most Federalists in 1808, the only proper methods of nomination were by mass-meetings, or by personal friends of the candidate." pp. 749-50.
14. Adams in a letter to Benjamin Rush, September 3, 1808. In Charles Francis Adams, ed., *The Works of John Adams, Second President of the United States* (Boston: Little Brown, 1850-56), IX, 602.

15. Cited by Nichols, op. cit., 260.
16. *The Autobiography of Martin Van Buren*, Annual Report of the American Historical Association for the Year 1918, II, 124. (Washington, D.C.: Government Printing Office).
17. Ibid., 193.

3. Posts of Honor, Places of Profit

1. John Taylor, *An Inquiry into the Principles and Policy of the Government of the United States* (1814) (New Haven: Yale University Press, 1950), 560.
2. Samuel Eliot Morison and Henry Steele Commager, *The Growth of the American Republic* (New York: Oxford University Press, 1946) I, 463.
3. Cited by M. Ostrogorski, *Democracy and the Party System in the United States* (New York: Macmillan, 1921), 12. A single-volume version of the Russian author's *Democracy and the Organization of Political Parties*, devoted exclusively to the growth of the party system in the United States.
4. Ibid.
5. Ibid., 13.
6. Ibid., 17, 19.
7. Arthur M. Schlesinger, Jr., *The Age of Jackson* (New York: Little Brown, 1945), 39. Schlesinger described Jackson at this time: "By 1829 he was technically a sick man—many thought dying. His head throbbed with splitting pains apparently produced by years of tobacco chewing, and his lean frame shook with a hacking consumptive cough."
8. Nichols, *Invention of American Political Parties*, 287.
9. Ibid., 278.
10. Ostrogorski, op. cit., 20.
11. Van Buren, *Autobiography*, 203, 271, 272. In old age Van Buren, Adams' former relentless enemy, grudgingly wrote of his admiration for Adams' "spirit and indomitable firmness." Referring to an early point in his career, Van Buren described him as "munificently endowed with genius and talents . . ."
12. See Schlesinger, Jr., op. cit., 83, 84.
13. Ibid., 83.
14. Richard B. Morris, ed., *Encyclopedia of American History* (New York: Harper & Brothers, 1953), 167.
15. Ostrogorski, op. cit., 21. "The vast popular army which marched triumphantly through the streets of Washington dispersed (after the inauguration) to their homes, but one of its divisions remained, the corps of marauders which followed it. This was composed of the politicians.

They wanted their spoils. By way of renumeration for their services they demanded places in the administration. They filled the air of Washington like locusts, they swarmed in the halls and lobbies of the public buildings, in the adjoining streets they besieged the residences of Jackson and his ministers. Jackson hastened to admit the justice of their claim."

16. Henry Steele Commager, ed., *Documents of American History*, 8th ed. (New York: Appleton-Century-Crofts, 1968), No. 139, 255.

17. Cited by Ostrogorski, op. cit., 24.

18. For another opinion, sample Arthur Schlesinger, Jr. "The spoils system, whatever its faults, at least destroyed peaceably the monopoly of offices by a class which could not govern, and brought to power a fresh and alert group which had the energy to meet the needs of the day.... There can be small doubt today that, whatever evils it brought into American life, its historical function was to narrow the gap between the people and the government—to expand popular participation in the workings of democracy."Op. cit., 47.

19. See page 36, footnote 14, citing 1828 election results; 1824 election returns were: Jackson 155,872, Adams 105,321, Crawford 42, 282, Clay 46,587, Nichols, op. cit., 278.

20. Schlesinger, Jr., op. cit., 424.

21. Ibid.

22. Martin Van Buren, *Inquiry into the Origin and Course of Political Parties in the United States* (New York: Augustus M. Kelley, 1967; reprint of Hurd and Houghton edition, 1867), 414.

23. Madison, *Notes*, 53.

4.   National Parties Appear on the Horizon

1. D. W. Brogan, in Foreword to Maurice Duverger, *Political Parties, Their Organization and Activity in the Modern State* (New York: Harper and Row, 1972), XI.

2. Alexis de Tocqueville, Democracy in America (New York: Knopf, 1972), I, 178.

3. Van Buren, *Inquiry*, 373.

4. Ostrogorski observed that the state-district-county convention system spread across the Union in the twenty-five years after Monroe's second administration, but was greeted with suspicion in the newly developing West. In Illinois it was viewed as a "Yankee contrivance destined to abridge the liberties of the people, by depriving individuals, on their own mere motion, of the privilege of becoming candidates, and depriv-

ing each man of the right to vote for a candidate of his own selection and choice." Cited by Ostrogorski, op. cit., 25.
5. Nichols, *Invention*, 307.
6. Ibid., 308.
7. Ibid., 309.
8. Morison and Commager, *Growth of American Republic*, 450.
9. Nichols, op. cit., 310.
10. Morris, *Encyclopedia*, 174.
11. Tocqueville, op. cit., 179.
12. Nichols, op. cit., 314-323.

5. The Political Party Coup

1. "Society," in Jacques Barzun, ed., *The Selected Writings of John Jay Chapman* (New York: Farrar, Straus and Cudahy, 1957), 246, 247.
2. "The haste to get rich was infecting the whole nation with such intensity that in point of fact the effective exercise of its political rights was becoming rather an embarrassment to it than otherwise. Yet the price and the consciousness of its strength which filled the new American democracy could not assent to a formal abdication. The American wanted at least the illusion of enjoying and using his rights." Ostrogorski, *Democracy and Party System*, 25.
3. Tocqueville, *Democracy*, 225.
4. Harold Syrett, *Andrew Jackson: His Contribution to the American Tradition* (Indianapolis: Bobbs-Merrill, 1953), 97, 98.
5. Nichols, *Invention*, 328-333.
6. Cited by William Harlan Hale, *Horace Greeley, Voice of the People* (New York: Harper & Brothers, 1950), 21.
7. Ibid., 55.
8. Daniel Webster in a letter to Edward Everett, February 16, 1840. Cited by Irving H. Bartlett, *Daniel Webster* (New York: Norton, 1978), 161.
9. Nichols, op. cit., 336.
10. Hale, op. cit., 59.
11. Cited by Morison and Commager, *Growth*, I, 556.
12. Ibid., I, 557.
13. Morris, *Encyclopedia*, 183.
14. Morison and Commager describe him as "an obstinate man of commonplace mind and narrow views." *Growth of American Republic*, 557.
15. Glyndon G. Van Deusen, *The Life of Henry Clay* (Boston: Little Brown, 1937), 343.
16. "The Address of Mr. Calhoun to his Political Friends and Supporters,"

in John C. Calhoun, *The Works of John C. Calhoun*, Richard K. Cralle, ed., VI, 247. Calhoun added, ". . . as objectionable as I think a Congressional caucus for nominating a President, it is, in my opinion, far less so than a Convention constituted as is proposed. The former had many things to recommend it. Its members, consisting of Senators and Representatives, were the immediate organs of the State Legislatures or the people, were, for the most part, of high character, standing and talents. . . . It was all that could be desired for a nominating body, and formed a striking contrast to the proposed Convention, and yet, it could not be borne by the people in the then purer days of the Republic."
17. Cited by Ostrogorsky, op. cit., 42.

6.   The Bold and the Violent

1. James K. Polk, *The Diary of James K. Polk, During His Presidency, 1845 to 1849*, Milo Milton Quaife, ed. (Chicago: A. C. McClurg & Co., 1910), IV, 232.
2. Tocqueville, *Democracy*, I, 225, 226.
3. Ibid., 226.
4. James Bryce, *The American Commonwealth* (New York: Putnam, 1959), II, 593.
5. Madison, *Notes*, 73.
6. Nichols, *Invention*, 361.
7. Charles Sellers, *James K. Polk, Continentalist, 1843-1846* (Princeton, N.J.: Princeton University Press, 1966), 164.
8. Cited by *Time* magazine, March 5, 1979, 6.
9. Ralph Waldo Emerson, *Essays by Ralph Waldo Emerson* (New York: Crowell, 1926), 402.
10. "The Life of Webster" (A sermon preached at the Melodeon, in Boston, Sunday, October 31, 1852) (Rochester, N.Y.: Printed at the Book and Job Office, 41 Main Street, 1852), 25, 26, 28.
11. Theodore Parker, address on "The Nebraska Question," at the Music Hall in Boston, February 12, 1854 (Boston: Benjamin B. Mussey and Co., 1854), 34, 35.

7.   The Birth of the Republican Party

1. John G. Nicolay and John Hay, eds., *Complete Works of Abraham Lincoln* (New York: Francis D. Tandy Company, 1905), I, 27.
2. Cited in Morison and Commager, op. cit., 621.
3. Bryce, op. cit., 319.

4. V.O. Key, Jr., *Politics, Parties and Pressure Groups* (New York: Crowell, 1947), 246.
5. Donald Bruce Johnson and Kirk H. Porter, compilers, *National Party Platforms*, 1840-1972 (Urbana: University of Illinois Press, 1973), 27.
6. Allen Nevins, *Fremont, Pathmarker of the West* (New York: Longmans, Green, 1955), 455.
7. Nichols, *Invention*, 375, 376.
8. Morris, *Encyclopedia*, 221.
9. Quincy, Ill., speech (October 13, 1858). In Abraham Lincoln, *The Collected Works of Abraham Lincoln*, Roy Baster, ed. (New Brunswick, N.J.: Rutgers University Press, 1953), III, 254.
10. Stephen Douglas debate with Lincoln in the summer of 1858. In Nicholay and Hay, op. cit., IV, 369, 370.
11. Cited by Morison and Commager, op. cit., I, 636.
12. Ibid.
13. Ibid.
14. Cited by Morris, op. cit., 227.

8. The Death of the Republican Party

1. Professor Randall's evaluation of the Radical Republicans, who had come to dominate the party as the war progressed, is cited in Malcolm Moos, *The Republicans, A History of Their Party* (New York: Random House, 1956), 98.
2. Ibid. 88.
3. By 1867, as political morality descended to one of its periodic lows, Cameron succeeded in buying the support of enough Pennsylvania legislators to purchase a Senate seat. Upon retirement, ten years later, he had no difficulty convincing his legislative claque to appoint his son in his place—a demonstration of the divine rights of kingmakers.
4. Nicolay and Hay, *Abraham Lincoln*, X, 263.
5. Ibid., X, 203.
6. Morison and Commager, *Growth of American Republic*, I, 732.
7. Carl Sandburg, *Abraham Lincoln—The Prairie Years and the War Years* (New York: Harcourt, Brace, 1954), 655.
8. Cited in Morison and Commager, op. cit., II, 33.
9. Ibid., 39.
10. Ibid., 41.
11. Bruce Catton, *U. S. Grant and the American Military Tradition*, Oscar Handlin, ed. (Boston: Little Brown, 1954), 49-54.
12. Morris, *Encyclopedia*, 249.

13. Vernon Louis Parrington, *Main Currents in American Thought* (New York: Harcourt, Brace, 1927), III, 29, 30.
14. William B. Hasseltine, *Ulysses S. Grant, Politician* (New York: Frederick Ungar, 1935), 171-178; Julia Dent Grant, *The Personal Memoirs of Julia Dent Grant,* John Y. Simon, ed. (New York: Putnam, 1975), 167 (footnote); Morris, op. cit., 250.
15. Morison and Commager, op. cit., II, 58.
16. Ibid., 66, 67.
17. Ibid., 112.
18. Ibid., 72.
19. *The New York Times,* January 22, 1872; 1, 7.
20. *The New York Times,* June 1, 1872; 1, 2.
21. Ibid.
22. Morison and Commager, op. cit., II, 71, 72.
23. *The New York Times,* February 26, 1873, 4.
24. Morison and Commager, op. cit., II, 72.
25. *The New York Times,* January 4, 1873, 1.
26. Parrington, op. cit., III, 29, 37.
27. Morison and Commager, op. cit., II, 112.

9.   How Hacks Produced Hacks

1. Attributed to William Marcy Tweed; possibly apocryphal.
2. J. Chal Vinson, *Thomas Nast, Political Cartoonist* (Athens, Ga.: University of Georgia Press, 1967), Illustration 38, originally printed in *Harper's Weekly,* June 10, 1871.
3. Morison and Commager, *Growth,* II, 74.
4. Frederick Burkhardt et al., *Concise Dictionary of American Biography* (New York: Scribner's, 1964), 1090. Referred to henceforth as *American Biography.*
5. From an interview which I taped with the former mayor on the floor of the convention. Wagner was a friendly individual who apparently viewed himself as essentially honest. Unlike many of his predecessors the scandals associated with his administration were not tied directly to him. However, his appointments to office (commissioners, deputies, heads of bureaus, consultants), and there were tens of thousands of them that were made outside of the civil service cadre, all had to be cleared with Carmine DeSapio and the other borough bosses. Professional politicians pretend to see nothing wrong with this arrangement. "As long as the people we appoint are qualified," I have heard the most corrupt of them say, "why should anyone care if they work for a political club?" Over-

looked in this rationalization is the fact that to limit the pool of talent available for government service to applicants from the clubhouse is to narrow the source of candidates to the lowest fraction of the total talent available in the country; members of that fraction have invariably been culled by the bosses for their weakest characteristics. To adopt a standard, as the leader of government, that you will appoint anyone who is merely *qualified*, as long as he is endorsed by a party chief, is to guarantee less than the best type of service, and, often, insure the worst.

10. An Opportunity to Inhibit Party Larceny

1. "Politics." In Ralph Waldo Emerson, *Essays, Second Series, (new and revised ed.)* (Boston: Houghton Mifflin, 1894), III, 201.
2. Cited by Morison and Commager, *Growth*, I, 775.
3. Ibid., II, 73.
4. Ibid., II, 76.
5. *American Biography*, 1068, 1069.
6. Samuel Eliot Morison, Henry Steele Commager, and William E. Leuchtenburg, *The Growth of The American Republic*, 6th ed. (New York: Oxford University Press, 1969), II, 154. Henceforth referred to as "Leuchtenburg."
7. Ibid., 151.
8. Cited by Morison and Commager, op. cit., II, 77.
9. Ibid.
10. *The New York Times*, November 20, 1876; 1, 7. Herein one finds a vivid description of the Democrats' voting practices in Mississippi. The *Times* "Occasional Correspondent" quotes from a letter written by "a prominent and influential lawyer of Mississippi" to substantiate his allegation that the election, in localities controlled by the Republicans, "was characterized by fraud and terrorism" which was "universal" and "unblushing." The statistics for Yazoo County, in paragraph VI, are particularly illuminating.
11. *American Biography*, 101.
12. Morison and Commager, op. cit., II, 78. A description of this midnight lobbying is attributed to Abram S. Hewitt, then Democratic leader of the House.
13. Leuchtenburg, op. cit., II, 154.
14. Cited by Theodore Clarke Smith, *The Life and Letters of James Abram Garfield* (New Haven: Yale University Press, 1925), I, 530.
15. Ibid. For an account of this affair, see pp. 530-543. So loath was Professor Smith to criticize the assassinated Garfield that one marvels to see so

much of the transcript of those damaging hearings in his sympathetic biography. A common fault in academicians has been their unwillingness to view presidents, when they are the subjects of their researches, with proper skepticism. They often function on the level of sportswriters, bugling the attributes of their home run hitters.

16. Ibid., 565, 566.
17. Morris, *Encyclopedia*, 256.
18. *The New York Times*, July 3, 1881; 1, 4.
19. Charles Guiteau, *The Truth and the Removal* (Washington, D.C.: Privately printed, 1882). The ultimate in vanity press publication.
20. Cited by Morison and Commager, op. cit., II, 222.
21. Thomas Reeves has uncovered Arthur's previously forgotten role in the corruption surrounding the 1880 election. As state party chairman in New York, Arthur sent letters to government employees—from washerwomen to judges—levying an "assessment" on each of them, appropriate to their station, debt to the party, and hope for the future. So ordinary was this practice that he did not hesitate to make his demands in his own handwriting. Thomas C. Reeves, "Chester A. Arthur and the Campaign of 1880," *Political Science Quarterly*, (December 1969), LXXXIV, 628-37.

11. Emergence of the One-Party System

1. Letter to William Giles, December 31, 1779. In *The Writings of Thomas Jefferson*, Paul Leicester Ford, ed. (New York, 1892-99), VII, 43.
2. Cited by Leuchtenburg, op. cit., II, 160.
3. Ibid.
4. *American Biography*, 619.
5. Henry Adams, *Democracy* (New York: Farrar, Straus and Young, 1952), 233, 238, 241.
6. Cited by Morison and Commager, op. cit., II, 217.

12. The Myth of the Imperial Presidency

1. Charles Francis Adams, ed., *Memoirs of John Quincy Adams, Comprising Portions of His Diary from 1795-1848* (Philadelphia: Lippincott, 1874), I, 249.
2. Theodore Roosevelt, Speech at Minnesota State Fair, September 2, 1901. In John Bartlett, *Familiar Quotations*, 14th ed., Emily Morison Beck, ed. (Boston: Little Brown, 1968), 847b.
3. *The New York Times*, August 8, 1912; 1, 8.
4. *The New York Times*, October 15, 1912; 1, 6.

5. John Wells Davidson, ed., Woodrow Wilson, *A Crossroads of Freedom—The 1912 Campaign Speeches of Woodrow Wilson* (New Haven: Yale University Press, 1956, 53.

6. Woodrow Wilson, *President Wilson's Great Speeches* (Chicago: Stanton and Van Vliet Co., 1919), 180.

13.   A Fool as President

1. Warren Gamaliel Harding, "Address of the President at the Luncheon of the Associated Press in New York, April 24, 1923" (Washington, D.C.: Government Printing Office, 1923), 91.

2. Francis Russell, *The Shadow of Blooming Grove* (New York: McGraw-Hill, 1968), 109.

3. Harry M. Daugherty, in collaboration with Thomas Dixon, *The Inside Story of the Harding Tragedy* (New York, Churchill Company, 1932), 5.

4. Cited by Russell, op. cit., 112.

5. Mark Sullivan, *Our Times: The United States 1900-1925* (New York: Scribner's, 1935), VI, 21.

6. Russell, op. cit., 166-171.

7. Ibid, Preface, IX.

8. Nan Britton, *The President's Daughter* (New York: Elizabeth Ann Guild, 1927), 6.

9. Cited by Russell, op. cit., 313.

10. *The New York Times*, May 30, 1920; 1, 8.

11. Cited by Russell, op. cit., 313.

12. Ibid.

13. Ibid., 314.

14. Britton, op. cit., 69.

15. Ibid., 75.

16. Cited by Russell, op. cit., 321.

17. Ibid., 331.

18. Ibid., 330.

19. Ibid.

20. Ibid.

21. Daugherty, op. cit., 15.

22. Ibid.

23. Ibid., 8.

24. Ibid., 18.

25. Cited by Russell, op. cit., 339.

26. Ibid., 341, 342. (Also see Sullivan's version, op. cit., VI, 37, 38, and *The New York Times*, June 13, 1920; 1, 7.)

27. The account of the convention, including statistics about the balloting,

was taken from *The New York Times,* June 1920, and Sullivan, op. cit., VI, 50-67.

28. Cited by Russell, op. cit., 356.
29. Ibid., 360.
30. Ibid., 361.
31. William Allen White, *The Autobiography of William Allen White* (New York: Macmillan, 1946), 584.
32. Cited by Sullivan, op. cit., VI, 128.
33. Ibid., 64.
34. Cited by Russell, op. cit., 383.
35. Ibid., 384.
36. Ibid.
37. Ibid.
38. Alice Roosevelt Longworth, *Crowded Hours* (New York: Scribner's, 1933), 311.
39. Ibid., 325.
40. Cited by Sullivan, op. cit., VI, 66.
41. Cited by Britton, op. cit., 136.
42. Cited by Morison and Commager, *Growth,* II, 517.
43. Cited by Russell, op. cit., 427.
44. Ibid., 432.

14.   The Criminal Administration

1. David Kin, ed., *Dictionary of American Maxims* (New York: Philosophical Library, 1955), 422.
2. Daugherty, *Inside Story,* 7.
3. Cited by Russell, *Shadow,* 524, 525.
4. Ibid., 556.
5. Britton, *President's Daughter,* 172, 173.
6. Ibid., 240.
7. Cited by Sullivan, *Our Times,* VI, 240.
8. Russell, op. cit., 405, 509.
9. Ibid., 521.
10. Ibid.
11. Daugherty, op. cit., 69.
12. Cited by Russell, op. cit., 511.
13. Ibid., 512.
14. Ibid., 567.
15. Ibid., 630.
16. Ibid., 502.
17. Cited by Sullivan, op. cit., VI, 250. The article's title, "A Calm View of a Calm Man."

18. Cited by White, *Autobiography*, 616. On page 618 White tells of Harding reminiscing with him in the president's office about how he and his printing competitors back in Marion used to rig the bidding for county printing contracts and then divided the profits. He was tormented by the thought that some "good friends of mine from Ohio," who were coming to see him that afternoon, were about to be indicted for "violating the antitrust law or some conspiracy law for doing exactly, in crockery, what I've done in printing for twenty years." Full of self-pity, he added, "My God, this is a hell of a job! I have no trouble with my enemies. I can take care of my enemies all right. But my damn friends—my God-damn friends, White, they're the ones that keep me walking the floor nights!"

15. The Institutionalizing of Presidential Incapacity

1. Cited by John Bradley et al., *The International Dictionary of Thoughts* (New York: J. C. Ferguson Publishing Co.), 540.
2. Cited by Leuchtenburg, op. cit., II, 413.
3. Morison and Commager, *Growth*, II, 521.
4. Leuchtenburg, op. cit., II, 420.
5. Russell, *Shadow*, 620.
6. Leuchtenburg, op. cit., 423.
7. John D. Hicks, "The Third Party Tradition in American Politics." *The Mississippi Valley Historical Review*, XX, (June 1933), 3-28. Hicks records: "In three-fifths of the presidential elections held during the last one hundred years, the candidates of significant, and at least temporarily powerful, third parties have been before the voters. In possibly half a dozen instances the third party vote has snatched victory from one major party ticket to give it to the other." p. 26.
8. Cited in William Allen White, A Puritan in Babylon (New York: Macmillan, 1938), 360.
9. Cited in Emmet John Hughes, *The Living Presidency* (New York: Coward, McCann & Geoghegan, 1972), 98.
10. John Kenneth Galbraith, *The Great Crash* (Boston: Houghton Mifflin, 1954), 22.
11. Cited by Leuchtenburg, op. cit., II, 427.
12. Ibid., 426.
13. Ibid.
14. Frederick Lewis Allen, *Only Yesterday* (New York: Harper & Row, 1931, 334. Chapter thirteen contains a lively description of the stock market crash.
15. Cited by Morison and Commager, op. cit., II, 545.
16. Cited by Allen, op. cit., 336.

17. Herbert Hoover, *The New Day: Campaign Speeches of Herbert Hoover,* 1928 (Stanford, Calif.: Stanford University press, 1929), 153, 155.
18. Cited by Galbraith, op. cit., 148.
19. Ibid., 182, 183.
20. Leuchtenburg, op. cit., II, 474.
21. Ibid.

16.   The Accident of Ability

1. Edward J. Flynn, *You're The Boss* (New York: Viking Press, 1947), 79. Boss Flynn drew his power from the iron control he exerted over the Bronx Democratic Organization. Roosevelt appointed him secretary of state after he was elected governor in 1928. Flynn's position had few duties, and mainly consisted of recommending people to F.D.R. for appointment to state jobs. Flynn commented: "Roosevelt in practically every instance appointed men and women recommended by the organizations." Op. cit., 78.
2. Arthur Schlesinger, Sr., eminent Harvard historian, took a 1948 poll of fifty-five of his fellows in the country's great universities and reported the consensus was ten occupants of the White House were "great" or "near great." They were: Lincoln, Washington, Franklin Roosevelt, Wilson, Jefferson, Jackson, Theodore Roosevelt, Cleveland, John Adams, and Polk. The only one on that list with whom I would argue is Cleveland, who seems pale when compared to the others. In terms of their ability I would add Madison and John Quincy Adams, two extraordinary men whose administrations were hobbled by circumstances. The poll is cited by Hughes, *Living Presidency,* 276.
3. James MacGregor Burns, *Roosevelt: The Lion and the Fox* (New York: Harcourt, Brace, 1956), 44. Professor Burns describes him thus: "Howe, with his dwarfish body, ferret-like features, and untidy clothes, looked like a troll out of a Catskill cave."
4. Foreword to Lela Stiles, *The Man Behind Roosevelt, The Story of Louis McHenry Howe* (New York: World Publishing Company, 1954).
5. Ibid., 20, 21.
6. Flynn, op. cit., 78.
7. Stiles, op. cit., 32.
8. A photocopy of the letter appears in Stiles' book, facing page 25.
9. Cited by Stiles, op. cit., 35.
10. A facsimile of the poster issued by Roosevelt appears in Burns, op. cit., 45. It is addressed "To Fruit Growers!" and contains what may well be the narrowest special interest issue ever presented in an American election. "I pledge myself to introduce and fight for the passage of an

amendment to the law making a Standard Fruit Barrel of 16½ inches."

11. Stiles, op. cit., 37.
12. Cited by Stiles, op. cit., 57.
13. Ibid., 58.
14. Ibid., 61.
15. Ibid., 63.
16. Ibid., 64.
17. Boss Flynn wrote of how the party organization really operated while publicly proclaiming it was only representing the people's interests. He first described William F. Kenney, "a man of considerable means who had been active in the Democratic party in New York City and who was one of its largest contributors. . . . Kenney was a contractor who had accumulated a great deal of money through building operations in New York City, where he had constructed many of the power houses of the New York Edison Company. On the roof of an office building he owned at the corner of Twenty-third Street and Fourth Avenue was a penthouse that consisted of one large room, famous in political circles as the 'Tiger Room.' It was so called because many members of the Democratic party, especially from Tammany, were in the habit of meeting there. It had a complete kitchen, and both luncheons and dinners were frequently served. There, of nights, politicians and financial leaders would gather to play cards, visit, and discuss conditions. The leaders of the various counties were often the beneficiaries of Kenney's hospitality. His interest in the Democratic party resulted in very generous contributions to all sorts of political activities. Many conferences, particularly while Hylan was Mayor, took place in this notable room. But Kenney's closest friend and the object of his complete admiration was Governor Smith. . . . As the likelihood of Smith's Presidential nomination increased, Smith made it a point to spend a great deal of his time at the 'Tiger Room,' where he held innumerable quiet meetings. It came to be a clearing house for state business and politics." Op. cit., 64, 65.

The symbiotic nature of the relationship between businessmen like Kenney and partymen such as Smith, Hylan, and Flynn is made understandable by Flynn's comment, "Political organizations, like any other organization, cannot exist without money. It is, to carry out the analogy of the machine, the fuel that keeps the motor going." Op. cit., 112.
18. Cited by Stiles, op. cit., 64.
19. Oscar Theodore Barck, Jr., and Nelson Manfred Blake, *Since 1900: A History of the United States in Our Times* (New York: Macmillan, 1947), 284.
20. Joseph P. Lash, *Eleanor and Franklin* (New York: Norton, 1971), 222.
21. Ibid., 226.

22. Ibid., 227.
23. Ibid., 256.
24. Stiles, op. cit., 73.
25. Ibid., 77.
26. Ibid., 78.
27. Ibid., 83.
28. Ibid., 82.
29. Ibid., 91.
30. Burns, op. cit., 93, 94.
31. Cited by Arthur M. Schlesinger, Jr., *The Crisis of the Old Order 1919-1933* (Boston: Houghton Mifflin, 1957), 104.
32. Cited by Stiles, op. cit., 110.
33. Flynn, op. cit., 67-79.
34. James A. Farley, *Behind The Ballots—The Personal History of a Politician* (New York: Harcourt, Brace, 1938), 66.
35. Ibid., 67.
36. Flynn, op. cit., 76.
37. Burns, op. cit., 104.
38. Cited by Stiles, op. cit., 119.
39. Ibid., 120.
40. Edward Robb Ellis, *The Epic of New York City* (New York: Coward-McCann, 1966), 540, 541. "Preferring pleasure to power, he [Walker] abdicated his responsibilities to the new Tammany boss, John F. Curry, and Tammany now fastened itself like an octopus on the city, as it had in the days of Boss Tweed. It controlled the mayor, all city departments, the courts, and every prosecuting agency within the five boroughs.

"Tammany relatives were put on city payrolls, while their unemployed neighbors had to go on relief. Businessmen paid tribute for services due them under the law. The granting of franchises became a political football and a common source of graft. Politicians allied themselves with criminals. Cops took bribes, beat up prisoners, framed innocents, terrorized the law-abiding. Much of Tammany's power lay in its concern for lawbreakers. By seeing to it that they stayed out of jail, Tammany won the gratitude, votes, and money of crooks of all kinds. . . . Judgeships were bought and sold. . . . A man seeking to become a judge paid a bribe of from $10,000 to $50,000, thus won Boss Curry's recommendation, and received his appointment from the mayor.

"Political hacks piled up incredible fortunes. Thomas M. Farley, sheriff of New York County and a Tammany sachem, earned only $8,500 a year but accumulated nearly $400,000 in 6 years. During the six years John Theofel served as Democratic leader of Queens, his net worth increased from $28,650 to $201,300. James J. McCormick, a Manhattan Democratic district leader and deputy city clerk, deposited his $384,788 in plunder in 30 different bank accounts."

41. A vivid description of F.D.R.'s reluctance to offend Tammany is given by Ellis, ibid., 542-548.
42. Cited by Stiles, op. cit., 126.
43. Burns, op. cit., 120.
44. Professor Burns commented on this aspect of F.D.R.'s shrewd political handling of Tammany. "Roosevelt evaded the net by the tactic of compromise. He took formal steps to enable the Republicans to investigate Tammany, but he never allowed a situation to arise where he was arrayed directly in an investigatory attack on Tammany." Op. cit., 121. In what might be considered Burns' summary of Roosevelt's political career in Albany, he wrote, "Indeed, Roosevelt played politics expertly and tirelessly throughout his gubernatorial days. While he occasionally donned the cloak of non-partisanship, he was essentially a party politician." Ibid., 118.
45. Interview with the author, December 12, 1974. Farley, obviously sharp and convivial, was still putting in a full day's work with the Coca-Cola Export Company, his major source of income since he retired from politics in 1940.
46. Cited by Stiles, op. cit., 135. Also cited by Burns, op. cit., 123.
47. Burns, op. cit., 123.
48. Ibid.
49. Ibid., 122.
50. Cited by Flynn, op. cit., 82.
51. Cited by Burns, op. cit., 129.
52. Stiles, op. cit., 140.
53. All the quotes from this letter are cited by Stiles, 146.
54. Ibid., 149.
55. Burns, op. cit., 130.
56. Ibid., 135, 136.
57. Cited by Stiles, op. cit., 183.
58. Cited by Burns, op. cit., 136.
59. James A. Farley, *Jim Farley's Story—The Roosevelt Years* (New York: McGraw-Hill, 1948), 19, 20.
60. Ibid., 22.
61. Alfred B. Rollins, Jr., *Roosevelt and Howe* (New York: Knopf, 1962), 4.
62. Cited by Stiles, op. cit., 185.
63. Ibid.
64. Ibid., 186. Also the Farley version in *Story*, op. cit., 22, 23. He described

Howe as "plotting the coralling of votes for 'Franklin' . . ." and pictures himself as guiding Howe with the whispered advice, "Texas is our only chance."

65. Cited by Stiles, op. cit., 186.
66. Schlesinger, Jr., *Crisis*, 309.
67. Cited by Stiles, op. cit., 187. (*The New York Times*, July 2, 1932; 1, 5, 8, and also for July 3, 1932; 1, 6 for an account of the Smith vs. McAdoo/Hearst "feud" and its contribution to Roosevelt's victory.)
68. *The New York Times*, July 3, 1932; 1, 8.
69. *The New York Times*, June 30, 1932; 1, 7.
70. Cited by Schlesinger, Jr., *Crisis*, 442, 423.
71. Cited by Burns, op. cit., 141.
72. *The New York Times*, January 18, 1933; 1, 8.

17.   The Decline of the Presidency

1. George E. Reedy, *The Twilight of the Presidency* (New York: World Publishing Company, 1970), XV.
2. Margaret Truman, *Harry S. Truman* (New York: Morrow & Company, 1973), 4.
3. Harry S. Truman, *Year of Decisions* (Garden City, N.Y.: Doubleday, 1955), I, 134.
4. Ibid., 136.
5. Ibid., 137.
6. Ibid.
7. Ibid., 138.
8. Ibid.
9. Ibid.
10. Ibid., 139.
11. Ibid.
12. Ibid., 140.
13. Ibid., 141.
14. Ibid., 137.
15. Ibid., 141.
16. *The New York Times*, July 18, 1944; 1, 1.
17. Cited by Leuchtenburg, op. cit., II, 605.
18. Truman, op. cit., I, 19.
19. Cited by Leuchtenburg, op. cit., II, 627.
20. For a description of this Democratic campaign to nominate the future Republican president, see the author's account in *The King Makers* (New York: Coward, McCann & Geoghegan, 1971), 1-7.

21. *The New York Times,* April 4, 1948; Section IV, 6e, 4.
22. Dwight D. Eisenhower, *Crusade in Europe* (Garden City, N.Y.: Doubleday, 1949), 444.
23. *The New York Times,* January 23, 1948.

18. The Honcho Presidents; One in Style, the Other in Substance

1. Cited by *The New York Times,* September 28, 1973: "Mr. Lippmann."
2. Fletcher Knebel, "Pulitzer Prize Entry—John F. Kennedy." In Eric Sevareid, ed., *Candidates 1960* (New York: Basic Books, 1959), 196, 197.
3. Ibid., 201, 202. Knebel discusses the loan of $500,000 made by Joseph P. Kennedy to the owner of the *Boston Post,* which came after the *Post* dramatically switched its editorial support from Lodge to Kennedy.
4. Ibid., 185. Rumors of John F. Kennedy's contact with underworld figures took on some substance during 1975 when congressional investigation of the Central Intelligence Agency developed evidence that the CIA had made contact with Chicago Mafia figures during Kennedy's administration, in an abortive attempt to arrange for Fidel Castro's assassination.

 In December 1975, Judith Campbell Exner, identified as a Mafia-connected figure, told the Senate Select Committee on Intelligence that she had been introduced to Kennedy by Frank Sinatra and had been the president's mistress, twenty times having rendezvoused with him in the White House. She had simultaneously been the girl friend of Chicago Mafia leader Sam Giancana, who was murdered in 1975 as this story began to surface. *The New York Times,* January 15, 1976, "Mrs. Exner Plans a Book on Kennedy Friendship," by John M. Crewdson.
5. Ibid., 204.
6. Ibid.
7. *The New York Times,* July 15, 1960; 1, 8. "Johnson Is Nominated for Vice President; Kennedy Picks Him to Placate the South," by W. H Lawrence.
8. Richard M. Nixon, *Six Crises* (Garden City, N.Y.: Doubleday, 1962), 318. One of the few memoirs of public figures which inadvertently reveal much of the true character of the subject.
9. Ibid., 340.
10. Ibid., 391 and 411, 412.
11. Cited by Knebel, op. cit., 187.
12. Cited by Robert L. Riggs, "The South *Could* Rise Again." In Sevareid, ed., op. cit., 298.
13. For a revealing account of this arrangement, see Kenneth P. O'Donnell

David F. Powers, Joe McCarthy, *Johnny, We Hardly Knew Ye* (Boston: Little Brown, 1970), 7, 189-200.

14. Reedy, *Twilight of Presidency*, 20.
15. George V. Higgins, "The Friends of Richard Nixon," *The Atlantic Monthly*, November 1974.
16. Cited by *Time* magazine, February 10, 1975, "L.B.J., Hoover and Domestic Spying," 16.
17. Ibid.
18. Ibid.
19. *The New York Times*, January 9, 1964; 1, 8.
20. Theodore H. White, *The Making of the President 1968* (New York: Atheneum, 1969), 102. After citing a series of Johnson lies which resulted in general doubts about his honesty, White commented, " 'Credibility gap' approached a phantasmagorical quality when in Korea he told the assembled troops, 'My great-great-grandfather died at the Alamo,' although his great-grandparents had not arrived in Texas until ten years after that massacre."
21. *The New York Times*, April 1, 1968; 1, 8. "President Steps Aside in Unity Bid—Says 'House' is Divided." by Tom Wicker.
22. In opposition to the current theory in some quarters that party organization is on the decline, I cite a judicious article by Cornelius Cotter and John Bibby in which they refer to "a clear pattern of increasing strength of national party institutions." This strength is most apparent in the presidential nominating process. Cornelius P. Cotter and John F. Bibby, "Institutional Development of Parties and the Thesis of Party Decline." *Political Science Quarterly*, (Spring 1980), Vol. 95, 1-27.

19.   How a Criminal Became President

1. Nixon, *Six Crises*, 402.
2. *The New York Times*, May 5, 1977, Section B, p. 11, col. 8. "Nixon, Conceding He Lied, Says 'I Let The American People Down!' " by James M. Naughton. Quote from text of David Frost television interview with Nixon.
3. William Costello, *The Facts About Nixon* (New York: Viking Press, 1960), 38.
4. Cited by Costello, op. cit., 39.
5. Helen Gahagan Douglas, interview with the author, June 6, 1973, which originally appeared in *The Impeachment of Richard Nixon* (New York: Berkley/Putnam, 1973), 43.
6. Murray Chotiner, interview with the author, August 4, 1971.

7. Cited by Costello, op. cit., 100.
8. *The New York Times,* September 24, 1952; 1, 8. "Nixon Leaves Fate to G.O.P. Chiefs," by Gladwin Hill.
9. Ibid.
10. Cited by Costello, op. cit., 118.
11. Merle Miller, *Plain Speaking* (New York: Berkley/Putnam, 1973), 135.
12. From the transcript of a television program with Ralph de Toledano and the author, "Biography of the President: The Man," Maryland Center for Public Broadcasting, Baltimore, October 14, 1971.
13. Chotiner, interview, August 4, 1971.
14. *The New York Times,* April 28, 1956; 1, 8. "Nixon Decides He Will Run—Delay Explained—Vice President Says He Took Time to Weigh 'All the Factors,'" by W. H. Lawrence.
15. Sherman Adams, *First Hand Report—The Story of the Eisenhower Administration* (New York: Harper & Brothers, 1961), 234. Invaluable.
16. Nixon, op. cit., 301.
17. Ibid., 321.
18. Ibid., 339.
19. Ibid., 375.
20. Herbert Klein, interview with the author, August 4, 1971.
21. Chotiner, interview, August 4, 1971.
22. *The New York Times,* November 6, 1964.
23. White, op. cit., 32.
24. Joe McGinniss, *The Selling of the President 1968* (New York: Trident Press, 1969), 89, 90. A sample transcript of a Nixon Vietnam commercial.
25. *Washington Post,* October 22, 1972. "AMA, Dairy Campaign Coffers Full." Cited by Morton Mintz and H. D. S. Greenway.
26. *The New York Times,* November 16, 1973. "3 More Corporations Tell About Illegal Aid to Nixon," by Eileen Shanahan.
27. Madison, op. cit., 172.
28. *The New York Times,* October 11, 1973; 1, 7 and 8. "Agnew Quits Vice Presidency and Admits Tax Evasion in '67; Nixon Consults on Successor—Judge Orders Fine, 3 Years' Probation," by James M. Naughton.
29. From notes taken by the author while watching the televised hearings, July 24, 1973.
30. *The New York Times,* March 30, 1973. "McCord Testifies His Fellow Plotters Linked High Nixon Aides to Watergate—Tells Senate Unit Mitchell Was Identified as 'Boss' of Political Espionage," by Walter Rugaber.
31. David Frost paid Nixon one million dollars, three years after his resigna-

tion, to appear on television and peripherally discuss his conduct. Text of his key interview appeared in *The New York Times*, May 5, 1977: "Nixon Looks Back on His Involvement in Watergate: 'I Brought Myself Down,'" Section B, 11, col. 6. *New York Magazine*, May 16, 1977, "From Prison: John Ehrlichman on 'The Nixon Interviews,'" 67.

32. Cited by *Time* magazine, April 8, 1974, 10.
33. *The New York Times*, October 20, 1974. "Ford, Campaigning in South, Urges G.O.P. to Adopt Truman's Fighting Spirit," by John Herbers.
34. Madison, *Notes*, 361.

20.   A Timid Supposition and A Simple Proposal

1. Nikolai Gogol, *Dead Souls* (New York: Penguin Books, 1978), 197, 198.

Selected Bibliography

Aaron, Daniel. *Men of Good Hope: A Story of American Progressives.* New York: Oxford University Press, 1951.

Adams, Henry. *Democracy.* New York: Farrar, Straus and Young, 1952.

―――. *The Education of Henry Adams.* Boston: Houghton Mifflin, 1961.

―――. *History of the United States, During the Administrations of Jefferson and Madison, 1801-1817* (abridged and edited by Ernest Samuels). Chicago: University of Chicago Press, 1967.

Adams, John. *The Works of John Adams.* Charles Francis Adams, ed. Boston: Little, Brown, 1850-1856. 10 vols.

Adams, John Quincy. *Memoirs of John Quincy Adams.* Charles Francis Adams, ed. Philadelphia: J. B. Lippincott, 1874-1877. 12 vols.

Adams, Sherman. *First Hand Report: The Story of the Eisenhower Administration.* New York: Harper, 1961.

Adams, Samuel Hopkins. *The Incredible Era: The Life and Times of Warren Gamaliel Harding.* Boston: Houghton Mifflin, 1939.

Alexander, DeAlva Stanwood. *Political History of the State of New York.* Port Washington, N.Y.: I. J. Friedman, 1969.

Alexander, Holmes Moss. *Aaron Burr: The Proud Pretender.* New York: Harper, 1937.

Allen, Frederick Lewis. *Only Yesterday.* New York: Harper, 1931.

Alsop, Stewart. *Nixon and Rockefeller: A Double Portrait.* Garden City, N.Y.: Doubleday, 1960.

———— "The Square Majority." *The Atlantic Monthly*, February, 1972.

Bancroft, Frederic. *The Life of William H. Seward*. Gloucester, Mass.: P. Smith, 1967. 2 vols.

Banner, James M. *To the Hartford Convention: The Federalists and the Origins of Party Politics in Massachusetts*. New York: Knopf, 1970.

Barck, Oscar Theodore, and Nelson Manfred Blake. *Since 1900: A History of the United States in Our Times*. New York: Macmillan, 1947.

Bartlett, Irving H. *Daniel Webster*. New York: Norton, 1978.

Barkley, Alben W. *That Reminds Me*. Garden City, N.Y.: Doubleday, 1954.

Bartlett, John. *Familiar Quotations*, Emily Morison, ed. (14th ed.). Boston: Little, Brown, 1968.

Bartlett, Ruhl Jacob. *John C. Frémont and the Republican Party*. Columbus: Ohio State University, 1930.

Bates, J. Leonard. "The Teapot Dome Scandal and the Election of 1924." *American Historical Review*, LX (January, 1955), 303-22.

Beard, Charles, and Mary R. *America in Mid-passage*. New York: Macmillan, 1939. 2 vols.

———— *Rise of American Civilization*. New York: Macmillan, 1942. 4 vols.

———— *The American Party Battle*. New York: Macmillan, 1928.

———— *An Economic Interpretation of the Constitution of the United States*. New York: Macmillan, 1935.

Becker, Carl L. *The Declaration of Independence*. New York: Knopf, 1942.

Beer, Thomas. *Hanna*. New York: Knopf, 1929.

Bell, Daniel. *The Radical Right*. New York: Doubleday, 1963.

Bellush, Bernard. *Franklin D. Roosevelt as Governor of New York*. New York: Columbia University Press, 1955.

Bemis, Samuel Flagg. *John Quincy Adams and the Union*. New York: Knopf, 1956.

Bendiner, Robert. "All Things to All Republicans." *The Reporter*, November 4, 1954.

———— "The Presidential Primaries: Haphazard, Unfair, and Wildly Illogical." *The New York Times Magazine*, February 27, 1972.

Benson, Lee. *The Concept of Jacksonian Democracy: New York as a Test Case*. Princeton, N.J.: Princeton University Press, 1961.

Billington, Ray Allen. *The Protestant Crusade, 1800-1860*. New York: Rinehart, 1952.

Bishop, Cortland F. *History of Elections in the American Colonies*. New York: Columbia College, 1893.

Blum, John M. *Joe Tumulty and the Wilson Era*. Boston: Houghton Mifflin, 1951.

Bolles, Blair. *Tyrant From Illinois: Uncle Joe Cannon's Experiment With Personal Power*. New York: Norton, 1951.

Bowers, Claude Gernade. *The Party Battles of the Jackson Period.* Boston: Houghton Mifflin, 1922.

———. *The Tragic Era: The Revolution After Lincoln.* Boston: Houghton Mifflin, 1929.

Boyd, Julian P. (ed.), Eyman H. Butterfield and Mina R. Bryan (assoc. eds.). *Papers of Thomas Jefferson.* Princeton, N.J.: Princeton University Press, 1950.

Bradley, John, *et al. The International Dictionary of Thoughts.* New York: Doubleday, 1969.

Brant, Irving. *James Madison.* New York: Bobbs-Merrill, 1941-1961. 6 vols.

Britton, Nan. *The President's Daughter.* New York: Elizabeth Ann Guild, 1927.

Brogan, D. W. *The Price of Revolution.* New York: Harper, 1951.

———. *Politics In America.* New York: Harper, 1954.

Brooks, Robert Clarkson. *Corruption in American Politics and Life.* New York: Dodd, Mead, 1910.

Brown, E. S. "The Presidential Elections of 1824-1825." *Political Science Quarterly,* Vol. 40, No. 3 (September, 1925), 384-403.

Bryce, James. *The American Commonwealth* (Louis Hacker, ed.). New York: G. P. Putnam's, 1959. 2 vols.

Buchanan, James. *The Collected Works of James Buchanan* (John Bassett Moore, ed.). Philadelphia: J. B. Lippincott, 1910.

Bullitt, Stimson. *To Be A Politician.* New York: Doubleday, 1959.

Burner, David. *The Politics of Provincialism: The Democratic Party in Transition, 1918-1932.* New York: Knopf, 1968.

Burnett, Edmund Cody. *The Continental Congress.* New York: Macmillan, 1941.

Burns, James MacGregor. *Four-Party Politics in America.* Englewood Cliffs, N.J.: Prentice-Hall, 1963.

———. *Roosevelt: The Lion and the Fox.* New York: Harcourt, Brace, 1956.

Byrdsall, Fitzwilliam. *The History of the Loco-foco or Equal Rights Party.* New York: B. Franklin, 1967 (reprint of 1842 edition).

Calhoun, John C. *The Works of John C. Calhoun.* Richard K. Cralle, ed. New York: Appleton, 1864.

Carleton, William G. "A Grass-Roots Guide to '58 and '60." *Harper's,* July, 1958.

Carroll, E. Malcolm. *Origins of the Whig Party.* Durham, N.C.: Duke University Press, 1925.

Cary, Edward. *George William Curtis.* Boston: Houghton Mifflin, 1894.

Chambers, William Nisbet. *Political Parties in a New Nation: The American Experience, 1776-1809.* New York: Oxford University Press, 1963.

Chambrun, Adolphe de. *Impressions of Lincoln and the Civil War: A Foreigner's Account*. New York: Random House, 1952.

Chapman, John Jay. *The Selected Writings of John Jay Chapman* (Jacques Barzun, ed.). New York: Farrar, Straus and Cudahy, 1957.

Charles, Joseph. *The Origins of the American Party System*. Williamsburg, Va.: Institute of Early American History and Culture, 1956.

Chase, Stuart. *The New Deal*. New York: Macmillan, 1932.

Chidsey, Donald Barr. *The Gentleman From New York: Roscoe Conkling*. New Haven: Yale University Press, 1935.

Cleaves, Freeman. *Old Tippecanoe: William Henry Harrison and His Times*. New York: Scribner's, 1939.

Cole, Arthur Charles. *The Irrepressible Conflict, 1850-1865*. New York: Macmillan, 1934.

———. *The Whig Party in the South*. Gloucester, Mass.: P. Smith, 1962.

Commager, Henry Steele, William E. Leuchtenburg, and Samuel Eliot Morison. *The Growth of the American Republic*. New York: Oxford University Press, 1969.

———. *Documents of American History*, (8th ed.). New York: Appleton-Century-Crofts, 1968.

———. *Theodore Parker*. Boston: Beacon Press, 1960.

Cotter, Cornelius P., and John F. Bibby. "Institutional Development of Parties and the Thesis of Party Decline." *Political Science Quarterly*, Vol. 95 (Spring, 1980), 1927.

Crawford, J. B. *The Crédit Mobilier of America*. New York: Greenwood Press, 1969.

Croly, Herbert. *Marcus Alonzo Hanna*. Hamden, Conn.: Archon Books, 1965.

Cunningham, Noble E. *The Jeffersonian Republicans: The Formation of Party Organization, 1789-1801*. Chapel Hill: University of North Carolina Press, 1957.

———. *The Jeffersonian Republicans in Power: Party Operations, 1801-1809*. Chapel Hill: University of North Carolina Press, 1963.

———. "John Beckley: An Early American Party Manager," *William and Mary Quarterly*, XIII (January, 1956), 40-52.

Curley, James Michael. *I'd Do It Again*. Englewood Cliffs, N.J.: Prentice-Hall, 1957.

Curti, Merle. *The Growth of American Thought*. New York: Harper, 1943.

Dallinger, Frederick William. *Nominations for Elective Office*. New York: Longmans, Green, 1897.

Daugherty, Harry M., and Thomas Dixon. *The Inside Story of the Harding Tragedy*. New York: Churchill, 1932.

David, Paul T., Ralph M. Goldman, and Richard C. Bain. *The Politics of National Party Conventions.* Washington, D.C.: Brookings Institution, 1960.

Dean, John. *Blind Ambition: The White House Years.* New York: Simon and Schuster, 1976.

Degler, Carl N. "American Political Parties and the Rise of the City: An Interpretation." *Journal of American History,* LI (June, 1964), 41-59.

Diamond, William. "Urban and Rural Voting in 1896." *American Historical Review,* XLVI (January, 1941), 281-305.

Donovan, Herbert D. *The Barnburners.* New York: New York University Press, 1925.

Donovan, Robert J. *Eisenhower: The Inside Story.* New York: Harper, 1956.

Dorfman, Joseph. *Thorstein Veblen and His America.* New York: Viking, 1934.

Draper, Theodore. *The Roots of American Communism.* New York: Viking, 1957.

Dumond, Dwight Lowell. *Roosevelt to Roosevelt.* New York: Holt, 1937.

Duverger, Maurice. *Political Parties, Their Organization and Activity in the Modern State.* New York: Harper, 1972.

Eisenhower, Dwight D. *Crusade in Europe.* Garden City, N.Y.: Doubleday, 1949.

———. *Mandate for Change, 1953-1956.* New York: Doubleday, 1963.

Ellis, Edward Robb. *The Epic of New York City.* New York: Coward-McCann, 1966.

———. *A Nation in Torment: The Great American Depression.* New York: Coward-McCann, 1970.

Emerson, Ralph Waldo. *Essays. (Second series, new and revised edition).* Boston: Houghton Mifflin, 1894.

Farrand, Max (ed). *The Records of the Federal Convention of 1787.* New Haven: Yale University Press, 1911-1937. 4 vols.

———. *Framing of the Constitution of the United States.* New Haven: Yale University Press, 1913.

Ferguson, Russell J. *Early Western Pennsylvania Politics.* Pittsburgh: University of Pittsburgh Press, 1938.

Fine, Nathan. *Labor and Farmer Parties in the United States, 1828-1928.* New York: Rand School of Social Science, 1928.

Fite, Emerson David. *The Presidential Campaign of 1860.* New York: Macmillan, 1911.

Fitzpatrick, John C. (ed.). *The Writings of George Washington from the Original Manuscript Sources, 1745-1799.* Washington, D.C.: Government Printing Office, 1940.

Flick, Alexander Clarence. *Samuel Jones Tilden.* Port Washington, N.Y.: Kennikat Press, 1963.

Flippin, Percy Scott. *The Royal Government of Virginia, 1624-1775.* New York: Columbia University, 1919.

Flynn, Edward J. *You're The Boss.* New York: Viking, 1947.

Foulke, William Dudley. *Fighting the Spoilsmen: Reminiscences of the Civil Service Reform Movement.* New York: G. P. Putnam's, 1919.

Fox, Dixon Ryan. *Decline of Aristocracy in the Politics of New York, 1801-1840.* Robert V. Romini, ed. New York: Harper, 1965.

Fraser, H. R. *Democracy in the Making: The Jackson-Tyler Era.* Indianapolis: Bobbs-Merrill, 1938.

Fuess, Claude Moore. *Daniel Webster.* Boston: Little, Brown, 1930. 2 vols.

Galbraith, John Kenneth. *The Great Crash.* Boston: Houghton Mifflin, 1954.

Gammon, Samuel Rhea. *Presidential Campaign of 1832.* Baltimore: The John Hopkins Press, 1922.

Goodman, Paul. *The Democratic Republicans of Massachusetts in a Young Republic.* Cambridge: Harvard University Press, 1964.

––––––. *The Federalists vs. the Jeffersonian Republicans.* New York: Holt, Rinehart and Winston, 1967.

Gordy, John Pancoast. *Political History of the United States with Special Reference to the Growth of Political Parties.* New York: Holt, 1904. 2 vols.

Gosnell, Harold Foote. *Champion Campaigner: Franklin D. Roosevelt.* New York: Macmillan, 1952.

––––––, and Norman Gill. "Analysis of the 1932 Presidential Vote in Chicago." *American Political Science Review,* XXIX (December, 1935), 967-84.

––––––, and Charles Edward Merriam. *The American Party System* (4th ed.). New York: Macmillan, 1949.

––––––. *Boss Platt and the New York Machine.* New York: Russell & Russell, 1969.

Grant, Julia Dent. *The Personal Memoirs of Julia Dent Grant* (John Y. Simon, ed.). New York: G. P. Putnam's, 1975.

Goldman, Eric F. *Rendezvous with Destiny.* New York: Knopf, 1952.

Guiteau, Charles. *The Truth and the Removal.* Washington, D.C.: Privately printed, 1882.

Gunderson, Robert G. *The Log-Cabin Campaign.* Lexington: University of Kentucky Press, 1957.

Hale, William Harlan. *Horace Greeley, Voice of the People.* New York: Harper, 1950.

Hamilton, Holman. *Zachary Taylor.* Indianapolis: Bobbs-Merrill, 1941.

Hammond, Bray. *Banks and Politics in America: From the Revolution to the Civil War.* Princeton: Princeton University Press, 1957.

Hanna, William S. *Benjamin Franklin and Pennsylvania Politics.* Stanford, California: Stanford University Press, 1964.

Harrison, Selig S. "Nixon: The Old Guard's Young Pretender." *New Republic,* August 20, 1956.

Hasseltine, William B. *Ulysses S. Grant, Politician.* New York: Ungar, 1935.

Haworth, P. L. *The Hayes-Tilden Disputed Presidential Election of 1876.* Cleveland: Burrows, 1906.

Hayes, Rutherford Birchard. *Hayes: The Diary of a President, 1875-1881* (T. Harry Williams, ed.). New York: McKay, 1964.

Haynes, George Henry. *Charles Sumner.* Philadelphia: G. W. Jacobs, 1909.

Hendrick, Burton J. *Bulwark of the Republic.* Boston: Little, Brown, 1937.

Hibben, Paxton. *The Peerless Leader, William Jennings Bryan.* New York: Russell & Russell, 1967.

Hicks, John D. "The Third Party Tradition in American Politics." *The Mississippi Valley Historical Review,* XX (June 1933) 3-28.

Higgins, George V. "The Friends of Richard Nixon." *The Atlantic Monthly,* November, 1974.

Hofstadter, Richard. *The Age of Reform: From Bryan to F.D.R.* New York: Knopf, 1965.

———. *The Idea of a Party System, 1780-1840.* Berkeley, Calif.: University of California Press, 1969.

Holcombe, Arthur Norman. *The Political Parties of Today.* New York: Harper, 1925.

Hoover, Herbert. *The Memoirs of Herbert Hoover.* New York: Macmillan 1952. 3 vols.

———. *The New Day: Campaign Speeches of Herbert Hoover, 1928.* Stanford, Calif.: Stanford University Press, 1929.

Hosford, Hester Ella. *Woodrow Wilson and New Jersey Made Over.* New York: Knickerbocker Press, 1912.

Howe, Irving, and Lewis Coser. *The American Communist Party.* New York: Praeger, 1962.

Howe, George Frederick. *Chester A. Arthur: A Quarter-Century of Machine Politics.* New York: Ungar, 1935.

Hrebenar, Ronald J. *Parties in Crisis.* New York: John Wiley, 1979.

Hughes, John Emmet. *The Living Presidency.* New York: Coward, McCann & Geoghegan, 1972.

Hyman, Sidney. *The Politics of Consensus.* New York: Random House, 1968.

Ickes, Harold L. *The Secret Diary of Harold L. Ickes*. New York: Simon and Schuster, 1953. 3 vols.

Jackson, Robert H. *The Struggle for Judicial Supremacy*. New York: Knopf, 1940.

James, Marquis. *The Life of Andrew Jackson*. New York: Bobbs-Merrill, 1938.

Jefferson, Thomas. *The Writings of Thomas Jefferson* (Paul Leicester Ford, ed.). New York: G. P. Putnam's, 1892-99. 10 vols.

Johnson, Donald Bruce, and Kirk H. Porter (compilers). *National Party Platforms, 1840-1972*. Urbana: University of Illinois Press, 1973.

Johnson, Hugh S. *The Blue Eagle from Egg to Earth*. Garden City, N.Y.: Doubleday, Doran, 1935.

Johnson, Lyndon B. *The Vantage Point: Perspectives of the Presidency*. New York: Holt, Rinehart and Winston, 1969.

Johnson, Samuel. *The Works of Samuel Johnson*. New Haven, Yale University Press, 1965.

Josephson, Matthew. *The Politicos, 1865-1896*. New York: Harcourt, Brace, 1940.

––––––– *The President Makers, 1896-1919*. New York: Harcourt, Brace, 1940.

––––––– *The Robber Barons*. New York: Harcourt, Brace, 1934.

Kane, Harnett T. *Louisiana Hayride: The American Rehearsal for Dictatorship, 1928-1940*. New York: Morrow, 1941.

Kempton, Murray. *Part of Our Times: Some Ruins and Monuments of the Thirties*. New York: Simon and Schuster, 1955.

Key, V. O. Jr. *Politics, Parties and Pressure Groups*. New York: Crowell, 1947.

––––––– *Southern Politics in State and Nation*. New York: Knopf, 1949.

Kin, David (ed.). *Dictionary of American Maxims*. New York: Philosophical Library, 1955.

Klein, Philip S. *President James Buchanan*. University Park, Pa.: State University Press, 1962.

Krock, Arthur. *Memoirs: Sixty Years on the Firing Line*. New York: Funk & Wagnalls, 1968.

Kurtz, Stephan. *The Presidency of John Adams: The Collapse of Federalism, 1795-1800*. Philadelphia: University of Pennsylvania, 1957.

Labaree, Leonard Woods. *Royal Government in America: A Study of the British Colonial System Before 1783*. New Haven: Yale University Press, 1930.

Lambert, Oscar Doane. *Presidential Politics in the United States, 1841-1844*. Durham, N.C.: Duke University Press, 1936.

Lash, Joseph P. *Eleanor and Franklin*. New York: Norton, 1971.

Laski, Harold J. *The American Presidency, An Interpretation.* New York: Harper, 1940.

Lavine, Emanuel H. *Gimme: Or, How Politicians Get Rich.* New York: Vanguard, 1931.

Lincoln, Abraham. *Complete Works of Abraham Lincoln* (John Hay and John G. Nicolay, eds.). New York: Tandy, 1905. 12 vols.

———. *The Collected Works of Abraham Lincoln* (Roy Baster, ed.). New Brunswick, N.J.: Rutgers University Press, 1953.

Lindsay, A. D. *The Modern Democratic State.* New York: Oxford University Press, 1947.

Link, Arthur S. *Wilson: The Road to the White House.* Princeton, N.J.: Princeton University Press, 1947.

———. "What Happened to the Progressive Movement in the 1920s?" *American Historical Review,* LXIV (July, 1959), 833-51.

Link, Eugene P. *Democratic Republican Societies, 1790-1800.* New York. Octagon, 1965.

Lippmann, Walter. "The Wetness of Al Smith." *Harper's,* XLVI (January, 1928), 133-39.

Livermore, Shaw. *The Twilight of Federalism, 1815-1830.* Princeton, N.J.. Princeton University Press, 1962.

Lodge, Henry Cabot. *Daniel Webster.* Boston: Houghton Mifflin, 1883.

Longworth, Alice Roosevelt. *Crowded Hours.* New York: Scribner's, 1933.

Lurie, Leonard. *The King Makers.* New York: Coward, McCann & Geoghegan, 1971.

———. *The Running of Richard Nixon.* New York: Coward, McCann & Geoghegan, 1972.

———. *The Impeachment of Richard Nixon.* New York: Berkley/Putnam, 1973.

Lynch, Dennis Tilden. *Boss Tweed.* New York: Boni & Liveright, 1927.

Lynch, William Orlando. *Fifty Years of Party Warfare.* Indianapolis: Bobbs-Merrill, 1931.

McAdoo, William Gibbs. *Crowded Years.* Boston: Houghton Mifflin, 1931.

McBain, Howard Lee. *DeWitt Clinton and the Origin of the Spoils System in New York.* New York: Columbia University Press, 1907.

McClure, Alexander Kelly. *Our Presidents and How We Make Them.* New York: Harper, 1902.

McCormac, Eugene. *James K. Polk: A Political Biography.* Berkeley, Calif.: University of California Press, 1922.

McCormick, Richard P. *The Second American Party System: Party Formation in the Jacksonian Era.* Chapel Hill, N.C.: University of North Carolina, 1966.

———. "New Perspectives on Jacksonian Politics." *American Historical Review.* LXV (January, 1960), 288-301.

McCoy, Donald R. *Calvin Coolidge: The Quiet President.* New York: Macmillan, 1967.

McGinniss, Joe. *The Selling of the President 1968.* New York: Trident, 1969.

McLaughlin, Andrew Cunningham. *The Confederation and the Constitution, 1783-1789.* New York: Harper, 1905.

———. *A Constitutional History of the United States.* New York: Appleton-Century, 1935.

MacIver, Robert M. *The Web of Government.* New York: Macmillan, 1947.

Macy, Jesse. *Party Organization and Machinery.* New York: Century, 1904.

———. *Political Parties in the United States, 1846-1861.* New York: Macmillan, 1917.

Madison, James. *Notes of Debates in the Federal Convention of 1787.* Athens: Ohio University Press, 1966.

———. *The Writings of James Madison* (Gaillard Hunt, ed.). New York: G. P. Putnam's, 1901. 9 vols.

Main, Jackson Turner. *The Antifederalists, Critics of the Constitution, 1781-1788.* New York: Norton, 1961.

Malone, Dumas (ed.). *Dictionary of American Biography.* New York: Scribner's, 1928-36. 20 vols.

———. *Jefferson and His Time.* Boston: Little, Brown, 1948. 5 vols.

Merriam, Charles Edward. *Four American Party Leaders.* New York: Macmillan, 1926.

Merrill, H. S. *Bourbon Leader: Grover Cleveland and the Democratic Party.* Boston: Little, Brown, 1957.

Miller, Merle. *Plain Speaking: An Oral Biography of Harry S Truman.* New York: Berkley, 1973.

Milton, George Fort. *The Eve of Conflict: Stephen A. Douglas and the Needless War.* Boston: Houghton Mifflin, 1934.

Minnigerode, Meade. *The Fabulous Forties, 1840-1850.* New York: G. P. Putnam's, 1924.

Moos, Malcolm. *The Republicans, A History of Their Party.* New York: Random House, 1956.

Morison, Samuel Eliot. "The First National Nominating Convention, 1808." *American Historical Review,* Vol. 17, 4 (July, 1912), 744-63.

Morris, Richard B. *Encyclopedia of American History.* New York: Harper, 1953.

Morse, Anson Ely. *The Federalist Party in Massachusetts to the Year 1800.* Princeton: The University Library, 1909.

Mushkat, Jerome. *Tammany: The Evolution of a Political Machine, 1789-*

1865. Syracuse, N. Y.: Syracuse University Press, 1971.

Muzzey, David Saville. *James G. Blaine: A Political Idol of Other Days*. New York: Dodd, Mead, 1934.

Myers, Gustavus. *The History of Tammany Hall*. New York: Boni & Liveright, 1917.

Nevins, Allan. *Frémont, Pathmarker of the West*. New York: Longmans, Green, 1955.

———. Grover Cleveland: *A Study in Courage*. New York: Dodd, Mead, 1932.

———. *John D. Rockefeller: The Heroic Age of American Enterprise*. New York: Scribner, 1940. 2 vols.

Nichols, Roy F. *The Democratic Machine, 1850-54*. New York: Columbia University Press, 1924.

———. *The Invention of the American Political Parties*. New York: Macmillan, 1967.

———. *Franklin Pierce*. Philadelphia: University of Pennsylvania Press, 1931.

Nixon, Hannah. "A Mother's Story." *Good Housekeeping*, June, 1960.

"Nixon's New Role." *U.S. News and World Report*, December 6, 1957.

Nixon, Richard Milhous. *Six Crises*. Garden City, N.Y.: Doubleday, 1962.

Novak, Michael. *Choosing Our King: Powerful Symbols in Presidential Politics*. New York: Macmillan, 1974.

O'Donnell, Kenneth P., David F. Powers, and Joe McCarthy. *"Johnny We Hardly Knew Ye": Memories of John Fitzgerald Kennedy*. Boston: Little, Brown, 1972.

Ogg, Frederic A., and Orman P. Ray. *Introduction to American Government* (8th ed.). New York: Appleton-Century, 1945.

Olcott, Charles Sumner. *The Life of William McKinley*. Boston: Houghton Mifflin, 1916. 2 vols.

Opotowsky, Stan. *The Longs of Louisiana*. New York: Dutton, 1960.

Orcutt, William Dana. *Burrows of Michigan and the Republican Party*. New York: Longmans, Green, 1917. 2 vols.

Orth, Samuel P. *The Boss and the Machine*. New Haven: Yale University Press, 1919.

Ostrogorski, M. *Democracy and the Party System in the United States*. New York: Macmillan, 1921.

Parrington, Vernon Louis. *Main Currents in American Thought*. New York: Harcourt, Brace, 1927.

Perry-Link, Eugene. *Democratic-Republican Societies, 1790-1800*. New York: Octagon Books, 1965.

Phillips, Cabell. "One-Man Task Force of the GOP." *The New York Times Magazine*, October 24, 1954.

Poage, George Rawlings. *Henry Clay and the Whig Party*. Chapel Hill: University of North Carolina Press, 1936.

Polk, James K. *The Diary of James K. Polk During His Presidency, 1845 to 1849*. Milo Milton Quaife, ed. Chicago: A. C. McClurg, 1910.

Pringle, Henry F. *Theodore Roosevelt*. New York: Harcourt, Brace, 1931.

_____. *A. E. Smith: a Critical Study*. New York: Macy-Masius, 1927.

_____. *The Life and Times of William Howard Taft*. New York: Farrar & Rinehart, 1939.

Rayback, Joseph G. *Free Soil: the Election of 1848*. Lexington: The University Press of Kentucky, 1970.

Rayback, Robert. *Millard Fillmore*. Buffalo, N.Y.: H. Stewart, 1959.

Reedy, George E. *The Twilight of the Presidency*. New York: World, 1970.

Reeves, Thomas C. "Chester A. Arthur and the Campaign of 1880." *Political Science Quarterly*, LXXXIV (December, 1969), 628-37.

Remini, Robert V. *Martin Van Buren and the Making of the Democratic Party*. New York: Columbia University Press, 1959.

Robinson, William Alexander. *Jeffersonian Democracy in New England*. New Haven: Yale University Press, 1916.

Rollins, Alfred B. *Roosevelt and Howe*. New York: Knopf, 1962.

Roosevelt, Theodore. *Theodore Roosevelt—An Autobiography*. New York: Macmillan, 1913.

Roseboom, Eugene H. *A History of Presidential Elections: From George Washington to John F. Kennedy*. New York: Macmillan, 1964.

Ross, Earle Dudley. *The Liberal Republican Movement*. New York: AMS Press, 1971.

Rossiter, Clinton Lawrence. *1787—The Grand Convention*. New York: Macmillan, 1966.

_____. *Parties and Politics in America*. Ithaca, N.Y.: Cornell University Press, 1960.

_____. *The American Presidency*. New York: Harcourt, Brace, 1960.

Rovere, Richard H. "A Reporter At Large: The Campaign: Nixon." *The New Yorker*, October 13, 1956.

Russell, Francis. *The Shadow of Blooming Grove*. New York: McGraw-Hill, 1968.

Sabine, George H. *A History of Political Theory*. New York: Holt, 1937.

Sait, Edward McChesney. *American Parties and Elections* (Howard Rae Penniman, ed.) (5th ed.). New York: Appleton-Century-Crofts, 1952.

Salter, John Thomas. *Boss Rule: Portraits in City Politics*. New York: McGraw-Hill, 1935.

Scammon, Richard M., and Ben J. Wattenberg, *The Real Majority*. New York: Coward, McCann & Geoghegan, 1970.

Schachner, Nathan. *Aaron Burr*. New York: Stokes, 1937.

————. *Thomas Jefferson*. New York: Appleton-Century-Crofts, 1951. 2 vols.

Schlesinger, Arthur M., Jr. *The Age of Jackson*. New York: Little, Brown, 1945.

————. *The Crisis of the Old Order, 1919-1933*. Boston: Houghton Mifflin, 1957.

————. *The Coming of the New Deal*. Boston, Houghton Mifflin, 1958.

Schurz, Carl. *Henry Clay*. New York: Ungar, 1968. 2 vols.

Seager, Robert. *And Tyler Too: A Biography of John & Julia Gardiner Tyler*. New York: McGraw-Hill, 1963.

Sellers, Charles Grier. *James K. Polk*. Princeton: Princeton University Press, 1966. 2 vols.

Sevareid, Eric. *In One Ear*. New York: Knopf, 1952.

————. (ed.). *Candidates 1960*. New York: Basic Books, 1959.

Shannon, David. *The Socialist Party of America: A History*. New York: Macmillan, 1955.

Shannon, William V. *The American Irish*. New York: Macmillan, 1963.

————. "The Nixon Story," New York *Post*, October 17-22, 1955.

Sirmans, Marion Eugene. *Colonial South Carolina: A Political History, 1663-1763*. Chapel Hill: University of North Carolina Press, 1966.

Smith, Theodore Clarke. *The Liberty and Free Soil Parties in the Northwest*. New York: Longmans, Green, 1897.

————. *Parties and Slavery: 1850-1859*. New York: Harper, 1906.

————. *The Life and Letters of James A. Garfield*. New Haven: Yale University Press, 1925. 2 vols.

Smith, William Ernest. *The Francis Preston Blair Family in Politics*. New York: Macmillan, 1933. 2 vols.

Spitz, David. *Patterns of Anti-Democratic Thought: with Special Reference to the American Political Mind in Recent Times*. New York: Macmillan, 1949.

Steffens, Lincoln. *The Autobiography of Lincoln Steffens*. New York: Harcourt, Brace, 1931.

————. *Shame of the Cities*. New York: Sagamore Press, 1957.

Stevenson, Adlai E. *Major Campaign Speeches 1952*. New York: Random House, 1953.

Stiles, Lela. *The Man Behind Roosevelt, The Story of Louis McHenry Howe*. New York: World, 1954.

Stoddard, Lothrop. *Master of Manhattan: the Life of Richard Croker*. New York: Longmans, Green, 1931.

Sullivan, Mark. *Our Times, The United States 1900-1925*. New York: Scribner's, 1935.

Sward, Keith. *The Legend of Henry Ford*. New York: Rinehart, 1948.

Syrett, Harold. *Andrew Jackson, His Contribution to the American Tradition*. Indianapolis: Bobbs-Merrill, 1953.

Taylor, John. *A Definition of Parties*. Philadelphia: Francis Bailey, 1794.

———. *An Inquiry Into the Principles and Policy of the Government of the United States, 1814*. New Haven: Yale University Press, 1950.

Taylor, John M. *Garfield of Ohio*. New York: Norton, 1970.

Thayer, George. *Who Shakes the Money Tree? American Campaign Financing Practices from 1789 to the Present*. New York: Simon and Schuster, 1973.

Thayer, Theodore George. *Pennsylvania Politics and the Growth of Democracy, 1740-1776*. Harrisburg, Pa.: Pennsylvania Historical and Museum Commission, 1953.

Tinkcom, Harry Maslin. *Republicans and Federalists in Pennsylvania, 1790-1801*. Harrisburg, Pa.: Pennsylvania Historical and Museum Commission, 1950.

Tocqueville, Alexis de. *Democracy in America*. New York: Knopf, 1972. 2 vols.

Truman, Harry S. *Memoirs*. New York: Doubleday, 1955-1956. 2 vols.

Truman, Margaret. *Harry S Truman*. New York: Morrow, 1973.

Turner, Lynn. "The Electoral Vote Against Monroe in 1820—An American Legend." *Mississippi Valley Historical Review*, XLII (September, 1955), 250-73.

Tyler, Lyon Gardiner. *The Letters and Times of the Tylers*. Richmond, Va.: Whittet & Shepperson, 1884-96. 3 vols.

Van Buren, Martin. *Autobiography*. Washington, D.C.: Government Printing Office, Annual Report of the American Historical Association for the Year 1918.

———. *Inquiry into the Origin and Course of Political Parties in the United States*. New York: Augustur M. Kelley, 1967 (reprint of Hurd and Houghton edition), 1867.

Van Der Linden, Frank. *The Turning Point: Jefferson's Battle for the Presidency*. Washington: R. B. Luce, 1962.

Van Deusen, Glyndon Garlock. *The Life of Henry Clay*. Boston: Little, Brown, 1937.

———. *Thurlow Weed, Wizard of the Lobby*. Boston: Little, Brown, 1947.

Van Devander, Charles W. *The Big Bosses*. New York: Howell, Soskin, 1944.

Van Doren, Carl. *Benjamin Franklin.* New York: Viking, 1938.

Vinson, J. Chal. *Thomas Nast, Political Cartoonist.* Athens: University of Georgia Press, 1967.

Warfel, Harry R. *Noah Webster, Schoolmaster to America.* New York: Macmillan, 1936.

Warren, Charles. *The Making of the Constitution.* Boston: Little, Brown, 1937.

Weed, Harriet A. ed., A Life of Thurlow Weed: Boston: Houghton, Mifflin, 1883, 1884. 2 vols.

Weston, Florence. *Presidential Election of 1828.* Washington, D.C.: Ruddick, 1938.

Whalen, Richard J. *The Founding Father: The Story of Joseph P. Kennedy.* New York: New American Library, 1964.

"The White House Transcripts." (Truncated by Richard Nixon, but still useful.) *Submission of Recorded Presidential Conversations to the Committee on the Judiciary of the House of Representatives by President Richard Nixon.* New York: Bantam Books, 1974.

White, Theodore H. *The Making of the President 1960.* New York: Atheneum, 1961.

————— *The Making of the President 1964.* New York: Atheneum, 1965.

————— *The Making of the President 1968.* New York: Atheneum, 1969.

————— "Razor's Edge for Nixon and the GOP." *Harper's,* February, 1961.

White, William Allen. *A Puritan in Babylon: The Story of Calvin Coolidge.* New York: Macmillan, 1938.

————— *Autobiography of William Allen White.* New York: Macmillan, 1946.

Williams, C. R. *The Life of Rutherford B. Hayes.* Boston: Houghton Mifflin, 1914. 2 vols.

Wills, Garry. *Nixon Agonistes.* New York: Houghton Mifflin, 1970.

Wilson, Woodrow. *President Wilson's Great Speeches.* Chicago: Stanton and Van Vliet, 1919.

————— *A Crossroads of Freedom—The 1912 Campaign Speeches of Woodrow Wilson* (John Wells Davidson, ed.). New Haven: Yale University Press, 1956.

Wiltse, Charles Maurice. *John C. Calhoun.* Indianapolis: Bobbs-Merrill, 1944-1951. 3 vols.

————— *The Jeffersonian Tradition in American Politics.* New York: Hill and Wang, 1960.

Witcover, Jules. *Marathon.* New York: Viking, 1977.

Woodburn, James Albert. *The Life of Thaddeus Stevens.* Indianapolis: Bobbs-Merrill, 1913.

_____. *American Politics: Political Parties and Party Problems in the United States* (3rd ed.). New York: G. P. Putnam's, 1924.

Young, Alfred F. *The Democratic Republicans of New York: the Origins, 1763-1797.* Chapel Hill: The University of North Carolina Press, 1967.

Index